Gazing into the Oracle

The Delphi Method and its Application
to Social Policy and Public Health

of related interest:

Welfare and Culture in Europe
Towards a New Paradigm in Social Policy
*Edited by Prue Chamberlayne, Andrew Cooper, Richard Freeman
and Michael Rustin*
ISBN 1 85302 700 6

Community Care Practice and the Law
Second Edition
Michael Mandelstam
ISBN 1 85302 647 6

Law, Rights and Disability
Edited by Jeremy Cooper
ISBN 1 85302 836 3

Disabled Children and the Law
Research and Good Practice
Janet Read and Luke Clements
ISBN 1 85302 793 6

Immigration Controls, the Family and the Welfare State
A Handbook of Law, Theory, Politics and Practice for Local Authority,
Voluntary Sector and Welfare State Workers and Legal Advisors
Steve Cohen
ISBN 1 85302 723 5

Errata

Peter Goldschmidt's affiliation on the contents page should read:
Peter Goldschmidt is President of the World Development Group Inc.
(WDG) Bethesda, Maryland.

p.89 An additional footnote to p.89 should read:
This paper was submitted in 1991.

p.119, para 2 should read:
Conclusion
Central questions
These findings are remarkably fresh today, even though the study was
completed 15 years ago.

Gazing into the Oracle

The Delphi Method and its Application to Social Policy and Public Health

Edited by Michael Adler and Erio Ziglio

Jessica Kingsley Publishers
London and Philadelphia

First published in the United Kingdom in 1996
by Jessica Kingsley Publishers Ltd
116 Pentonville Road
London N1 9JB, England
and
325 Chestnut Street
Philadelphia, PA 19106, USA

www.jkp.com

Copyright © Jessica Kingsley Publishers 1996
Printed digitally since 2002

Library of Congress Cataloging in Publication Data
Gazing into the oracle : the Delphi method and its application to
social policy and public health / edited by Michael Adler and Erio Ziglio
p. cm
Includes bibliographical references and index
ISBN 1-85302-104-0 (alk. paper)
1. Social planning. 2. Social policy. 3. Human services-
-Planning. 4. Health planning. 5. Delphi method. I. Adler,
Michael. II Ziglio, Erio.
HN29.G39   1996   96-40745
361.6'1--dc20   CIP

British Library Cataloguing in Publication Data
Adler, Michael
Gazing into the Oracle
I. Title
306.4

ISBN 1 85302 104 0

Contents

Acknowledgements

We would like to acknowledge the support of the Commission of the European Communities (D.G.V. Public Health Unit) which, in the early 1990s, sponsored an expert meeting in Luxembourg to examine the Delphi Method and its potential utilisation in public health. This book is a direct outcome of that meeting.

The book should have been completed some time ago. We take full responsibility for the delay and would like to thank all the contributors and our publisher, Jessica Kingsley, for their patience and forbearance. It is our good fortune that, despite the delay, the book has not become dated in any way.

We would also like to thank three people without whose help the book would not have been published. Sharon Ruwart (formerly at the World Health Organisation in Copenhagen) and Zoe Irving (formerly at the Department of Social Policy in Edinburgh) both put a great deal of work into preparing the papers for publication and we are very grateful to them. Rose Pipes' contribution was quite exceptional. We would like to thank her for editing the manuscript in such an efficient and professional manner and, in the nicest and most friendly way, making it impossible for us to leave the task unfinished. Thank you, Rose.

Michael Adler
Erio Ziglio
Edinburgh and Copenhagen

Preface

Michael Adler and Erio Ziglio

Why a Book on the Delphi Method Now?

The mid-1970s saw the publication of two seminal books on the Delphi Method (Delbecq, Van de Ven, and Gustafson 1975; Linstone, and Turoff 1975). At about the same time, the theoretical and methodological questions which were posed by Sackman (1974) in his critique of the Delphi Method were given convincing and satisfactory answers by Goldschmidt (1975). Unfortunately, since then there have been no major publications which have sought either to address fundamental theoretical, methodological and practical issues relating to the Delphi Method or to describe new applications of the technique.

The fact that the major publications on the Delphi Method were all written in the 1970s does not mean that, since that time, the technique has not been used. In the last two decades, the Delphi Method has found a wide range of applications in planning, evaluation, forecasting and issue-exploration in many areas. However, in spite of this, there have been few applications in social policy or public health. One consequence of this is that in these two fields the Delphi Method is not as well-known as it ought to be.

It is our hope that this book will redress some of these omissions. In it, we address methodological and practical issues raised by the Delphi Method and bring together a number of more recent Delphi applications in different areas of health and social policy.

The Aims of the Book

The book is directed first at policy makers, professionals, researchers and management consultants in public health and social policy, and second at academics and postgraduate students in these fields. It should be particularly useful to health and social planners in national and international organisations. The book aims to introduce the Delphi Method to this audience, to illustrate by means of examples what can be achieved with it, and to discuss some important theo-

retical, methodological and practical issues which need to be faced if
the technique is to be applied successfully. It is our belief that applications of the Delphi Method and other similar techniques will
greatly benefit from the exploration of these issues and that they will
greatly enhance informed decision-making in social policy and public
health.

The Structure of the Book

The book is divided into two parts. Part 1 deals with theory and
methods. The opening chapter by Ziglio provides an introduction to
the Delphi Method, an analysis of the methodological problems
associated with it and an assessment of its contribution to decision-
making. The next two chapters advocate a number of methodological
refinements in the technique. In Chapter 2, Rotondi and Gustafson
outline a set of techniques for strengthening communication between
participants in group problem solving, and in Chapter 3, Turoff and
Hiltz describe some of the exciting implications of interactive computer systems for group communications and thus for the Delphi
Method.

Part 2 comprises a selection of case studies, all but one carried out
in the last decade in various fields of social policy and public health.
These include applications of the Delphi Method to planning for the
future and to formulating policies and programmes in the following
areas: biomedical and behavioural research (Goldschmidt, Chapter
4); mental health and mental health care (Bijl, Chapter 5); services for
the elderly (Bertin, Chapter 6); the organisation of social security
services (Adler and Sainsbury, Chapter 7); accidents and injuries (van
Beeck, Chapter 8) and family planning services (Niero and Robertson,
Chapter 9). Part 2 concludes with an assessment by the editors of
what can be learned from the case studies and an indication of the
potential of the Delphi Method for more informed decision-making
in public health and social policy.

The applications not only cover a wide range of issues and policies
in health and social policy but are also drawn from four different
countries (Italy, the Netherlands, the United Kingdom and the United
States of America). By bringing contributions from several countries
to a wider audience, we seek both to enlighten and inform colleagues
in different policy fields of the important contribution that the Delphi
Method can make to the achievement of more informed and more
effective decision-making.

Although it is clear that the use of the Delphi Method is already
quite widespread, it is equally evident that it has been rather

sporadic. However, it is our hope that, with the publication of this book, its usefulness can be better appreciated and its potential more fully realised by individual researchers, local and national governments, and by international organisations in Europe and beyond.

References

Delbecq, A.L., Van de Ven, A.H. and Gustafson, D.H. (1975) *Group Techniques for Program Planning: A Guide to Nominal Group and Delphi Processes*. Glenview, IL: Scott Foreman and Co.

Linstone, H.A. and Turoff, M. (eds) (1975) *The Delphi Method: Techniques and Applications*. Reading, MA: Addison-Wesley.

Sackman, H. (1974) *Delphi Critique: Expert Opinion, Forecasting and Group Process*. Lexington, MA: D.C. Heath

Goldschmidt, P. (1975) 'Scientific inquiry or political critique? Remarks on Delphi assessment, expert opinion, forecasting, and group process by H. Sackmann.' *Technological Forecasting and Social Change 7*, 195–213.

Part 1

Theory and Methods

Chapter 1

The Delphi Method and its Contribution to Decision-Making

Erio Ziglio

Introduction

The objective of most Delphi applications is the reliable and creative exploration of ideas or the production of suitable information for decision-making. The Delphi Method is based on a structured process for collecting and distilling knowledge from a group of experts by means of a series of questionnaires interspersed with controlled opinion feedback.

Delphi is used to support judgmental or heuristic decision-making, or, more colloquially, creative or informed decision-making. The central element of this situation is described by Delbecq *et al.* (1975, p.5) as:

> the lack of agreement or incomplete state of knowledge concerning either the nature of the problem or the components which must be included in a successful solution. As a result, heterogeneous group members must pool their judgements to invent or discover a satisfactory course of action.

In the fields of social policy and public health, the need for creative or judgmental problem solving occurs frequently. Linstone and Turoff (1975, p.4) identify some specific features of the judgmental decision-making context in which the Delphi Method has proved to be effective. From the work of these two authors, three considerations are important for Delphi applications to issues related to social policy and public health:

1. *the problem does not lend itself to precise analytical techniques* but can benefit from subjective judgements on a collective basis, for example, possible impact of the single European market on migration, education policy, employment linked fringe benefits, etc.;

2. *the problem at hand has no monitored history nor adequate information on its present and future development* (e.g. public health and environmental effects of the Chernobyl nuclear disaster; or of the greenhouse effect);

3. *addressing the problem requires the exploration and assessment of numerous issues connected with various policy options* where the need for pooled judgement can be facilitated by judgmental techniques (e.g. possible common public health measures in the member States of the European Union in the areas of preventing the spread of AIDS/HIV or the trafficking of illicit drugs).

The need to improve the use of informed judgement in the fields of social policy and public health is practically unlimited and is mainly due to the already mentioned problem of taking decisions under conditions of uncertainty (Brouwer and Schreuder 1986; STG 1992; WHO 1994). This uncertainty is usually related to the nature of the problem and/or to policy measures to resolve it effectively and efficiently.

Pill (1971; see also Goldschmidt 1975) notes that there are two options when one is working on a problem under conditions of uncertainty determined by insufficient data on the problem under investigation and incomplete theory on both its cause and effects. The first option is to wait (perhaps indefinitely) until we have an adequate theory based on tested scientific knowledge enabling us to address the problem concerned. Of course, this option is not feasible if the problem needs urgent attention and action. Furthermore, many social and health problems are not amenable to solution by pure positivistic or 'scientific' methods (Goldschmidt 1975, p.199).

The second alternative is to make the most of what is, admittedly, an unsatisfactory situation, and to try to obtain the relevant intuitive insights of experts and use their informed judgement as systematically as possible. According to Dalkey (1967), the rationale and use of the Delphi Method represents a systematic effort within the second alternative. It is within this latter perspective that it is suggested that the method can be applied in the fields of social policy and public health with the aim of generating new insights and future scenarios; assessing the desirability and feasibility of policy alternatives; and contributing to problem solving and informed decision-making.

Where Does the Delphi Method Come From?

The Delphi Method is not new. The basic notion, theoretical assumptions and methodological procedures originated in the 1950s and

1960s at the RAND Corporation. In their chapter, Turoff and Hiltz rightly note that the name 'Delphi' was never a term with which either Helmer or Dalkey (the founders of the Method) were particularly happy. Dalkey acknowledged that it was rather unfortunate that the set of procedures developed at the RAND Corporation, and designed to improve methods of forecasting, came to be known as 'Delphi'. He argued that the term implies 'something oracular, something smacking a little of the occult – whereas, as a matter of fact, precisely the opposite is involved; it is primarily concerned with making the best you can of a less than perfect fund of information.' (Dalkey 1968)

One of the very first applications of the Delphi Method carried out at the RAND Corporation is illustrated in the publication by Gordon and Helmer (1964). Its aim was to assess the direction of long-range trends, with special emphasis on science and technology, and their probable effects on society. The study covered six topics: scientific breakthroughs; population control; automation; space progress; war prevention; weapon systems (Gordon and Helmer 1964; Linstone and Turoff 1975, pp.10–11). The first Delphi applications were in the area of technological forecasting and aimed to forecast likely inventions, new technologies and the social and economic impact of technological change.

Public sector use of the Delphi Method has been reviewed by Preble (1983), McGaw *et al.* (1976) and Niero (1987). Initial applications of the Delphi Method aimed to explore the impact of new land use policy; information systems relevant for planning purposes; the future role and organisational arrangements of hospitals, and other health services. In public health and social policy, the Method has been used to generate future scenarios likely to occur in the fields of social services, health care, accidents, spread of AIDS/HIV and in the assessment of the probable impact on the population's health of environmental, social and economic and urban policies (Ley and Anderson 1975; Sing and Webbe 1979; Hollender and Becker 1987; WHO/STG 1988; 1989; Garrett 1994; 1995). In social work, nursing and medical education, the Delphi Method has been used to design new curricula and to predict the impact of socio-economic developments on future school systems, training and research needs (McGaw *et al.* 1976; Ventura *et al.* 1981; Bond and Bond 1982; Garrett 1994).

The Need for Creative and Structured Communication

Dalkey (1969a) describes various types of information which can be represented as points on a continuum. One extreme of the continuum can be labelled 'knowledge'. According to Dalkey (1969a) knowledge is that kind of information which is thoroughly substantiated by solid empirical evidence. This is the kind of information which is usually produced in the natural sciences, tested and confirmed by experiment. This kind of knowledge is very often harder to achieve in the field of public health. At the other extreme of the continuum, Dalkey identifies 'speculation' as the type of information which is based on little or no foundation.

Dalkey (1969a; see also Dahl 1974) argues that between knowledge and speculation is a grey area which is often called 'wisdom', 'insight' or 'informed judgement'. Informed judgement is central to the theoretical assumptions of the Delphi Method. According to the pioneering work of Dalkey (1968, 1969) and Rescher (1969), the theoretical assumptions of the Delphi Method make it impossible to label everything that is not knowledge as mere speculation. The methodological procedure used in the Delphi Method aims at structuring and distilling the vast mass of information for which there is some evidence (but not yet knowledge) in order to achieve and improve informed judgement and decision-making.

The results of a Delphi study can undoubtedly be used to enrich traditional face-to-face meetings. For example, the efficiency of face-to-face meetings can be increased by a supplementary group communication process obtained via Delphi. In other cases the Delphi Method can be used when time and cost constraints make frequent face-to-face meetings difficult to arrange. This could be the case when experts are dispersed geographically. The Delphi Method may also be used when the heterogeneity of the participants must be preserved and anonymity assured to avoid the domination of the communication process by one particular profession, vested interest or strong personality.

The Delphi Method as a Tool for Knowledge Building

There is an increasing commitment to social policy and public health issues on the part of international as well as national and local authorities and organisations. This has brought about a wider range of functions, new institutions, the setting up of *ad hoc* committees and other decision-making bodies involving civil servants, experts, politicians, administrators and the lay community. The relationships and exchanges of experience and information amongst these 'partners' are often far from ideal. Opportunities and practical tools for improving the exchange of information, supporting social policy and public health-related agencies and various decision-making bodies, are becoming more and more of a necessity and a challenge at every level of policy making.

In social policy and public health agencies, both at national and local levels as well as internationally, it is not uncommon to have twenty or more individuals in one committee or working group. In this context, a complete, effective and free exchange of views is often too time consuming (or downright impossible). Deadlines have to be met and the pressure to get through all the items on typically heavy agendas often make communication exchanges and informed decision-making difficult. A great deal of creativity and technical support is needed, given the complexity of many social policy and public health issues, ranging from policies for drug use reduction to the prevention of AIDS/HIV; from regulatory measures for quality standards of medical devices and pharmaceutical products to facilitating means for health promotion and training; from assessment of social security measures to investment in housing and education, policies which enhance individual welfare and the quality of life. Delphi is one method (amongst others) for improving the generation of critical ideas, and the structured collection and processing of information gathered from experts.

A Delphi exercise could be commissioned with the intention of using the information generated as an input to a committee activity. Once a Delphi exercise has been accomplished, the committee may utilise the results to establish all the differing positions advocated on a given issue and the principal pros and cons of each of those positions. Even in those cases where the experts involved in the Delphi process are themselves members of the committee, the technique has the advantage of eliminating a major bottleneck in most group dynamics by providing opportunities for a clear delineation of differing views in a non-threatening environment.

In the assessment of policy issues in social policy and public health, adaptation of the Delphi Method in the form of a Policy Delphi can be of particular value. Turoff (1970) maintains that the Policy Delphi (i.e. the application of the Delphi Method to the exploration and evaluation of policy issues) is particularly useful in situations where there is no clear-cut resolution of a given policy issue. In this situation, experts become advocates for the effectiveness and efficiency of a particular resolution of that policy issue and must compete with the advocates of other concerned interest groups who are affected by the final policy decision (Turoff 1970; Dahl 1974 Ch. 3). This is a very common situation characterising policy making in social policy and public health.

The Delphi Method, and similar techniques such as Policy Delphi, Committee Delphi and Nominal Group Technique (NGT), represents an organised method for collecting views and information pertaining to a specific policy area. Because in many Delphi applications the contributions and viewpoints elicited by respondents are reported in an anonymous way, fears of potential repercussions are removed and no single individual need commit him/herself publicly to a particular view until all the alternatives have been put on the table (Dahl 1974, pp.50–52; see also Linstone 1984, Ch. 13).

To sum up, the results of a Delphi exercise can serve any one or any combination of the following purposes:

- to ensure that all the major possible options concerning a particular issue have been put on the table for consideration;

- to estimate the impact (e.g. in terms of technical and economic feasibility) and consequences of any particular option; and

- to examine the acceptability (e.g. in terms of political or ethical desirability) of any given option.

Of course, it must be absolutely clear that the use of the Delphi Method should not in any way be perceived as an attempt to remove the policy formulation or decision-making responsibility from those who must exercise it. Thus, Delphi designers should work in close cooperation with civil servants and those who will eventually utilise the information provided by the application of the Delphi Method. Such cooperation is indispensable in order to ensure that the real intent and purpose of the Delphi application are correctly understood by all interested parties and seen as an impartial tool for assisting decision-making.

As illustrated by the case studies described in Part 2, the Delphi Method and similar techniques can be used as tools for improving data collection, generation of ideas, exploration of future scenarios and informed decision-making in social policy and public health. The Delphi Method can, therefore, provide a very important tool for decision-makers facing uncertainty by: exploring the nature of a particular social policy or public health problem; assessing its magnitude; and evaluating different possible ways of addressing it. The results of proper applications of the Delphi Method can greatly assist policy makers to improve creativity in their decision-making when accurate information is unavailable.

The Basics of the Delphi Method

The Delphi Method is an exercise in group communication among a panel of geographically dispersed experts. The technique allows experts to deal systematically with a complex problem or task. The essence of the technique is fairly straightforward. It comprises a series of questionnaires sent, either by mail or via computerised systems, to a pre-selected group of experts. These questionnaires are designed to elicit and develop individual responses to the problems posed and to enable the experts to refine their views as the group's work progresses in accordance with the assigned task.

In most applications, the first questionnaire (Q1) (see Appendix 2) poses the problem in broad terms and invites answers and comments. The replies to Q1 are summarised and used to construct a second questionnaire (Q2) (see Appendix 4). Q2 presents the results of Q1 and gives the respondents an opportunity to re-evaluate their original answers in the light of comprehensive feedback on the responses of the whole group. During this interactive process, which can be repeated as many times as are judged appropriate in the circumstances, issues can be clarified, areas of agreement and disagreement can be identified, and an understanding of the priorities can be developed.

In virtually every use of the Delphi Method, two phases can be identified. The first can be labelled as the 'exploration phase'. It usually characterises Q1, sometimes also Q2, where the subject under discussion is fully explored and additional information is provided. The second phase (the 'evaluation phase') involves the process of assessing and gathering the experts' views (there may be consensus or disagreement) on various ways of addressing the issues under investigation. Generally speaking, the evaluation phase characterises Q2 and Q3. If there is significant disagreement, then this can be explored further (e.g. in Q4) to bring out the underlying reasons for the differences among experts and possibly to evaluate them (Linstone and Turoff 1975, pp.5–6; Delbecq, Van de Ven and Gustafson 1975, Ch. 4).

Main Stages and Outcomes in a Delphi Process

The first stage of a Delphi process, i.e. Q1, is of crucial importance. If respondents do not understand the aim of the Delphi exercise, they may answer inappropriately or become frustrated and lose interest (Delbecq *et al.* 1975). It is worth reassuring people selected for a Delphi panel who are not familiar with the technique that they will be able to accomplish the tasks required by the technique. To this end,

individual contact with Delphi panellists and the provision of appropriate background material on the technique can prove very effective
(Ziglio 1985 pp.85–86; see also Chapter 2 in this book).

Generally speaking, the second questionnaire (Q2) asks participants to review the items identified in Q1 as summarised by the
Delphi team responsible for the analysis. As in Q1, experts can argue
in favour of or against each item. It is common at Q2 stage to ask
respondents to rank items and to establish preliminary priorities
amongst them according to the instructions given.

The benefits which can reasonably be expected at the Q2 stage are
the initial identification of areas of agreement and disagreement
amongst panellists as well as issues requiring further clarification.
Delbecq *et al.* (1975) point out four positive outcomes of Q2:

Areas of agreement: these are identifiable in the light of the
comments and priority voting made by experts.

Areas of disagreement: the items in Q2 indicate the initial position of participants. Comments and reactions to the items can
further clarify those positions. Based on this information, the
analysis of Q2 can indicate, to some degree, why differences can
occur.

Areas needing clarification: items in Q2 where respondents are
unclear as to the meaning can be identified. Then in Q3 and, if
necessary, subsequent questionnaires, these items can be recon-
structed so that misunderstanding does not distort final voting.

Understanding: Q2 is the beginning of a dialogue between participants. Questions can be raised. Statements of support and
criticism can be made. Results will be relayed to all participants
through Q3, allowing respondents to consider these further clarifications and vote accordingly. The aim is to help participants to
understand each other's position and to move towards an accurate judgement concerning the relative importance of items.

Finally, another important, and perhaps the least understood, property of the Delphi Method is the ability of members of a group to
participate in an asynchronous manner. As pointed out in Chapter 3,
this property of asynchronous interaction has two main characteristics:

1. experts may choose to participate in the group
   communication process when they feel they want to, and
2. they may choose to contribute to that aspect of the problem
   for which they feel best qualified.

When to Use the Delphi Method

Delphi and similar methods have not been developed to be used in routine meetings, or meetings set up, for example, specifically for coordination, bargaining or negotiation.

Before deciding whether or not the Delphi Method should be used, it is very important to consider thoroughly the context within which the method is to be applied (Delbecq *et al.* 1975). A number of questions need to be asked before making the decision of selecting or ruling out the Delphi technique:

- What kind of group communication process is desirable in order to explore the problem at hand?
- Who are the people with expertise on the problem and where are they located?
- What are the alternative techniques available and what results can reasonably be expected from their application?

Only when the above questions are answered can one decide whether the Delphi Method is appropriate to the context in which it will be applied. Failure to address the above questions may lead to inappropriate applications of Delphi and discredit the whole creative effort. Moreover, one has to recognise that the decision to use the Delphi Method does not guarantee, by itself, that Delphi will work. On the surface, the Delphi Method appears to be a straightforward and easy method. As pointed out in Chapter 2, it is often very common, even today, for people to come to a wrong view of the Delphi Method that reflects a misconception of what the technique can achieve, and the process involved. The risk is, therefore, that of jumping at the technique without carefully examining its requirements and considering alternative approaches.

Techniques Similar to Delphi:
NGT and Cross Impact Analysis

Several techniques are similar to the Delphi Method. Amongst these, the most important are Cross Impact Analysis and the Nominal Group Technique (NGT).

When the Delphi Method is used to forecast future events, one of its drawbacks is that it tends to treat each component of the analysis individually as an independent variable. Cross Impact Analysis minimises this drawback. Here, events, or other components of the analysis, are not only independently assessed but evaluated in relation to each other. For example, event 'A' as well as event 'B' may have a relatively low probability of occurrence, but the probability of event 'B' may be increased if event 'A' is realised. Cross Impact Analysis therefore provides analytical depth in forecasting as well as sensitivity and consistency of the analysis (Coates 1974; Duval *et al.* 1974).

In soliciting experts' judgement, NGT involves a process similar to the Delphi Method. It comprises phases of independent idea generation, structured feedback, and independent mathematical judgement (Gustafson *et al.* 1973; Scholters 1990). A structured group meeting of an NGT application generally proceeds along the lines summarised in Table 1.1.

Table 1.1 Stages in an NGT Process

(1) Silent generation of ideas in writing.

(2) Round-robin feedback from group members to record each idea in a terse phrase on a flip chart.

(3) Discussion of each recorded idea for clarification and evaluation.

(4) Individual voting on priority ideas with the group decision being mathematically derived through rank-ordering or rating.

(5) Discussion of the preliminary vote.

(6) Final vote and outcome of the meeting.

Source: Adapted from Delbecq *et al.* 1975, Ch. 3

Like the Delphi Method, NGT is used for aggregating group judgement and for distilling information on highly complex problems characterised by uncertainty. NGT refers to processes which bring experts together and combines both non-verbal and verbal stages within a highly structured communication procedure. In the last two decades, NGT has gained extensive recognition and has been widely applied in industry, education, government and, increasingly, in public health (Delbecq *et al.* 1975; Bertin 1990; Scholters 1990).

The seminal work of Delbecq *et al.* (1975) still remains the best literature source for conducting an NGT process. Readers interested in NGT processes are therefore recommended to refer to this publication.

Finally, it should be noted that NGT and Cross Impact Analysis as well as simulations and surveys can be used in combination with the Delphi Method. Some of the Delphi applications described in Part 2 of this book (see Chapters 6 and 9) are examples of effective combined use of these techniques.

Methodological Considerations in the Delphi Process

Any research method inevitably generates criticism as well as consensus. The Delphi Method has been criticised (often unfairly) for not using 'scientific' procedures in terms of sampling and testing of results through conventional experimental control.

The most extensive critique of the Delphi Method was made by Sackman (1974). In his report Sackman raises an indignant voice: 'The future is far too important for the human species to be left to fortune tellers using new versions of old crystal balls. It is time for the oracle to move out and science to move in.'.

Goldschmidt (1975) successfully demonstrated that most of the criticisms made by Sackman were unfair. In his meticulously researched article, Goldschmidt agrees that there have been many poorly conducted Delphi projects. For example, Delphi questionnaires are often poorly constructed, not pre-tested and often include ambiguous questions. Goldschmidt, however, warns that it is a fundamental mistake to equate the applications of the Delphi Method with the Delphi Method itself, as too many critics do. There is, in fact, an important conceptual distinction between evaluating a technique and evaluating an application of a technique.

Linstone (1975, p.573) argued against Sackman's criticism that the very nature of the Delphi Method is somehow unscientific. He maintained that:

> Science to Sackman means psychometrically trained social scientists...it is in the same vein as the illusion that science is 'objective', that only Lockean or Leibnizian inquiring systems are legitimate, and that subjective or Bayesian probability is heretical. Orthodoxy faced with new paradigms often responds with sweeping condemnations and unwitting distortions.

While Delphi designers may be accused of ignoring experimental scientific rigour, they are meeting a demand that cannot otherwise be met (Turoff 1975). There is no reason why the Delphi Method should be less methodologically robust than techniques such as interviewing, case study analysis or behavioural simulations, which are now widely accepted as tools for policy analysis, and the generation of ideas and scenarios.

It is, however, important to avoid hailing the Delphi Method as a panacea. The limits as well as the strong points of the Method must be understood. A number of methodological considerations are, therefore, worth exploring before using the technique.

Selection of Panellists and Expert Group Size

In most cases, the criterion for deciding on sample size for constructing a Delphi panel is not (and cannot be) a statistical one. The size of
the expert panel will be variable. The literature on this subject suggests that with a homogeneous group of experts good results can be
obtained even with small panels of 10–15 individuals. In situations
where various reference groups are involved, the size of the sample
may be considerably larger (Delbecq *et al.* 1975, Ch. 4; see also Helmer
and Rescher 1959; Goldschmidt 1975; see also Chapter 4 below).

The effect of group size on the outcome of a Delphi exercise is, of
course, a crucial question in the application of the Delphi Method.
Experiments carried out in the 1950s and 1960s show that there is a
reduction in group error (or, in other words, an improvement in the
quality of the group outcome) with increasing group size (Delbecq
1968; Dalkey 1969a, 1969b). It should be noted, however, that above
a certain threshold, including more and more individuals provides
only marginal benefit to the distillation process resulting from the use
of the Delphi Method (Dalkey and Helmer 1963; Helmer 1967).

The selection of 'appropriate experts' must not, of course, be a
matter of mere personal preference. On the contrary, it must follow a
procedure governed by explicit criteria. These criteria may vary from
one application to another, depending on the aims and context within
which the Delphi process is carried out. Nevertheless 'expertise' is
usually the key requirement in selecting members for a Delphi panel.
The first component of expertise is, of course, knowledge and practical engagement with the issues under investigation. Another criterion is the capacity and willingness of selected experts to contribute
to the exploration of a particular problem. Other criteria for selection
include assurance from experts that sufficient time will be dedicated
to the Delphi exercise. Skill in written communication and in expressing priorities through voting procedures can also represent criteria
for selection.

Finally, it should be noted that the definition of 'experts' varies
according to the context and field of interest in which the Delphi
Method is going to be applied. Being an expert entails the acquisition
of experience, special skill in or knowledge of a particular subject.
Experts selected for participation in a Delphi process do not necessarily need to have standard academic qualifications such as First
Class Honours degrees and PhDs.

What Delphi Method designers must ensure is that the experts
selected will produce responses which are rather more meaningful
than if just anyone filled out the questionnaire (Goldschmidt 1975).
Let us assume, for example, that the aim of the Delphi exercise is to

identify and prioritise criteria for assessing the quality of hospital care. In this context the judgement of both providers and receivers of care is salient. Thus, a panel comprising members with medical expertise and of lay patients (i.e. individuals who have been through the experience of hospitalisation) may be selected. Patient-defined criteria for quality of care can be quite different (yet salient to the purpose of the Delphi exercise) from those identified by medical experts. Both types of expertise (lay and medical) are meaningful for developing quality of care indicators which go beyond narrowly defined clinical criteria.

Reliability of Delphi Outcomes

Users of the Delphi Method recognise a need for structuring a group communication exchange in order better to explore or assess the nature of a problem and possible policies to address it. In the introduction to their book, Linstone and Turoff (1975, p.5) point out that underlying the decision to use the Delphi Method and similar group judgmental techniques lies a deeper question: 'Is it possible, via structured group communications, to create any sort of collective human intelligence?' In other words, how can one tell that results and considerations resulting from the Delphi process are superior to those made by single experts or individuals involved in unstructured group communication?

There are no cut-and-dried answers to these questions (which are dealt with in Chapters 2 and 3). The theoretical assumption of the Delphi Method is that informed group judgements, achieved through the methodological procedures associated with the Delphi Method, are more reliable than individual judgement (Helmer 1963 and 1964; Brown and Helmer 1964; Dalkey 1969a and 1969b).

The issues of reliability and the definition of expert were addressed at the RAND Corporation, mainly by the work of Helmer (1963 and 1964); Brown and Helmer (1964); Rescher (1969); and Dalkey (1969a, 1969b and 1969c). The key question here was whether the process used in a Delphi exercise produces better quality in terms of informed judgement than, for example, traditional face-to-face interactive groups.

A number of experiments, carried out mainly in the 1960s and 1970s, have demonstrated that for subject matter where the best available information is the judgement of knowledgeable individuals, the Delphi Method has distinct advantages over traditional group discussions, conferences, brainstorming and other interactive group processes (Dalkey 1969a, 1971 and 1975; Dalkey and Rourke 1971;

Dahl 1974; Scheibe *et al.* 1975). This is because the Delphi Method involves a systematic process of querying and aggregating experts' judgements. Some of these experiments have been reviewed by Riggs (1983) and Pill (1971).

Unfortunately, since the mid-1970s very few experiments comparing the outcome of Delphi applications with other techniques have been reported in the literature. Thus, most publications on this subject are by now quite out of date. In the last decade there has been practically no major publication addressing fundamental theoretical, methodological and practical issues associated with Delphi processes. This is despite the fact that over the years there have been many developments in inquiry strategies, scaling and rating methods and in information technology of considerable significance for the Delphi Method.

There are several reasons for this apparent 'academic silence' on the Delphi Method. One of these reasons is probably related to a concomitant change in research priorities and the preference for discipline-oriented research grants in both the USA and Europe. As the Delphi Method does not belong to any specific branch of science, it has proved difficult to secure funding for researchers working on group processes such as Delphi. Dahl (1974) rightly points out that from the 1950s throughout the 1960s and early 1970s there was a much greater institutional interest in group techniques and processes – small group techniques in particular. This interest was reflected in the availability of research grants, the development of experiments, the publication of books and articles, and the organisation of conferences, workshops and training seminars. It was during this period that small group techniques for decision-making such as, for example, T-Group and Transactional Analysis, were tested (Strodtbeck and Hare 1954). In the same period Nominal Group Technique (Delbecq *et al.* 1975) and Delphi (Dalkey and Helmer 1963; Dalkey 1967, 1969c) and variants of Delphi such as Policy Delphi (Turoff 1970, 1975) and Committee Delphi (Dahl 1974) were also developed.

Another reason for the lack of experimental work on Delphi versus other techniques is that Delphi processes are, by definition, concerned with the utilisation of experts' opinions. Experts are rarely available as experimental laboratory subjects. Delphi applications, therefore, are carried out almost entirely without experimental controls. There is undoubtedly room for further investigation and experimental work in this area. One can agree with Helmer (1975, pp.19–20) when he concludes that:

> Further solidification of the Delphi technique, based on careful experimentation, clearly would be desirable, especially in view

of far-reaching applications... Amongst these, particular attention is deserved by the following two... The first such application
consists in the employment of Delphi surveys to provide judgmental input data for use in studies in the social science area, in
cases where hard data are unavailable or too costly to obtain...
The other major application of the Delphi...is to the process of
gathering expert opinions among the nation-wide 'advice community' on which governmental decision-makers frequently rely.
In this mode of application, Delphi can be of considerable utility,
both systematising the process and by lending greater objectivity
to its 'adversary' aspects.

Instructions to Experts

Clear instructions to experts involved in responding to a Delphi
questionnaire can help increase the reliability of their responses.
Instructions such as those in Table 1.2 are often used to provide a way
of collecting information on the extent to which experts feel confident
about the various tasks assigned in a given Delphi exercise (e.g. the
probability of occurrence of a specific event; the probability of resolving a given policy issue; the relevance of comments made; etc.). Thus,
they indirectly offer a measurement of experts' perceived reliability
and accuracy in performing assigned tasks in Delphi questionnaires.

Table 1.2 Expert's self-reported confidence in fulfilling the assigned tasks

For each response given to the items in the questionnaire, please rate your
subjective judgement, i.e. your confidence of being accurate in the contribution you have made.
The following scale is designed to guide your subjective judgements.

(1) Very Probable 99–80% confidence of being right	**(2) Probable** 79–60% confidence of being right
(3) Either Way 59–40% confidence of being right	**(4) Improbable** 39–20% confidence of being right
(5) Very Improbable 19–0% confidence of being right	**(6) No Judgement**

Source: Adapted from Jillson 1975

When the Delphi Method involves experts from different countries a problem may arise due to language. Although the great majority of experts in the fields of public health and social policy are usually very fluent in English, the choice of the language to be used is a crucial one. If the Delphi designers (i.e. the team in charge of developing and analysing the Delphi questionnaires) can cater for excellent and readily available translation facilities, experts could be allowed to give responses in their own mother tongue. However, it is seldom possible to offer this freedom of response either because of time constraints or cost.

Table 1.3 Example of instructions for improving homogeneity of language

Dear Panellist,
In your comments you are free to make any judgement you think appropriate. In order to increase the homogeneity of the judgmental task some key-words are suggested below.

Certain	*Risky*
• Low risk of being wrong.	• Substantial risk of being wrong.
• Most inferences drawn from this will be true.	• Not willing to make a decision on this alone.
	• Many incorrect inferences can be drawn.
Reliable	*Unreliable*
• Slight risk of being wrong.	• Great risk of being wrong.
• Willingness to make a decision based upon this.	• Worthless as a decision basis.
• Assuming this to be true but recognising the possibility of a small margin of error.	
	Not pertinent
	• Whether assertion is certain or unreliable, it has no significance for the basic issue.
	No judgement
	• No knowledge to judge this issue.

Source: Adapted from Turoff 1975

In running a Delphi process it is important to minimise possible misunderstandings or 'fuzzy' contributions. The effectiveness of information exchanges and the reliability of the assessments requested from experts can be increased by providing key words and clear instructions for carrying out the tasks required. Instructions such as those in Table 1.3 are often given for the reason that they both allow experts to think about the degree of confidence with which they accomplish certain required tasks in the Delphi process, and increases the homogeneity of language used.

Key words and instructions for rating items on the Delphi questionnaires are particularly important for the Policy Delphi. In the Policy Delphi, many tasks requested from experts are related to an assessment of the desirability and feasibility of resolving a given policy issue. The work of Turoff (1975), Jillson (1975), and Ziglio (1985) provide examples of scales for rating desirability and feasibility. Some of these scales are reported in Appendix 6 (see also the Delphi application described in Chapter 7 below).

In using the Delphi Method it should always be remembered that the characteristics of the design of the process (e.g. the methods of collecting experts' opinions, the scales used, the feedback provided, etc.) can have important effects on both the nature of the communication process amongst panellists and final outcomes (Scheibe *et al.* 1975). Hence, instructions, scales and any other device used to collect experts' judgements should be properly pre-tested. The same should be done for different ways available to the Delphi team of providing feedback to the experts on their responses to previous Delphi questionnaires.

New Tools for the Delphi Technique

Since its first use, many innovations are now available to enrich Delphi processes ranging from the use of fax machines to computerised Delphi as a substitute for traditional mail questionnaires. Furthermore, as demonstrated in several case studies in Part 2, experience has been gained in combining the Delphi technique with other research methods such as social surveys, NGT, Cross Impact Analysis and various types of simulations.

A Delphi process should provide experts with opportunities for a deep understanding of each other's thinking, assessments and forecast assumptions. In other words, in order to be effective, a Delphi process needs to facilitate in-depth conversation among experts. This need is even greater for Delphi applications aiming to generate information for problem solving and the exploration of policy options.

In-depth conversation is, however, a big challenge in any form of communication – Delphi processes included. In any group exchange there are problems in fostering deep mutual understanding caused by differing status, assumptions, values, backgrounds and areas of expertise of group members. In Chapter 2 below, Rotondi and Gustafson rightly point out that due to the nature of a Delphi process, the necessity of relatively brief written comments and long delays between responses can limit the chances for critically exploring participants' ideas and revealing their underlying rationale. A key challenge for those engaged in applying the Delphi Method is, therefore, to find ways of promoting enough depth of communication amongst experts so as to create the understanding needed to produce high quality contributions to the process.

According to Rotondi and Gustafson (Chapter 2 below, see also Gustafson *et al.* 1992), in order to increase the chance that a group's conversation will be creative and lead to synergistic thinking, the members should be united in their efforts to accomplish their task. They suggest that a 'straw model' should be developed to promote deep conversation in a Delphi process. A straw model defines the parameters of the task and presents a perspective on how the task can be accomplished. It allows better identification of the underlying assumptions and values in operation during the Delphi process.

Although the Delphi Method is commonly applied using a paper-and-pencil communication process among groups in which the members are dispersed in space and time, an additional opportunity has now been introduced in the form of Computer-Mediated Communication Systems (Hiltz and Turoff 1978; Rice and Associates 1984; Turoff 1989, 1991). As explained in Chapter 3, these are computer systems that support group communications either in a synchronous (Group Decision Support Systems) or an asynchronous (Computer Conferencing) manner. Methodological procedures that were developed and refined in the evolution of the Delphi Method (e.g. anonymity, voting) are incorporated as basic features of many of these computer-based systems.

Conclusions

The Delphi Method represents a method for structuring a communication process amongst experts. It allows a group of experts, as a whole, to deal with a complex problem systematically. Linstone and

Turoff (1975, p.3) point out that to accomplish this 'structured communication' the Delphi Method allows for: feedback of individual contributions; assessment of group judgement; opportunity for experts to revise views and reassess previous contributions; and, if necessary, provision of some degree of anonymity for the individual responses. These elements are generally not available in traditional face-to-face interactive meetings (Dahl 1974, pp.47–48; Goldschmidt 1975).

This chapter has argued that the Delphi Method has numerous applications in the fields of public health and social policy. It can produce very useful information and support decision-making in either the paper and pencil mode or computer-mediated format. Delphi results can be utilised in combination with face-to-face meetings and NGT, simulations, Cross Impact Analysis, policy and decision conferencing and the like.

In concluding this chapter the following points can be made:

- The Delphi Technique attempts to draw on a wide reservoir of knowledge, experience and expertise in a **systematic manner** instead of relying on *ad hoc* communications with selected individuals.

- The Delphi Method should be used when the primary source of information sought is **informed judgement.** In other words, where there is uncertainty on both the nature of the problem under investigation and the possible policy measures for addressing it effectively and efficiently; and where existing information on the magnitude of the problem is not available or is too costly to provide.

- There are many instances in social policy and public health where decisions would require knowledge which is not readily available. In these situations decision-makers must rely on the **opinion of experts**. A challenge for decision-makers is how to secure such expert opinion, and how to reconcile different opinions about the subject matter. Delphi processes are one way of meeting this challenge.

- A Delphi exercise, properly managed, can be a **highly motivating task** for respondent experts. If Delphi designers are imaginative in their analysis, feedback and construction of the sequential questionnaires, the Delphi Method can provide a novel and interesting way of exchanging and distilling information from the experts involved.

- **Anonymity** in carrying out the Delphi exercise and a number of measures can be adopted to improve group response and to allow a sharing of responsibility that can be refreshing and release respondents from inhibitions.

- In almost every application of the Delphi Method, concerns arise regarding its value and usefulness as a tool for inquiry. These concerns centre mainly around the **credibility of the results** arrived at through the Delphi process. While these concerns are real and valid, they do not apply exclusively to the Delphi Method, but to any form of exchange of information from interactive meetings to interviewing; from conferences to *ad hoc* working groups. In generating new ideas, exploring future scenarios and improving informed judgement on particular problems characterised by uncertainty, the Delphi Method, if properly conducted, usually generates a better outcome than traditional face-to-face interactive communication.

- The Delphi Technique has some **specific merits** in eliciting and processing judgmental information. According to the literature (Dahl 1974, Ch. 3; Delbecq *et al.* 1975 Ch. 4; Goldschmidt 1975; Turoff 1975; Linstone 1984, pp.227–229), the merits of the Delphi Method can be summarised as follows:

  it focuses attention directly on the issue under investigation;

  it provides a framework within which individuals with diverse backgrounds or in remote locations can work together on the same problem;

  it minimises the tendency to follow-the-leader and other psychological and professional barriers to communication;

  it provides an equal opportunity for all experts involved in the process; and

  it produces precise documented records of the distillation process through which informed judgement has been achieved.

- Recent developments both in the area of **computer-mediated communication** and in the methods for building **straw models** can have a tremendous impact on minimising some of the weaknesses of the Delphi Method. In particular, these development can: reduce the time-consuming activities involved in a Delphi process; improve facilities for including explicit procedures for synthesising experts' contributions; and increase the opportunities for allowing side conversations amongst experts.

References

Bond, S. and Bond, J. (1982) 'A Delphi survey of clinical nursing research priorities.' *Journal of Advanced Nursing 7*, 565–575.

Brouwer, J.J. and Schreuder, R.F. (eds) (1986) *Scenarios and Other Methods to Support Long-Term Health Planning: Theory and Practice.* Proceedings and Outcome of a STG/WHO workshop, Noordwijk, the Netherlands, 14–16 October, 1986. Rijswijk: STG (Stuurgroep Toekomstscenario's Gezondheidszorg. Steering Committee on Future Health Scenarios).

Brown, B. and Helmer, O. (1964) *Improving the Reliability of Estimates Obtained from Consensus of Experts*, p.2986. Santa Monica, CA: The RAND Corporation.

Coates, J.F. (1974) 'Some methods and techniques for comprehensive impact assessment.' *Technological Forecasting and Social Change 6*, 341–357.

Dahl, A.W. (1974) 'Delphic and interactive committee processes in a comprehensive health planning advisory council: a comparative case study.' Unpublished PhD thesis. Baltimore, MD: Johns Hopkins University School of Hygiene and Public Health.

Dalkey, N.C. (1967) *Delphi*. Santa Monica, CA: The RAND Corporation (P-3704).

Dalkey, N.C. (1968) *Predicting the Future.* Santa Monica, CA: The RAND Corporation (P-3948).

Dalkey, N.C. (1969a) 'An experimental study of group opinion: the Delphi Method.' *Futures 1*, 5, 408–426.

Dalkey, N.C. (1969b) 'Analysis from a group opinion.' *Futures 1*, 6, 541–551.

Dalkey, N.C. (1969c) *The Delphi Method: An Experimental Study of Group Opinion.* Santa Monica, CA: The RAND Corporation (Rm 5888-PR).

Dalkey, N.C. (1971) *Comparison of Group Judgement Techniques with Short-Range Predictions and Almanac Questions.* New York: The RAND Corporation (R-678).

Dalkey, N.C. (1975) 'Toward a theory of group estimation.' In H.L. Linstone and M. Turoff (eds) (1975) *The Delphi Method: Techniques and Applications.* Reading, MA: Addison-Wesley.

Dalkey, N.C. and Helmer, O. (1963) 'An experimental application of the Delphi Method to the use of experts.' *Management Science 9*, 458–467.

Dalkey, N.C. and Rourke, D.I. (1971) *Experimental Assessment of Delphi Procedures with Group Value Judgements*. Santa Monica, CA: The RAND Corporation.

Delbecq, A.L. (1968) 'The world within the span of control.' *Business Horizons*, August.

Delbecq, A.L., Van de Ven, A.H. and Gustafson, D.H. (1975) *Group Techniques for Program Planning: A Guide to Nominal Group and Delphi Processes*. Glenview, IL: Scott-Foreman and Co.

Duval, A., Fontela, E. and Gabus, A. (1974) *Cross Impact Analysis: A Handbook of Concepts and Applications*. Report No. 1, Dematel Innovative Methods, Geneva: Batelle Research Centre.

Garrett, M.J. (1994) 'National future studies: an introduction for policy-makers in the health sector.' *World Health Statistics Quarterly 47*, 3/4, 101–117.

Garrett, M.J. (1995) 'National 21st century studies.' In B. Lloyd (ed) *Framing the Future: A 21st Century Reader*. London: Adamantine and New York: Praeger.

Goldschmidt, P. (1975) 'Scientific inquiry or political critique? Remarks on Delphi assessment, expert opinion, forecasting and group process by H. Sackman.' *Technological Forecasting and Social Change 7*, 195–213.

Gordon, T.J. and Helmer, O. (1964) *Report on a Long-Range Forecasting Study*. Santa Monica, CA: The RAND Corporation (P-2982).

Gustafson, D.H., Cats-Baril, W.L. and Alemi, F. (1992) *Systems to Support Health Policy Analysis*. Ann Arbor, MI: Health Administration Press.

Gustafson, D.H., Shukla, R.M., Delbecq, A.L. and Walster, G.W. (1973) 'A comparative study of differences in subjective likelihood estimates made by individuals, interacting groups, Delphi groups and nominal groups.' *Organizational Behaviour and Human Performance 9*, 280–291.

Handy, C. (1992) *The Age of Unreason*. London: Arrow Business Books.

Hare, A.P. (1976) *Handbook of Small Group Research*. New York: Free Press.

Helmer, O. (1963) *The Systematic Use of Expert Judgement in Operations Research*. Santa Monica, CA: The RAND Corporation.

Helmer, O. (1964) *Convergence of Expert Consensus through Feedback*. Santa Monica, CA: The RAND Corporation.

Helmer, O. (1967) *Analysis of the Future: The Delphi Method*. Santa Monica, CA: The RAND Corporation.

Helmer, O. (1975) 'Foreword'. In H.A. Linstone and M. Turoff (eds) (1975) *The Delphi Method: Techniques and Applications*. Reading, MA: Addison-Wesley.

Helmer, O. and Rescher, N. (1959) 'On the epidemiology of the inexact sciences.' *Management Science 6*, 11, 25–52.

Hiltz, S.R. and Turoff, M. (1978) *The Network Nation: Human Communication via Computer*. Reading, MA: Addison-Wesley.

Hollander, C.F. and Becker, H.A. (1987) *Growing Old in the Future: Scenarios of Health and Aging 1984–2000*. Dortrecht: Martinus Nijhoff.

Jillson, I.A (1975) 'The national drug-abuse Policy Delphi: progress report and findings to date.' In H.L. Linstone and M. Turoff (eds) *The Delphi Method: Techniques and Applications*. Reading, MA: Addison-Wesley.

Ley, D.F. and Anderson, G. (1975) 'The Delphi Technique in urban forecasting.' *Regional Studies 9*, 243–249.

Linstone, H.L. (1975) 'Eight basic pitfalls: a check list.' In H.L. Linstone and M. Turoff (eds) *The Delphi Method: Techniques and Applications*. Reading, MA: Addison-Wesley.

Linstone, H.L. (1984) *Multiple Perspectives for Decision-Making*. New York: North Holland/Elsevier.

Linstone, H.L. and Turoff, M. (eds) (1975) *The Delphi Method: Techniques and Applications*. Reading, MA: Addison-Wesley.

McGaw, B., Brown, R.K. and Rees, P. (1976) 'Delphi in education: review and assessment.' *Australian Journal of Education 20*, 1, 59–76.

Niero, M. (1987) *Paradigmi e Metodi di Ricerca Sociale*. Vicenza: Nuovo Progetto.

Pill, J. (1971) 'The Delphi Method: substance, contexts, a critique and an annotated bibliography.' *Socio-Economic Planning Sciences 5*, 57–71.

Preble, J.F. (1983) 'Public sector use of the Delphi Technique.' *Technological Forecasting and Social Change 23*, 75–88.

Rescher, N. (1969) *Delphi and Values*. Santa Monica, CA: The RAND Corporation (P-4182).

Rice, R.E. and Associates (1984) 'Knowledge reorganization and reasoning style.' In *Developments in Expert Systems*. M.J. Coombs (ed). New York: Academic Press, 159–176.

Riggs, W.E. (1983) 'The Delphi Technique: an experimental evaluation.' *Technological Forecasting and Social Change 23*, 89–94.

Sackman, H. (1974) *Delphi Critique: Expert Opinion, Forecasting and Group Process*. Lexington, MA: D.C. Heath.

Scholters, P.R. (1990) *The Team Handbook: How to Use Teams to Improve Quality*. Madison (WISC) Joiner Associates Inc.

Sing, R.N. and Webbe, B.R. (1979) 'Use of Delphi methodology to assess goals and social impacts of a watershed project.' *Water Resources Bulletin 15*, 2, 136–143 (American Water Resources Association).

Strodbeck, F.L. and Hare, A.P. (1954) 'Bibliography of small group research: from 1900–1953.' *Sociometry 17*, 107–178.

Turoff, M. (1970) 'The design of a Policy Delphi.' *Journal of Technological Forecasting and Social Change 2*, 2, 149–172.

Turoff, M. (1975) 'The Policy Delphi.' In H.L. Linstone and M. Turoff. *The Delphi Method: Techniques and Applications.* Reading (Mass): Addison-Wesley.

Turoff, M. (1989) 'The anatomy of a computer application innovation: computer mediated communications (CMC).' *Journal of Technological Forecasting and Social Change 36*, 107–122.

Turoff, M. (1991) 'Computer mediated communication requirements for group support.' *Organising Computing 1*, 1, 85–133.

Ventura, M.R. and Waligora, S. (1981) 'Setting priorities for nursing research.' *Journal of Nursing Administration*, June, 30–34.

WHO/STG (1988) *Summary of the scenario report on accidents in the year 2000.* Rijswijk, the Netherlands: Ministerie van Welzijn, Volksgezondheid en Cultuur.

WHO/STG (1989) *The Impact of Aids.* WHO/STG Project, Steering Commitee on Future Health Scenarios. Rijswijk, the Netherlands: Ministerie van Welzijn, Volksgezondheid en Cultuur.

World Health Organisation (1994) *Health in Europe.* Copenhagen: WHO Regional Office for the European Region.

Ziglio, E. (1985) 'Uncertainty and innovation in health policy: the Canadian and Norwegian approaches to health promotion.' Unpublished PhD thesis. Edinburgh: University of Edinburgh Faculty of Social Science.

Appendix 1

Example of Instructions for Q1

Dear Panellist,

The present is the first of a series of Delphi Questionnaires. The aim of this Delphi exercise is to explore and assess the numerous issues involved in pursuing a common policy for outcome evaluation of health education programmes fostered at European level.

The Delphi exercise sets out to provide an organised method for correlating views and information pertaining to specific issues in developing a European policy for outcome evaluation of health education programmes.

In this first Delphi questionnaire you are asked to do 5 things:

1. REVIEW all the issues on the questionnaire.

2. MAKE COMMENTS on any issue you wish. Feel free to suggest clarifications, argue in favour of or against issues, ask questions.

3. RATE the level of *desirability* and *feasibility* of each issue according to the rating scale herewith enclosed.

4. SELECT the 7 issues you feel are the most important for developing a European policy for outcome assessment of health education programmes. Assign a value of '7' to the most important. Assign a value of '6' to the next most important and so on, until the seventh issue (the least important of the seven) is assigned a value of '1'.

   (Note that this is merely a preliminary vote. You will have the opportunity to vote again in subsequent questionnaires.)

5. RETURN your response by .... (date)

Adapted from Delbecq *et al.* (1975) and from Ziglio (1985).

Appendix 2

First Delphi Questionnaire

Policy Issue Description	*Comments*	*Vote*
	Please insert your comments here	Your vote here

Issue No. 1
Set up specific training .... D (1) (2) (3) (4) (5)
in project methodology .... F (1) (2) (3) (4) (5)
for health and other pro- ....
fessionals ....

Issue No. 2
Social sciences should be .... D (1) (2) (3) (4) (5)
involved in the evalu- .... F (1) (2) (3) (4) (5)
ation, which should be ....
broader than a mere ex- ....
amination of the effects
of health education cam-
paigns

Issue No. X .... D (1) (2) (3) (4) (5)
.... F (1) (2) (3) (4) (5)
....

Appendix 3

Examples of Instructions for Q2

Dear Panellist,

This is the second Delphi questionnaire aimed at exploring and assessing the numerous issues involved in pursuing a common policy for outcome evaluation of health education programmes fostered at European level.

As you can see, this questionnaire is based on the responses (review, comments, priority vote, etc.) obtained in the first questionnaire.

In this second Delphi questionnaire you are asked to do 5 things:

1. REVIEW all the issues on the questionnaire.

2. MAKE COMMENTS on any issue you wish. Feel free to suggest clarifications, argue in favour of or against issues, ask questions.

3. RATE the level of *technical feasibility* (TF) and *political feasibility* (PF) of each issue according to the rating scale herewith enclosed.

4. SELECT the 5 issues you feel are the most important for developing a European policy for outcome assessment of health education programmes. Assign a value of '5' to the most important. Assign a value of '4' to the next most important, and so on, until the fifth issue (the least important of the five) is assigned a value of '1'.

5. RETURN your response by .... (date)

Adapted from Debecqu *et al.* (1975) and Ziglio (1985)

Appendix 4

Second Delphi Questionnaire

Policy Issue Description	*Summary of previous comments*	*Previous vote*
Issue No. 1		
Set up specific training in project methodology for health and other professionals	In Q1 experts felt that the resolution of this policy was both desirable and feasible. Some of the comments, however, pointed to the complex nature of evaluation of health education:	2; 2; 2; 2; 3; 3; 3; 3; 3; 5=28

'I think this is important but it depends upon the willingness to multiply training at national and local level.'

'A European training could be very difficult to provide given the heterogeneity of context in which health education is implemented in Europe.'

Please insert your comments here	**Your vote here**
....	TF (1) (2) (3) (4) (5)
....	PF (1) (2) (3) (4) (5)
....	

Issue No. 2		
Social sciences should be involved in this evaluation, which should be broader than a mere examination of the effects of health education campaigns.	In Q1 experts felt that the resolution of this policy was both desirable and feasible. From the comments made in Q1, two additional issues should be added to the present questionnaire. These are identified as Policy Issues 2a and 2b.	1; 1; 1; 2; 3; 3; 5; 5=21

Please insert your comments here	**Your vote here**
....	TF (1) (2) (3) (4) (5)
....	PF (1) (2) (3) (4) (5)
....	

Issue No. 2a

| Need for building a con-
sensus on the different
types of data required
for outcome evaluation
of programmes devel-
oped for national and lo-
cal levels. | **Please insert your com-
ments here**

....
....
.... | **Your vote here**

TF (1) (2) (3) (4) (5)
PF (1) (2) (3) (4) (5) |

Issue No. 2b

| Need for agreement on
European baseline data
from which to compare
the outcome of different
programmes. | **Please insert your com-
ments here**

....
....
.... | **Your vote here**

TF (1) (2) (3) (4) (5)
PF (1) (2) (3) (4) (5) |

Issue No. 3

| | **Please insert your com-
ments here**

....
....
.... | **Your vote here**

TF (1) (2) (3) (4) (5)
PF (1) (2) (3) (4) (5) |

...

Issue No. X

Rating Scale for Technical Feasibility

Please rate the technical feasibility of resolving the issues listed in the questionnaire according to the following scale.

(1) **Definitely Feasible**

- Can be implemented.
- No further research and development required.
- Necessary resources (financial, labour etc.) are presently available.

(2) **Probably Feasible**

- Some indication that this can be implemented.
- Some research and development still required.
- Available resources would have to be supplemented.

(3) **May or may not be implemented**

- Contradictory evidence that this can be implemented.
- Indeterminable research and development effort needed (existing resources may be inadequate).
- Increase in available resources would be needed.

(4) **Probably Unfeasible**

- Some indication that this cannot be implemented.
- Major research and development effort needed (existing resources are inadequate).
- Large scale increase in available resources would be needed.

(5) **Definitely Unfeasible**

- Cannot be implemented.
- Basic research needed.
- Unprecedented allocation of resources would be needed.

Adapted from Turoff (1975), Jillson (1975) and Ziglio (1985).

Appendix 6

Rating Scale for Political Feasibility

Please rate the political feasibility of resolving the issues listed in the questionnaire according to the following scale.

(1) **Definitely politically feasible**
- No major political obstacles.
- Will be acceptable to the general public.

(2) **Probably Politically Feasible**
- Some minor political obstacles.
- Further consideration may have to be given to public reaction, although some indication exists that the proposed resolution of this issue may be acceptable.

(3) **May or may not be implemented politically**
- Political obstacles.
- Some indication that this may not be acceptable to a large proportion of the general public.

(4) **Probably Politically Unfeasible**
- Major political obstacles.
- Not acceptable to a large proportion of the general public.

(5) **Definitely Politically Unfeasible**
- Politically unacceptable.
- Completely unacceptable to the general public.

Adapted from Turoff (1975), Jillson (1975) and Ziglio (1985).

Chapter 2

Theoretical, Methodological and Practical Issues Arising out of the Delphi Method

Armando Rotondi and David Gustafson

Introduction

This chapter presents a number of methods to improve communication during a Delphi exercise. Most of them can be applied to any Delphi process whether it is for the purpose of generating new ideas, problem solving or forecasting. However, this chapter is particularly tailored to Delphi applications in the context of problem solving. In such a context, the emphasis is on eliciting key information and insights for organisational and policy change. Though the search for consensus is not necessarily the primary aim in all Delphi processes, it is very relevant in problem solving.

The methods described in this chapter are based on a theory of communication in group problem solving which is outlined in the following section. This theory grew out of experiences with and observations of successful and unsuccessful problem-solving groups, using both face-to-face and Delphi group processes. Based on these observations, a number of generalisations emerged about the character of 'successful' problem solving groups. These include:

- Groups which gain an understanding of the lines of reasoning behind members' opinions have a greater tendency for their thinking to converge than groups which do not.

- When a group's thinking begins to converge, a synergistic group perspective often emerges.

- The creation of a synergistic perspective in a group, and the insights which accompany its development, are more likely to occur when the participants understand the foundation for one another's ideas and perspectives.

- Groups which develop a group perspective are more likely to develop a consensus solution which the entire group can strongly support than groups which do not.

The approach of this chapter is based on the assumption that creativity, synergy and consensus are desirable outcomes in a Delphi application. This is not always so, of course, but these are often important in a Delphi exercise. In order to promote these outcomes, the methods described in this chapter facilitate:

- a more in-depth conversation than typically occurs during a Delphi exercise;
- the development of a synergistic group perspective;
- the development of a consensus solution.

The chapter should be viewed as presenting a 'toolbox' of methods from which one can pick and choose to suit the purposes and needs of a particular Delphi exercise.

The Need for In-Depth Conversation in the Delphi Process

One of a group's strengths is its ability to combine the efforts of individuals with diverse experiences, expertise and wisdom, and to direct these efforts toward the achievement of a common goal. When the individual members of a group unite their efforts and think as a single, coherent unit, their potential for insight and creativity increases markedly over the sum of the potentials of the individuals alone. This added potential which a group offers stems in part from a relationship between synergy and insight. When the perspectives of two or more members of a group combine to yield a third, synergistic perspective, the new perspective invariably yields insights which are advances over what either of the individual perspectives provided on their own. When this happens, a group's thinking develops a life of its own, which is able to take a group in directions outside any single member's perspective, and beyond what any member's perspective could have anticipated. But how is the development of a synergistic or group perspective facilitated during group problem solving, and how can its development be promoted in a Delphi process?

To begin with, a group needs to have an 'in-depth' conversation; in other words, a conversation which provides the participants with a deep understanding of each other's thinking. This means that a group's conversation must go beyond the mere exchange of opinions, biases and beliefs to reveal the conceptual basis for those beliefs; the reasons, causes, rationale and the how and why of each participant's views. This is important in establishing a synergistic group perspective because members' stated opinions, biases, and ideas for implementation may be too far apart to form a common ground for the development of a new group perspective. Opinions and biases are merely abstractions of one's underlying network of concepts. Experimentation (Stillwell *et al.* 1987) and experience have shown that underlying rationales and lines of reasoning between people are often far more similar than their stated opinions might indicate. It is this deeper level of thinking which will form the basis for developing a synergistic group perspective.

A group's communications should thus endeavour to reveal this deeper level of thinking. This point is illustrated by a proverb about a group of blind persons, each of which is grasping a different part of an elephant. In this situation each member of the group knows the part he or she is grasping, each believes that the whole looks like the part he or she is holding, and each feels that his or her understanding of the whole is the correct one. Only when this or any other group's conversation helps each member to understand every member's 'vision' in the light of his or her own can a group build a synergistic vision which encompasses and transcends all of the individual members' perspectives. A group process should thus help the participants to understand one another's perspective in order to realise a group's full potential for creativity, insight and synergy.

To promote the development of a synergistic perspective, a Delphi application needs to facilitate an in-depth conversation among the participants. This can be a challenge for a typical Delphi process. Due to the nature of the exchanges – for example, the necessity of relatively brief written comments, long delays between responses and the limited number of exchanges – the process can lack the continuity and duration needed to establish a conversation deep enough to explore critically participants' ideas and reveal their underlying rationale. Without this vital depth, however, a group is likely to miss the opportunities for new directions in thought and synergy which each participant's ideas offer. A crucial question, therefore, which this chapter will try to answer, is that given the nature of a Delphi process, coupled with the inherent barriers to communication between individuals – differing assumptions, values, motives, backgrounds, and areas of expertise – how can a Delphi exercise promote sufficient depth of communications to create the understanding needed to unleash a group's potential for synergistic thinking?

The next section of this chapter presents a number of methods to promote the development and facilitate the continuation of in-depth conversations in a Delphi application.

Promoting Mutual Understanding in a Group

At the start of a Delphi process, members are often unfamiliar with one another and they may therefore feel out of touch with and isolated from the group. Because mutual understanding is necessary for an in-depth conversation to develop, it is important to help the members gain a good understanding of each other. A certain amount of familiarity and understanding will of course develop during the normal course of a Delphi exercise. However, by the time this happens, a typical Delphi exercise may be over. It can therefore be helpful to employ methods which will facilitate camaraderie, trust and mutual understanding among the members of a group. Two such procedures are presented below.

Team building

The objective of team building is to remove barriers between the members of a group which may inhibit the development of open and in-depth communication. This is usually accomplished by having the members of a group perform a series of activities with each other. There are several relatively simple face-to-face team building procedures (Scholters 1988) which could be conveniently used in a Delphi exercise. The procedure presented here is meant as an example. The activities which are best suited to any particular group will depend on a number of factors, including what is to be accomplished during the Delphi process, the personalities in the group, how well the members know each other and the amount of anonymity which needs to be preserved. This example assumes that the group's members know very little about each other.

This team building exercise consists of a semi-structured group conversation – which could take place using computers as the medium of communication, via the telephone, or even face-to-face (see Chapter 3 in this book). The session begins with members introducing themselves to the group. A simple guideline is to have the members reveal the things which they might like to know about the other members in their group. Following a discussion of these, the members can list their expectations for the Delphi project, i.e. their concerns about the outcome, and what they would like to see the Delphi project achieve and avoid. This session could conclude with a discussion of what the members think the group could do to realise their hopes, and to prevent their fears from coming true.

Team building can increase participants' enthusiasm for a project and help individuals feel closer to each other. This helps to create an environment with fewer barriers to the development of an in-depth conversation.

Reduced participant anonymity

One potential strength of the Delphi method is the anonymity which it affords participants. This can increase the chance that the participants will be truthful, and make it possible for them to express opinions which might otherwise jeopardise their position or credibility. However, absolute anonymity – not allowing the participants to know anything about the other members of the group – can cause participants to feel isolated and make it difficult for them to judge how best to formulate their ideas so that others will understand them.

When conditions permit, there are a number of ways to lessen a group's anonymity in order to help promote in-depth conversation. For example, a biographical sketch of each member could be provided to the group which includes general background information, a summary of the reasons why each member was chosen, and a description of their expertise. This will give the participants a better understanding of their group. If appropriate, each participant could even be identified by name. In situations where greater anonymity is required, the information could be provided in purely general terms. For example, it could reveal that a member is the director of a 500-bed medical facility in the midwestern United States, that she has a masters degree in statistics, etc.

Another method for reducing anonymity could be to assign each participant a unique code, such as a name or a letter of the alphabet. Thus, for example, if a group had 12 members each would be assigned a letter from 'A' to 'L'. Each member's code would be used to label all of his or her contributions during the process. It would make it possible for a group's comments to be presented in a slightly different format than typically occurs. Instead of presenting the ideas from each round of a Delphi exercise using summary statements which make no reference to the contributor(s), it would be possible to identify members with their ideas using the code. This would make it more convenient to provide participants' actual comments or very close paraphrases, rather than combining similar ideas from different members into summary statements, as is often done in a Delphi exercise. This format would allow a group to gain a better understanding of each member's train of thought.

This format would allow a group's contributions to be presented in a form which promotes greater dialogue among the participants by more closely resembling a conversation (see discussion of Conversation Histories). This type of organisation would allow the participants to express more detailed and complex ideas than might otherwise be possible, and thus would help a group to gain more insight into the similarities and the differences amongst members' ideas. This can make it easier for a group to understand where and why they agree and disagree, and help the participants accurately to focus their contributions. The increased understanding of each member's thinking which can result would form the basis for more in-depth exchanges.

It must be pointed out, however, that even identifying members by code has potential pitfalls. If anonymity is important, there are risks in providing quotes or close paraphrases from the participants. The participants may be able to pick up hints about the identity of other members by the way they phrase their ideas. The level of anonymity which is appropriate in a Delphi process requires a good deal of thought. Though it is true that the participants can feel more isolated from each other, and perhaps it is more difficult to develop an in-depth conversation when the process is anonymous, in some situations the advantages may outweigh the disadvantages. It is not, however, always an advantage to conduct a Delphi exercise under absolute anonymity, and there can be clear advantages to reducing or eliminating anonymity.

The Motivation to Participate

Because of the time and effort required to complete a Delphi exercise, it is important that the members of a group are motivated to participate. In general, the more motivated the participants, the more willing they will be to invest the time necessary to complete a Delphi exercise. A number of methods to increase participants' motivation are presented below.

Tension for change

The participants should feel a 'tension' for change, meaning they should be dissatisfied with the current situation around which the Delphi exercise focuses. They should believe that change is essential generally, as well as in their own situation. Tension for change is felt all the more urgently if in addition there is clear evidence that the current situation may deteriorate.

Perceived need of the group

The members should feel that the Delphi group can help them deal with their problem. This means that they truly believe that the situation can change for the better, that they are not sure of the most effective way to change the status quo on their own, and that they feel that a group will help them bring about change.

Thus, members of a group should believe that alone they are unable to bring about the necessary changes to improve the status quo. If the members believe that they can cope with the situation on their own, they will be less motivated to work with a group and devote the time and energy which is required.

Timing

The participants need to believe that the Delphi process is not just an academic exercise or they may be less enthusiastic in their participation. Participants should also believe that this group is in a unique position to change the current situation. It is not necessary that they believe that no other group could do what their group will, just that no other group currently exists which is in the same position as theirs is. Finally, the participants should believe that this is a good time to attempt to change the current situation. This means that the social conditions favour a change in the status quo, the constituents and power brokers are willing to support the implementation of a change, and the resources (time, money, and expertise) are or can be made available.

Ensuring these conditions apply will help improve the participants' confidence that the Delphi exercise is a legitimate vehicle to bring about changes which will alleviate the discomfort felt in the current situation (for a practical example see Chapter 6). A Delphi application works particularly well when a group has a mandate for change from influential individuals, powerful organisations, political parties, etc., and it is helpful if it can include those who are in positions to influence whether the group's recommendations are actually implemented.

Potential for personal and professional growth

One reason for devoting the effort necessary to have an in-depth group conversation is that the participants hope and believe that as a result of their participation in a Delphi exercise they will grow and change personally and/or professionally. These could be relatively small changes; for example, an increase in knowledge or certainty of belief or a change in values, attitudes, or behaviour.

The changes might also be of a less personal nature; for example, a participant may believe that a Delphi exercise offers an opportunity to enhance his or her ability to influence an organisation or the current situation. A person who believes that he or she has good ideas and a valuable perspective on a problem, but lacks organisational power or is not in a position to have his or her ideas realised, may see a Delphi process as an opportunity to exert greater influence than would normally be possible.

There are several ways in which the participants could experience positive change through a Delphi exercise, and it would help to motivate them if one of their objectives is to grow and change as a result of their participation.

Respect for other participants

The participants should have respect for one another's experience and their ability to contribute to the development and/or implementation of changes which can significantly improve the current situation. Thus, not only should the members of a group have confidence in one another's intellectual abilities, they should also have confidence that the group's members will be listened to outside the group, because they have prestige, are outstanding members of their fields, and/or are people who command authority and influence.

Concern for reputation

The participants should be concerned with how they appear to the other members of the group. It should be important to each member to look good to the group. It would increase the participants' motivation if they believed that their personal performance and that of the group could influence how they might be evaluated in the future.

Ability to meet requirements of the Delphi process

The members should believe that they are capable of following through with the Delphi exercise's activities. This means that they must understand how the process works. They need to have a precise schedule of the activities which the group will follow and to understand the strategy which will be used to develop the group's product.

Advantages of the Delphi Method over Other Processes

Not only is it important for participants to understand how the Delphi Method works, but they should also believe that a Delphi exercise is the best way for the group to accomplish its task. This means that the advantages of a Delphi process should be made clear to the participants. They could include any or all of the following:

- For reasons of cost, time, and geographical separation, it is possible to convene a group of people that are of higher quality using the Delphi method than could otherwise be assembled.

- The process allows participants time to think through their ideas, and forces them to write their ideas down before they present them to the group. This is a useful way of having the participants synthesise their ideas because it promotes careful and in-depth thinking.

- Similarly, the process allows the participants enough time to digest a group's comments carefully and thoroughly before responding.

- The process provides a record of a group's thoughts which can be reviewed as needed.

- The anonymity of the participants allows them to express opinions and take positions which they might otherwise not be able to express because doing so in the open could jeopardise their position in an organisation, or their ability to accomplish certain objectives.

- The process has proven to be very effective in a variety of problems and situations. Examples of successful outcomes could be provided to the participants to increase their confidence in the Delphi process.

Because a Delphi exercise can take from several weeks to several months to be completed, it can be difficult for participants to sustain their enthusiasm and concentration if they are not convinced that their efforts will lead to a successful outcome. The participants should thus be confident that the Delphi is an appropriate method for the group to accomplish its task. Helping participants to understand its advantages will help to assure them that the results will justify the time spent.

Developing a Straw Model to Unify Perspectives

If the members of a group have different perspectives on what their task is, how it should be accomplished, or what the final outcome should be, the extra potential for creativity which a group offers will not be realised.

To increase the chances that a group's conversation will be creative and lead to synergistic thinking, the members should be united in their efforts to accomplish their task. A method to help accomplish this is described below. This methodology is based on a process originally created to facilitate the development of quantitative models in face-to-face meetings (Gustafson *et al.* 1991). The methodology has two phases. First, participants are provided with a common background from which to view their task. Next, their individual perspectives on how to solve the problem are used to develop an initial 'group perspective'. This perspective is used to start a group's Delphi conversation, and help guide the participants' efforts during a Delphi exercise. This perspective, termed a 'straw model', is developed from conversations with each of the participants.

What is a straw model?

A straw model is a conceptual model of a group's task. It defines the parameters of the task and presents a perspective on how the task can be accomplished. A straw model can take on many forms, depending on the situation and the task. Two examples are: a flow diagram or decision tree which presents the major decisions involved in the treatment of a patient's cancer pain; and a list of the most important variables, with possible scales for measuring the variables, and bench marks for each scale, for developing a model to predict the chances that a seventh grade student will be a problem user of alcohol by the time he or she is in the tenth grade. It is expected, however, that a straw model will contain areas which are incomplete, inaccurate assertions, and important omissions. This model helps to make a group aware of the areas where they must concentrate their effort during the Delphi process. It is intended to be a target for a group to focus on and direct their efforts.

Purposes of a straw model

When Delphi panellists are involved in a problem-solving exercise, there are at least four main reasons for developing a straw model.

1. It allows the participants to begin their Delphi conversation with a common perspective on their task. This helps the participants to work together toward a common goal.

2. The intellectual diversity of the participants as it relates to the group's task is made visible. The participants are able to see one another's perspective and thus know what they do and do not understand, and where they are and are not in agreement. This provides the starting point for a group's discussion. For example, an oncologist and a surgeon might have different perspectives on which procedures to use in the treatment of cancer pain, and thus they would each emphasise different procedures in their treatment. A straw

model helps to make this clear to the group. Once the members of a group accurately understand each other's thinking, at the level of causes and explanations, they will have an opportunity to develop their collective thinking and thus achieve new insights and synthesise new visions.

3. The straw model is developed from all of the members' contributions. It is a vision of the task which is uniquely the group's and different from any single member's vision, but it has its roots in every member's perspective. Because it is an integrative model, it provides a view of the diversity of thinking present in a group. The straw model establishes for each member that the group's perspective is different, and more comprehensive than any individual member's perspective. It helps to develop the attitude that each member is an important resource for a group, and that the group has the potential to develop a solution superior to that of any individual. The result is a foundation for the members to see the Delphi method as an opportunity to develop a better understanding of each other, and use this understanding to work synergistically to develop a superior outcome.

4. The straw model provides an example of the type of outcome that should be produced and the depth of thinking needed to produce it. The straw model leads directly into the first questionnaire by setting the stage for a group's task. The group must now decide what needs to be conveyed, compared to what the straw model conveys. Once the group determines this, they can begin to move from the straw model to the finished product.

Providing participants with a common background

The members of a group should begin their problem solving effort with a common understanding of the problem, which will serve as a foundation for them to work together. In developing a straw model, most participants are contacted by telephone during the solicitation process. This provides an excellent opportunity to discuss or make an appointment to discuss the group's task. This conversation will help to 'jump start' a Delphi process by giving each participant some background about the task, and by starting each participant thinking about the task.

During the first part of the conversation, the group's task should be thoroughly explained to each participant. For example, if the Delphi exercise aims to develop a solution to a problem, then the specifics of the problem and the solution should be discussed. This might include: why it is a problem; for whom; how serious the problem is; how long it has been a problem; the urgency of alleviating the problem; why this group is being formed to solve the problem and can have a significant effect on the problem; and what type of solution is expected.

Each participant should be given an opportunity to discuss any questions he or she might have about the group's task, including doubts about the Delphi process and curiosity about who the other participants are. All participants should be brought to the same general understanding about the problem. They should realise that the problem is serious, why it is a problem, that the current situation needs to change, and that the Delphi group is a legitimate vehicle to develop a change and/or provide key information towards the resolution of the problem under investigation.

Eliciting information to build a straw model

The information collected during this part of the conversation will be used to develop a straw model, and to establish for the participants the intellectual depth which the group's Delphi conversation will aim for. First, each participant's ideas are elicited about what he or she believes are the 'components' of an ideal solution to the group's task. If the group's task is to develop a solution to a problem, for example creating a protocol to be used to guide the treatment of cancer pain, then each member would indicate what he or she believes to be the ideal cancer pain treatment protocol. If the group's task is to determine the most important unanswered questions preventing policy makers from developing optimal health policies, then each participant should discuss his or her thoughts about what are the most important of these questions.

Second, besides listing their ideas, the participants should also discuss the rationale or line of reasoning for each of their ideas. For instance, in the pain treatment example mentioned above, this would include discussing why each item mentioned is important for an effective cancer pain treatment protocol and how each operates to alleviate a cause of the problem.

This part of the interview could be accomplished in a number of ways. For example, to create a cancer pain treatment protocol each member of the group could be put in a behavioural or operational context. If a member were a health care professional such as a physician, the interviewer could tell the member to imagine that he or she has been contacted by a colleague and asked to give recommendations for the treatment of the cancer pain of one of the colleague's patients. The interviewer then asks the physician for the information which he or she needs to make treatment recommendations for the patient. Once the physician has identified the information, the interviewer would go through the list and find out why each item is important for the physician's decision-making, and how it relates to other items. The process of first listing items and then discussing them should continue until the physician has discussed all the information which is involved in his or her decision-making about the treatment of cancer pain.

This part of the conversation is designed to reveal a participant's underlying thinking on a topic in order to bring the participant, and ultimately the group, to a deeper level of thinking than might otherwise emerge. Especially when members of a group disagree, or have different approaches to solving a problem, they will want to know, for example, 'Why is his or her judgement or approach different from mine?'; 'What causes this person to hold these opinions?'. This type of information will help to identify where members are different, and provide them with the knowledge of why they are different. This knowledge will form the basis for developing the first questionnaire and allow a group to begin its Delphi discussion at a deeper level than might otherwise be possible.

Third, the information collected from interviewing the panellists, including rationales and explanations, is used to develop a straw model or preliminary solution to the group's task.

As an example of a straw model, consider the problem of developing a protocol to guide the treatment of cancer pain mentioned earlier. As a result of talking to all the group members, a relatively coherent and comprehensive approach to the treatment of cancer pain should begin to emerge. This might include:

- a flow diagram representing the decision process;
- six major decision points, including assessment of the severity of a patient's pain, matching the strength of analgesic medication to the severity of the pain, determination of the mechanism(s) for the pain(s), assessment of the need for adjunctive non-analgesic medication, etc.;
- a number of minor decision points associated with each of the major decision points;
- explanations of why each of the decision points is important to the management of cancer pain;
- a rationale which justifies this approach to managing cancer pain, and;

- a set of principles to apply to the problem, e.g. (i) trust the patient's pain reports, (ii) determine the patient's needs and expectations.

The members are sent a copy of this model of cancer pain management. The straw model should come as close as possible at this stage in the process, to what the group might develop by the end of their Delphi exercise. It should be constructed to provide an example of the conceptual nature of the final product, the form of the product, and the intellectual depth that the group's conversation is aiming for.

Side-Conversations

During group discussions it often proves helpful if participants are able to discuss their thoughts with other members of their group. At times, the topics of these conversations, though relevant to the task, will be of little interest to the majority of the group, whereas at other times they might concern an issue that benefits the entire group. In face-to-face meetings, though such discussions might prove to be of great value to the participants, it would be inconvenient and disruptive if 'side-conversations' occurred simultaneously with other discussions. The Delphi Method can provide opportunities for side-conversations to take place without disrupting a group's main conversation. The physical separation of the participants in a Delphi exercise creates a perfect setting for two or more participants to have side-conversations simultaneously with and independently of the primary conversation (i.e. the Delphi questionnaire) or other side-conversations.

A side-conversation would be initiated by a participant sending a comment to one or more members of a group. For example, if the members have some knowledge of one anothers' backgrounds a participant might direct a comment to participant 'X' and participant 'Y' such as, 'I would like to clarify what has been said on such and such an issue, in the light of my own understanding of this particular issue. I have a few questions which you might be able to answer'. The comment would be delivered to each of these two members' facsimile or computer mail boxes (discussed later in the chapter). It would indicate that it was a comment from participant 'B', directed specifically to 'X' and 'Y'. Though this could be 'delivered' with the regular Delphi correspondence, it would be more effective if it was delivered independently so that it would not be restricted to the relatively long cycle time of the main questionnaire. For example, within a short period of time after delivery, possibly one or two days, an entire side-conversation could take place between a few members of a group if the members were allowed to send messages at will. Of course, as explained in Chapter 3, side-conversations can easily and effectively be developed in computer-mediated Delphi.

There are many ways in which side-conversations could prove useful to the development of in-depth conversation during a Delphi exercise. First, they provide a channel which enables each member to speak specifically to one or more members and raise questions, solicit information, obtain further clarification, bounce an idea off specific participants or help a member clarify his or her thinking on an issue. This is especially useful if each member is familiar with every other member's background and expertise. Second, the facilitator could suggest topics for a conversation between two or more members on an issue which the group needs to explore in greater depth. Thus, if a facilitator sees a need to encourage the conversation to go in a particular direction, perceives an area where the participants do not really understand each other, or sees an important topic which is being neglected, he or she could initiate a side-conversation to encourage discussion and clarify the issues. The facilitator could do this by asking, for example, participants 'A', 'B', and 'C' to respond to a specific inquiry relating to the facilitator's concerns. This request would be 'delivered' to these three participants, but the rest of the group would also be allowed to contribute to the conversation.

It is important that these conversations take place with the full knowledge of the entire group. Their purpose is not to exclude members, but rather to encourage and facilitate participation and in-depth exchanges. Any participant should be able to join a side-conversation at any time. The facilitator should be responsible for synthesising the ideas and summarising the conversation for the rest of the participants. After reading the summary, the other participants should be able to access the entire conversation if they want.

Side-conversations allow members to explore thoughts in greater depth than might otherwise be possible. They provide a mechanism for members explicitly to direct comments to one or more participants and for the facilitator to promote greater depth of conversation. The mechanism for carrying out these conversations should be similar to the mechanism used for the main Delphi conversation. All contributions could go through a facilitator and be routed to all members of the group. The time allowed for these could be relatively brief, however, because generally they would cover less material and would not need to wait for every participant to provide input.

Conversation Histories

During a Delphi exercise, participants' responses to each questionnaire are processed before they are sent to the group. During the processing, ideas may be combined, summarised, or paraphrased in order to develop a coherent document. The ideas on a given issue will often be processed in one of two ways. Different ideas on the same issue may be presented as separate and independent ideas. Often when there are differences of thinking on a single issue, there is no convenient mechanism to present these ideas in a form which preserves the group's richness of thinking. This can have the effect of making the group's thinking appear to be further apart than it may actually be. Another strategy which may be employed is to combine a number of similar positions into a single summary idea. This can have the effect of masking subtle differences between members' thinking and thus making the group's thinking appear to be more similar than it actually is. At first glance, a number of participants' ideas may appear similar, but upon deeper investigation they will often prove to be as different as the members are themselves.

When either of these methods is employed before the participants have had an opportunity to study and react to each other's ideas, a group's opportunities for synthesis and synergistic thinking are diminished. A group needs time to explore and understand its own diversity of thinking in order to benefit from it. Thus, a group should be involved in the decision to combine or separate ideas, as part of their problem-solving process. It need not be undertaken covertly by a facilitator.

To promote synergy, a group's richness and diversity of thinking on a given issue needs to be preserved to allow exploration of the similarities and the differences between the members' thinking. 'Conversation histories' are one way to preserve a group's diversity of thinking in a way which can promote synergy during a Delphi exercise. A conversation history is a record of all the comments and thoughts that a group has had on a given issue. Its purpose is to provide a mechanism for members to present more complex and in-depth thinking, and to help make visible the points where members agree and disagree in order to promote exchanges which have enough depth to reveal the rationale behind participants' positions. A conversation history can be organised like a transcript, or a conversation from a drama, in order to represent the flow of thinking.

For example, in round 1, participants 'A' and 'B' might make comments about the same part of the straw model. These would both appear in a conversation history as comments linked to the issue they are referring to in the straw model. Each would have its own code to distinguish it from all other comments, and each code would identify the member of the group who made the comment. In subsequent rounds, thoughts concerning either of these participants' comments would be linked to them. The process would continue from round to round with the goal of allowing the group to reach consensus on these issues. The facilitator would provide synopses and comments after each round to help to resolve the issues being discussed, and to promote the development of consensus.

Conversation histories can help to facilitate the development of greater depth in a Delphi conversation in at least four ways:

1. they provide a mechanism to establish, systematise, and sustain a conversation among the members of a group from round to round;

2. they help to preserve continuity of thought on a given topic;

3. they help to preserve a group's diversity of thinking on a given topic;

4. they allow the participants to present ideas with more complexity and depth than is typically possible.

All four of these help to promote synergy.

Promoting Participation

In the methodology presented in this chapter, the participants in a Delphi process might be identified either with a name or a code, and the discussions would be organised in a dialogue format. Both of these methods are meant to increase the continuity of a group's discussions in order to improve the Delphi Method's ability to support in-depth conversations.

The importance of continuity to the development of depth in a group's conversation brings up important issues for member participation. In the early stages of the discussion of a topic, because some members of a group will have greater expertise or more interest in a given topic than others, those members would be expected to play a larger role in the discussion. However, participants are often at liberty to contribute or not to the various topics which are being discussed, as they see fit. In this respect, participation is by and large unfacilitated during a typical Delphi exercise. Whether participants respond to or even read any given part of the generated material is left entirely up to them. There is nothing inherently wrong with this set-up of course; however, member participation is so crucial to the quality of the Delphi outcome that it should not be left to chance. Simply because a group is not a face-to-face group does not mean that facilitation plays a lesser role, or that it can be neglected.

For a number of reasons member participation should be closely facilitated by the management team. First, if consensus is an important outcome then each member should become involved in the discussion of each topic before recommendations are finalised, because it is more likely that she or he will support the conclusions which she or he has been involved in developing. Second, when all the members of a group are involved, the discussion may be improved as a result of each participant's influence on the discussion. This is not necessarily true, and members should be allowed to play a minor role in discussions which they do not feel confident about; however, the involvement of reluctant, and what might be called 'naive' participants, often improves the quality of a discussion.

Naive participants can also play the valuable role of asking the 'dumb' questions which reveal the implicit assumptions and foundations upon which the arguments of the more expert participants are based. Often these assumptions are so fundamental to the experts' perspective that they do not enter into discussion. Yet these assumptions can lie at the heart of agreements and disagreements among the participants. It can take a naive member to ask fundamental questions which are so important in opening up the avenues leading to the development of consensus. Finally, consistent participation is important for maintaining the continuity of a discussion. In any conversation, whether it is face-to-face, computer mediated or by mail it can be disruptive to have participants continually entering and dropping out.

In order to maintain the continuity needed to sustain conversations, it is important for each participant to respond to other members' comments, especially if the comments are a response to ideas which he or she has contributed, or involve the discussion of an issue in which the member has participated. It should be, of course, the facilitator's responsibility to orchestrate participation. He or she can direct the members to certain issues, and encourage them to focus attention on selected topics. However, the participants should not have the impression that participation is optional. Without everyone's involvement the group will not achieve maximum results.

Monitoring Participant Satisfaction

If a participant begins to lose interest or feels that his or her opinions are not being fully understood during a Delphi exercise, or has suggestions for improving the process, the individual should be able to discuss these concerns with the facilitator. A mechanism for such discussions will help the Delphi Method to adapt to the needs of different groups, to change as a group's needs change, and to let the members know that their involvement and contributions are important enough to allow them to influence the process. Feedback about the effectiveness of the process will help the facilitator to keep the process efficient and focused.

Monitoring the members of a group is not an easy task however, even when a facilitator is in face-to-face contact with a group, because the members are often reluctant to say what they do not like about a meeting or about the group's dynamics. Among the reasons for this are that members feel they will be viewed as 'complainers'; they do not want to waste the group's time on such 'relatively unimportant' issues; they may not devote time to thinking about these issues – especially if they are not asked about them; they may simply not know how to articulate their feelings about the process; or they could be generally happy with the process.

Thus, unless a participant is so dissatisfied that he or she wants to leave the group, it is unusual for individuals to speak out on these issues. This is an area where the Delphi Method can offer advantages over other group processes. In a Delphi exercise, it is not necessary to communicate individual concerns about the process to the entire group. Suggestions and comments can be transmitted only to the facilitator, and these can even be anonymous. The group should, however, have a forum to discuss the issues which arise. In a computerised Delphi process, this would be easy to arrange by having a sub-conversation or a 'conference' dedicated to the discussion of process issues (see Chapter 3). In a paper-and-pencil Delphi exercise, the facilitator could summarise the members' thoughts on these issues after each round, and present them in a special section designated for the discussion of process issues.

Even if these communications are anonymous, it may be difficult to get participants to be forthcoming with comments about the process for the reasons mentioned above. There are a number of ways in which a group can be prompted to think about and discuss these issues. One method is to have participants answer a questionnaire about the Delphi exercise, and allow the group to discuss the results. Another is to contact one or a few members and elicit their impressions. Their reactions could form the basis for a group-wide discussion.

The Medium of Communication

One obstacle to the development of depth and synergy during a Delphi exercise is the lack of continuity during discussions. A contributing factor is the time lag between members' comments and subsequent feedback. Clearly, the postal system can be a slow medium for communication in situations where continuity is important to the process. As numerous successful examples in this book show, it is certainly possible for the facilitator to lessen the impact which postal communication can have on a conversation's continuity by skilled facilitation and careful development of the questionnaires. Computer-based communication is one tool which can help to speed up communications in a Delphi process (see Chapter 3).

Another powerful tool is facsimile (fax) machines. These are simple to use, permit lengthy and hand-written communications, allow figures, graphs, tables, and even pictures to be sent effortlessly, and reduce turn-around time. After receiving and processing a group's fax communications, the facilitator can send the results back to each member via fax, thus considerably shortening the time lag.

Fax is an ideal medium for side-conversations as well. Comments from one member to another can be sent via fax to the facilitator who can then process them if necessary and send them on to the appropriate members. Alternatively, the members could send these comments directly to other participants, and send a copy to the facilitator. In either case the facilitator would be responsible for summarising each side-conversation for the rest of the group.

Computers are excellent tools to store the results of a Delphi exercise as it progresses. The facilitator can send the results from each round to the members by fax to start the group on its task as soon as possible. At the same time each member could be sent a copy of the results via electronic mail to his or her computer. Material generated from a Delphi exercise, including the results from each main questionnaire, conversation histories, and side-conversations, could be organised and stored on computer and referenced for future use. For example, statements from one round which are commented on in subsequent rounds, or in one of the side-conversations, could be referenced so that the group could access this information.

Conclusions

A group facilitator is often in a position to gain insight into the processes which individual members of a group go through in order to develop a perspective which allows them to see eye-to-eye on issues which they were at odds over at the start. It is probably not necessary for every group to go through exactly the same process to develop its own synergistic perspective, but many problem solving groups exhibit a number of striking similarities.

To begin with, the members must be motivated to complete the group's task. This will give them the drive to continue to work with other members even when the going gets tough. They must also develop a conversation which allows the members to explore the reasons behind one another's opinions. Members' underlying rationales for their opinions will often be compatible enough to allow a group to gain insight from different perspectives. The insight members gain from such a conversation will enable a group to develop its own perspective on a task. This perspective will allow a group to reach consensus on issues upon which its members may previously have disagreed. When a group develops a perspective of its own, its conversation is more capable of developing a direction which is able to take its thinking in directions which yield new insights and innovative solutions. For this to occur in a Delphi exercise, the process needs to develop a conversation which can reveal the causes and rationale for each member's opinions and beliefs.

This chapter has discussed a number of aspects of the communication process and how it can be facilitated during a Delphi exercise to bring about certain results. Many of the methods presented here, such as conversation histories and side-conversations, lend themselves to fax and computer-mediated Delphi processes, but these methods are not limited in their effectiveness to high-technology Delphi applications – most methods outlined here could work in mail-mediated Delphi exercises as well.

For example, side-conversations could take place between the members in a mail-based exercise, though participants might be required to mail their comments simultaneously to each other and the facilitator to save time, rather than circulating a single response or mailing the comments to the facilitator for distribution. Also, the discussion might have to be less complex, depending on the time allotted for the entire process, but side-conversations, and most of the other methods presented in this chapter, could be adapted to many different media and circumstances.

It is not necessary to use all of the methods presented in this chapter simultaneously for any single method to be effective. The methods which will be most useful will vary with the conditions of a given exercise. Variables which may affect a method's usefulness will include the number of participants, the duration of the exercise, the number of rounds of questionnaires, the purpose of the process the use which the results will be put to and the levels of anonymity or security that are desired.

References

Gustafson, D.R., Cats-Barrel, W. and Alemi, F. (1991) *Systems to Support Policy Analysis: Theory, Models, and Uses in Health Care*. Ann Arbor, MI: Health Administration Press.

Scholters, P.R. (1988) *The Team Handbook: How to Use Teams to Improve Quality*. Madison, WI: Joiner Associates Inc.

Stillwell, W.G., Winterfeldt, R. von, and Richards, J. (1987) 'Comparing hierarchical and non-hierarchical WGTW: methods for eliciting multi-attribute value models.' Unpublished paper (presented at TIMS/ORSA National Meeting, New Orleans, May).

Chapter 3

Computer-Based Delphi Processes

Murray Turoff and Starr Roxanne Hiltz

Introduction

The name 'Delphi' was never a term with which either Olaf Helmer or Norman Dalkey (the founders of the method) was particularly happy. Since many of the early Delphi studies focused on utilising the technique to make forecasts of future occurrences, the name was first applied by some others at The RAND Corporation as a joke. However, the name stuck. The resulting image – of a priestess sitting on a stool over a crack in the earth, inhaling sulphur fumes and making vague and jumbled statements with many possible interpretations – did not exactly inspire confidence in the Delphi Method.

The straightforward nature of utilising an iterative survey to gather information 'sounds' so easy to do that many people have done one Delphi, but not a second. Since the name gives no obvious insight into the method, and since the number of unsuccessful Delphi studies probably exceeds the successful ones, there has been a long history of diverse definitions and opinions about the method. Some of these misconceptions are expressed in statements found in the literature, such as the following:

- Delphi is a method for predicting future events.
- It is a method for generating a quick consensus by a group.
- It is the use of a survey to collect information.
- It is the use of anonymity on the part of the participants.
- It is the use of voting to reduce the need for long discussions.
- It is a method for quantifying human judgement in a group setting.

While some of these statements are sometimes true, others, such as the focus on 'generating consensus', may actually be contrary to the purpose of a Delphi exercise. It is common for people to view the Delphi Method in a way that reflects a particular application with which they are familiar. In fact, the Delphi Method is a communications structure aimed at producing detailed critical examination and discussion, not at forcing a quick compromise. Certainly, quantification is a property of the method, but only insofar as it serves the goal of quickly identifying agreement and disagreement in order to focus attention on significant issues. Linstone and Turoff (1975) proposed a view of the Delphi Method that they felt best summarised both the technique and its objective: 'Delphi may be characterised as a method for structuring a group communication process, so that the process is effective in allowing a group of individuals, as a whole, to deal with complex problems.' (p.3)

The essence of the Delphi Method, then, is the structuring of the group communication process. Given that there had been much earlier work on the means of facilitating and structuring face-to-face meetings, the other important distinction of the Delphi Method is that it was commonly applied utilising a paper-and-pencil communication process in groups in which the members were dispersed in space and time. Also, Delphi methodology was often used with groups of a size (30 to 100 individuals) that could not function well in a face-to-face environment, even if they could find a time when they could all get together.

Additional possibilities for applying the Delphi Method have been generated by the introduction of Computer-Mediated Communication Systems (CMCs) (Hiltz and Turoff 1978; Rice and Associates 1984; Turoff 1989; Turoff 1991). These are computer systems that support group communications in either a synchronous (Group Decision Support Systems, DeSanctis and Gallupe 1987) or an asynchronous manner (Computer Conferencing). Techniques that were developed and refined as the Delphi Method evolved, such as anonymity and voting, have been incorporated as basic elements of many of these computer-based systems, which can thus be used to carry out some form of a Delphi process or Nominal Group Technique (NGT) (Delbecq et al. 1975; Rohrbaugh 1981).

The proliferation of applications and techniques of the Delphi Method has resulted in confusion due to different names being used to describe the same processes. In addition, there is a basic lack of knowledge on the part of many people as to what has been researched and learned in terms of how Delphi techniques may be properly employed, and their potential impact on the communication process. There seems to be a great deal of 'rediscovery' and repeating of earlier misconceptions and difficulties.

Given this situation, the primary objective of this chapter is to review the specific properties and methods employed in the design and execution of Delphi exercises, and to examine how they may best be translated into a computer-based environment.

Asynchronous Interaction

Perhaps the most important and least understood property of the Delphi Method is the ability of members of a group to participate in an asynchronous manner. This property of asynchronous interaction has two characteristics:

1. A person may choose to participate in the group communication process when he or she chooses.

2. A person may choose to contribute to that aspect of the problem to which he or she feels best able to contribute.

It does not matter what time of the day or night Delphi participants think of good ideas to include in their responses; the Delphi survey may be completed or their computer terminals activated to receive a response at any time. Furthermore, participants can revise and add to their responses over time before sending them to the group monitor for dissemination to others in the group.

A good Delphi survey attempts to address an issue from many different perspectives. For example, questions can be included in a Delphi survey which approach the problem both from 'bottom-up' and from 'top-down' perspectives. This allows individuals in the group to approach the problem in whatever way they feel most comfortable. It contrasts with ordinary face-to-face meetings, and with the environment characterised by face-to-face Group Decision Support Systems, wherein all members of the group are forced into a lockstep treatment of a problem. When the group is considering the subject of 'goals', those who have difficulty dealing with 'abstraction' may feel at a disadvantage, while those who deal better with 'abstractions' may not feel they can contribute effectively to discussions on specific solution approaches. To illustrate: a typical model of a group problem-solving process involves the following steps:

- recognising the problem
- defining the problem
- changing the representation of the problem
- developing the goals associated with solving the problem
- determining the strategy for generating the possible solutions
- choosing a strategy
- generating the evaluation criteria to be applied to solutions
- evaluating the solution criteria
- generating the solutions
- evaluating the solutions.

With all these different tasks involved, it is not surprising that the literature on human cognitive abilities and problem solving approaches confirms that individuals differ considerably in their ability to deal with different aspects of a problem solving situation (Benbasat and Taylor 1982; Streitz 1987). Their approaches depend upon such psychological dimensions as the ability to deal with abstractions, searching for data, operating without data, grasp of concepts, and inductive and deductive cognitive abilities.

In most face-to-face approaches, the group as a whole is forced to take a sequential path through a problem-solving process. The Delphi Method, by contrast, takes advantage of the fact that individuals bring to a group different perspectives, cognitive abilities and problem solving skills to contribute to the solution of a complex problem. The Delphi process attempts to design a communications structure that allows individuals to choose the sequence in which to examine and contribute to the problem solving process. Therefore, the single most important criterion by which we should evaluate the design of a Delphi-oriented communication structure is: Does it allow the individual to exercise personal judgement about what part of the problem to deal with at any time in the group problem-solving process?

Time has shown that providing this level of individual choice in a Delphi exercise is easier to accomplish using a computer system than with the original paper-and-pencil-based Delphi studies. The 'round' structure and the need to limit the physical size of any paper-and-pencil survey place severe constraints on the degree to which one can provide choice at all points in the process. Hence, paper-and-pencil Delphi exercises are usually limited by the 'top-down/bottom-up' dichotomy rather than allowing more complete parallel entry to all aspects of the problem. For example, in a single Delphi application, one might in the first round of surveying explore 'goals' (a top view) and specific 'consequences' (a bottom view). Relating goals to consequences requires developing the relationships inherent in alternative actions and states of nature. These would be put off to a later round. In a computerised environment, individuals could be free to tackle any aspect of the problem according to their personal preferences.

This particular objective of Delphi design – providing choices to participants in the sequence of their responses – is also characterised by two other practices commonly applied to Delphi studies. First, it should be clear to participants that they do not have to respond to every question, but can decide to take a 'no judgement' view. Second, the survey may ask participants to rate their confidence in their judgements, particularly quantified judgements. Allowing the respondents to estimate their own degree of expertise on the judge-ments they are supplying has been found to improve the quality of the estimates made in Delphi exercises (Dalkey 1970). The fact that contributions can be made anonymously also means a person need not be embarrassed if he or she does not feel able confidently to contribute to a specific aspect of the problem.

This advantage of the Delphi Method comes at an obvious price. With material being supplied in parallel, it is clear that a primary requirement is the need to structure and organise it in a way that makes sense to the group (Turoff 1974, 1991; Hiltz and Turoff 1985). The need to define carefully the total communication structure and put it into a framework that produces both a group view and a synchronisation of the group process is the most difficult part of a good Delphi design. We will deal with this in following sections. In paper-and -pencil Delphi exercises, the design team must address this issue in processing the results of each round and producing a sum-mary. In a computer-based Delphi process, this has a somewhat different connotation in that the round structure disappears, and is replaced by a continuous feedback process which may or may not involve human intervention for the processing of responses.

The most significant observation resulting from the above consid-erations is that most of the attempts to understand the group prob-lem-solving process in the computer-based environment are still based on models developed from studying face-to-face group meet-ings. Thus, what are often considered to be 'ideal' group problem-solving structures are based upon the 'sequential' treatment of a problem by a group (Turoff 1991). There has been little work to date in developing models of the group problem-solving process based on parallel and asynchronous activities by individuals within a group. There is a need for a model which integrates the individual problem-solving process with the group process. It is only within the context of such a model that we can come to a deeper understanding of the design process that goes beyond the trial and error evolution of the method that has occurred to date.

Anonymity

Perhaps the property that most characterises the Delphi Method in most people's minds is the use of anonymity. Typically, in paper-and-pencil Delphi exercises, contributors of specific material or evaluative judgements are not identified. This should not be considered a hard-and-fast rule for all aspects of a Delphi exercise, however. Moreover, the computer makes possible variations in anonymity (e.g. use of pen names, required roles, multiple roles, etc.) which are impossible in a paper-and-pencil environment. Before we explore these, we should look at the primary reasons for anonymity:

1. Individuals should not have to commit themselves to initial expressions of an idea that may not turn out to be suitable.

   • If an idea turns out to be unsuitable, no one loses face from having been the one to introduce it.

   • Persons of high status are often reluctant to produce questionable ideas.

   • Committing one's name to a concept makes it harder to reject it or change one's mind about it.

   • Votes are more frequently changed when the identity of a given voter is not available to the group.

2. The consideration of an idea or concept may be biased due to the person who introduced it.

   • When ideas are introduced within a group where severe conflicts exist in either 'interests' or 'values', the consideration of an idea may be biased by knowing it is produced by someone with whom the individual agrees or disagrees.

   • The high social status of an individual contributor may influence others in the group to accept a given concept or idea.

   • Conversely, lower status individuals may not introduce ideas, for fear that the idea will be rejected outright.

In essence, the objective of anonymity is to allow the introduction and evaluation of ideas and concepts by removing some of the common biases normally occurring in the face-to-face group process. Sometimes the use of anonymity has been carried too far. For example, it is important that the members of a Delphi exercise believe that they are communicating with a peer group; individual participants must feel that the other group members will contribute valuable insights about the problem being examined. This is a primary factor in motivating participation (see Chapter 2). It is usual to inform the participants about who is actually involved in the group of Delphi respondents. Only when there are strong antagonisms among group members would one consider not doing this.

Delphi panellists are motivated to participate actively only if they feel they will obtain value from the information they receive as a result of the process. This value received needs to be at least equal, in their minds, to the effort expended to contribute information. This is one reason why blanket invitations to participate in a Delphi exercise that do not specify who will be involved, and what the feedback will be, often result in very low participation rates.

Conducting a Delphi application through a Computer-Mediated Communication System makes more options available for handling the process of anonymity. First, one can easily incorporate the use of pseudonyms (Hiltz, Turoff and Johnson 1986). Without identifying a person, the use of pseudonyms allows a person to be identified with a set of related contributions, giving other group members greater understanding of why specific individuals agree or disagree with certain concepts. For example, knowing all the arguments a person has made for or against a given position allows people better to tailor their own arguments in response, and also allows the expression of more complex individual viewpoints. This coherence is hard to observe or utilise when everything is anonymous.

As a result, it is probably desirable in most computer-based Delphi exercises to impose the default use of pseudonyms rather than anonymity on qualitative statements made in the discussion. In some cases it is also possible to allow respondents to choose when they wish to use pseudonyms as opposed to their real names. The more the individuals know one another and the greater their history as a 'social' group, the more likely that good results will be obtained from allowing participants to choose freely either real names, pseudonyms or anonymity, depending on the situation.

Studies of computer-based message systems have attempted to conclude that the use of anonymity leads to 'flaming' and antagonism (Kiesler, Siegel and McGuire 1984). Most such observations have been based on studies of groups of students with no shared history or knowledge of one another. Flaming and disinhibition have not been problems among groups that already have a social history or social structure.

When utilising a computer-based system with groups who are not familiar with one another, it may be important to provide a separate computer-based conference devoted to socialising among the group members. This would serve the same purpose as coffee breaks serve for groups working together in the same place. In the computer-based communications environment, it has been observed that social-emotional exchanges can help to facilitate consensus development and eliminate potential misunderstanding (Hiltz, Johnson and Turoff 1986).

While permitting a certain level of identification and familiarity among participants in a Delphi exercise, there remain certain aspects of the process, such as voting and estimating subjective quantitative information, where anonymity is probably desirable to maintain. It is also desirable, however, for the coordinator of a computer-based Delphi exercise to be able to identify people with extreme votes or estimates. In this way the facilitator can encourage individuals holding extreme views to explain them, which they may be reluctant to do if they perceive they are in a minority position.

In some cases it may be desirable to allow voters to be identified; for example, in the final stages of a budget-allocation task, everyone should perhaps assume accountability for the final recommendation. Even in face-to-face committees, committee reports where no identified individuals assume responsibility, have sometimes led to a lack of group commitment when it comes to implementing the results. Also, when no one is accountable, more risky recommendations may be made than would result if names were attached to them. The decision to identify voters must be based upon the nature of the application and the group. In any case, the identification of a member's voting position should apply only to the final evaluation phase of a group process.

Moderation and Facilitation

Just as in face-to-face meetings, Computer-Mediated Communication Systems require moderation and facilitation to conduct group-oriented communications. However, the nature of leadership in the on-line environment is different from that in the face-to-face environment. In the on-line environment it is much easier to separate the role of process facilitation from that of content leadership. It is also possible to appoint different leaders for different areas of a problem.

In the paper-and-pencil Delphi exercise, every contribution first goes to the coordinator of the exercise and is then integrated into a single summary provided for all participants. Clearly, this is not necessary in the computer-based environment, since individuals can update themselves before making further contributions. Deciding whether or not to screen or summarise contributions before permitting new contributions to be made is a function of the application and the nature of a particular contribution. For example, it may be desirable to withhold certain contributions until the group is at a suitable point in the process to deal with them. Also, information such as voting results should not be provided until a sufficient number of votes has been accumulated. In situations dealing with very strong controversies, it may be necessary to screen and edit the wording of certain contributions to minimise emotional biases and mitigate tactics such as name-calling and insulting remarks. In any case, the amount of duplication is minimised in a computer-based Delphi process.

While much of the material in an on-line Delphi exercise can be delivered directly to the group, specific decisions on disseminating information still need to be made by the person or team in control of the process. In Computer-Mediated Communications, the activity level and actions of a conference moderator can be critical to the success of an asynchronous conference. Specific guidelines for moderators can be found in the literature (Hiltz 1984).

In many Delphi applications, material has been summarised based on the breakdown of the respondents into various specialised expert sub-groups or differing interests and perspectives. In the computer-based environment it becomes possible to consider multiple group environments, or separate communications structures for each sub-group, with the information being synthesised or filtered for passage between groups. This allows very large numbers of respondents to be engaged in common task objectives. A practical example of this is multiple industrial standards groups which must be informed of what is arising from other groups if it has an impact on their considerations, but do not need to be involved in details of the sub-group deliberations in other areas.

There are many Delphi applications where respondents actually engage in taking on roles (e.g. Stakeholder Analysis, Linstone 1984; Lowe 1985) to deal with certain situations. This requires moderator supervision and direction. Associated with role playing is the employment of gaming situations where groups may be in competition with one another and communication is regulated by the game director (Hsu 1989). In the area of policy analysis it could be productive to allow sub-groups which agree about a resolution to have a private computer-mediated conference to discuss possible responses to the material in the main Delphi. Sub-groups could also be formulated dynamically, based on the content of their responses.

Multiple-group Delphi exercises in a computer environment represent a relatively new development and there are no hard-and-fast rules for setting up communication structures in this area. As group-oriented Computer-Mediated Communication Systems become more widely used, there will be much opportunity to experiment with this opportunity for structuring communications at both the inter- and intra- group level.

Structure

The heart of the Delphi Method is the structure that relates all the contributions made by individuals in the group and which produces a group view or perspective. In a computer-based Delphi, the structure reflects continuous operation and contributions. This is somewhat different from the paper-and-pencil mode where the structure must be divided into three or more discrete rounds. As an example, we will describe potential transformations of two simple structures often utilised in paper-and-pencil Delphi applications for use in a computerised environment.

The Policy Delphi

The first example is the Policy Delphi (Turoff 1970). The objective of this Delphi structure is not to produce a consensus, but to expose the strongest arguments for and against possible resolutions of a policy issue. This form of policy analysis provides a decision-maker with the strongest arguments on each side of an issue. Usually, individuals with strongly opposing views are used as respondents. The structure of a Policy Delphi is very simple, as shown below:

Policy Delphi structure

Type of Item	Voting Scales	Relationships
Resolution	Desirability Feasibility	Policy Alternatives
Argument	Importance Validity	For or against a given resolution Opposition to other arguments

In this structure, any respondent in the exercise is free to add a possible resolution (solution) to the basic policy issue, or to make a *pro* or *con* argument about one or more of the listed possible resolutions. He or she can do this at any time. Also, the respondent can vote at any time on the two types of voting scales associated with either of the items. Individuals may also choose to change their votes on a given item at any time. In this structure the two scales are needed to highlight situations where policy resolutions might be rated in such categories as desirable but unfeasible, and arguments may be rated as important but invalid. When making additions of a qualitative nature, participants must also indicate how that addition is related to the existing items.

The computer's role in the process is to organise everything so that the individual can follow what is going on and obtain a group view by:

- providing each member with new items that they have not yet seen;
- tallying the votes and making the vote distribution viewable when sufficient votes have been counted;
- organising lists of *pro* and *con* arguments about given resolutions;
- allowing individuals to view lists of arguments according to the results of the different voting scales (e.g. most valid to least valid arguments);
- allowing individuals to compare opposing arguments;
- providing status information on how many respondents have dealt with a given resolution or list of arguments.

While the role of the Delphi co-ordinator or human facilitator in such a well defined structure is minimal, he or she requires certain software capabilities and designated rights, such as:

- being able to freeze a given list when it is felt there are sufficient entries, so as to focus energies on the evaluation of items entered up to that point;
- being able to edit entries to eliminate or minimise duplications of resolutions or arguments;
- being able to call for final voting on a given item or set of items;
- being able to modify linkages between items when appropriate;
- reviewing data on participation to encourage participation via private messages.

It is also possible to develop rules to allow the computer to handle some of the above functions, but given today's technology, these functions are still better handled by a person. A group using this structure for the first time should go through a training exercise. The Policy Delphi structure can be designed to make it fairly easy to learn and utilise. The use of graphics to support visualisation of the structure of the discussion can also be helpful.

The Policy Delphi structure was first implemented in paper-and-pencil in 1970 and was later implemented in two separate computer versions (Turoff 1972; Conklin and Begeman 1987). It should be noted that the structure of items in a Policy Delphi may also be viewed as a representation of a specialised or tailored Hypertext system

(Conklin 1987; Nelson 1965). Hypertext is the ability of the reader to view the text in a non-linear manner by being able to branch out in various directions of thought at any point in the document. Most Delphi designs, when translated into a computer environment, depend upon semantic relationships among items being established and are utilised for browsing and presenting content oriented groupings of the material. A generalised approach to supporting Delphi relationships within a Hypertext environment may be found in the literature (Rao and Turoff 1990; Turoff, Rao and Hiltz, 1991).

Most Delphi structures can be considered to be types of item (i.e. nodes) which have various relationships (i.e. links) to one another. Therefore, it is possible to view a specific Delphi as a particular instance of a Hypertext system. Hypertext is the view of text fragments in a computer as the nodes within a graph or web of relationships making up a body of knowledge. Hypertext functionality is therefore useful for the support of automated Delphi processes.

The trend model

This Delphi process involves first choosing a specific trend of concern to the group; for example, deaths from AIDS or the amount of life extension expected from a particular medical treatment. One might include in a single study a set of related trend variables. For the purpose of this explanation we will focus on the use of one trend.

In the trend model exercise, participants are first asked to project where they think the time curve will go in the next five years. Then they are asked to list their assumptions in determining this trend, along with any uncertainties they have. Uncertainties are things participants do not think will occur, but if they did, they would cause changes in estimates of the trend.

Since some people's uncertainties are others' assumptions, these are compiled into a list of 'possible' assumptions and every individual is asked to vote on each possible assumption according to validity. To accomplish this validity estimation the group may be provided with an anchored interval scale which varies, for example, from 'definitely true' to 'definitely false', with a mid-point of 'maybe'. The resulting list of assumptions is automatically reordered by the group validity judgement. The ones the group agrees on as valid or invalid are set aside, and the subsequent discussion focuses on the assumptions that have an average vote of 'maybe'. The analysis of the voting has to point out which 'maybe' votes result from true uncertainty on the part of the respondents, and which result from wide differences in beliefs between sub-groups of respondents.

Clearly, in the computer environment, this process of listing, voting and discussing the assumptions can take place on a continuous basis. The voting serves quickly to eliminate from the discussion those items on which the group agrees. The remaining uncertain items are usually divided into two types:

1. those which can be influenced (e.g. improvements in knowledge about the proper use of condoms);

2. those that cannot be influenced (e.g. hospital facilities in the short term).

In the final stage, after the list has been completed and evaluated, the participants are asked to re-estimate their earlier trend estimate. One could observe that a statistical regression analysis might have produced a similar trend curve. However, the application of such a mathematical technique will not produce the qualitative model that represents the collective judgement of all the experts involved. It is that model which is important to understanding the projection and what actions can be taken to influence changes in the trend or in understanding the variation in the projection of the trend.

There is practically no planning task where the above trend analysis structure is not applicable. In the medical field, for example, examining trend curves for the occurrence of certain medical problems and the impact of various treatments is rather broadly applicable. This particular structure has been utilised in a significant number of corporate planning exercises. With graphic capabilities on workstations, it would be easy to implement in a computerised version. A similar structure may be applied to qualitative trends made up of a time series of related discrete events. An example would be AIDS cases triggering specific legal rulings and particular ethical dilemmas.

The above two examples were chosen because they are fairly simple and straightforward. However, there are literally dozens of different Delphi structures that have been demonstrated in the paper-and-pencil environment (Linstone and Turoff 1975) and are transferable to the computer-based environment. Many of these require the ability to utilise graphics to view the complexity of relationships among concepts. Others require extended facilities to utilise generalised Hypertext structures. However, one of the most significant potentials for the automation of the Delphi process is the incorporation of real-time analysis aids for the interpretation and presentation of the subjective information produced in a Delphi exercise. This will be considered in a following section.

Software structures

It should also be clear from the above examples that there are certain fundamental tools that apply across a wide range of Delphi structures. The ability of a group to contribute to building a specific list, to apply specific voting capabilities, and to sort the list by voting results represents a set of general tool capabilities. This is the approach we have taken in the development of the EIES 2 system (Turoff 1991) at the New Jersey Institute of Technology (NJIT) to support a wide variety of applications such as Group Decision Support, Delphi Design, Project Management, and Education (Hiltz 1986, 1990).

EIES 2 is a general-purpose Computer-Mediated Communication System that provides many features whereby an individual moderating a conference can tailor the group process. The moderator can create, at any point in the discussion, an 'activity' that may be attached to a comment. These activities are computer programmes that accomplish different specialised functions such as list collection and voting. However, the interface to all these activities is the same in the sense that the same basic generic commands apply. For example, one may 'do' the activity to make changes to it or 'view' the results of the activity. The conference moderator has the authority to introduce these activities whenever he or she feels they fit within the current discussion. Also, the moderator may choose to allow or deny anonymity for a given activity or conference.

EIES 2 also provides a general capability that can be tailored to notify the participants in a group process whenever any action occurs of which they need to be made aware. For example, a notification may let the members of a Delphi exercise know when the votes on a specific item are sufficient to allow viewing of the resulting distribution. EIES 2 is constructed so that any programmes or analysis routines developed in any language within the context of the UNIX operating system or a TCP/IP network can be integrated or made available through the EIES 2 interface. The major facility that must be added to basic computer conferencing to enhance Delphi processes is the provision of a collection of group support tools, including the ability of the group to build a common list of alternatives, and polling and voting structures.

In sum, the system must also include the privileges for a facilitator or group leader to decide on the dynamic incorporation of these tools in the group process.

Analysis

A principal contribution to the improvement of the quality of the results in a paper-and-pencil Delphi study is the analysis that the design and coordination team can perform on the results of each round. This analysis has a number of specific objectives:

- improving the understanding of the participants through analysis of subjective judgements to produce a clear presentation of the range of views and considerations;
- detecting hidden disagreements and judgemental biases that should be exposed for further clarification;
- detecting missing information or cases of ambiguity in interpretation by different participants;
- allowing the examination of very complex situations that can be summarised only by analysis procedures;
- detecting patterns of information and of sub-group positions;
- detecting critical items that need to be focused upon.

To accomplish the above, there is a host of analytic approaches that come from many different fields. Many of these are amenable to implementation as real-time computer-based support to a continuous Delphi process conducted via a CMC System. We will briefly address here some of the most significant types of these methods for supporting Delphi applications.

Scaling Methods

Scaling is the method of determining measuring instruments for human judgement. Clearly, one needs to make use of appropriate scaling methods in order to improve the accuracy of subjective estimation and voting procedures. While most of these methods were originally developed to measure human judgement, they are easily adaptable, in many cases, to providing feedback to a Delphi group on the consequences of the judgements being made by the group members.

For example, in many cases the appropriate judgement we wish to solicit from an individual is a ranking (i.e. ordinal scale measurement) of individual items. It is comparatively more accurate to ask individuals to rank order items, such as objectives or goals, than to ask for interval or ratio measures. A single person can estimate that a particular goal is more important than another one; but it is much more difficult for a group to estimate this consistently (i.e. Arrow's paradox). However, a scaling method such as Thurstone's Law of

Comparative Judgement (Torgenson 1958) can transform individual ranking judgements and produce analytically a group result which is an interval scale rather than a rank ordered scale. Providing the results to the group in terms of this interval scale allows the group members to detect in a much more reliable manner the extent to which certain objectives are clearly distinct from other objectives, and those which are considered in closer proximity. Merely providing an averaging of the ranking scale does not contribute this added insight to the group as a whole. Furthermore, standard averaging approaches can lead to inconsistencies in group judgements (i.e. Arrow's paradox). This can occur when there are disagreements underlying the averaging and when appropriate 'anchoring' of the scales is lacking.

Standard correlation analysis approaches can be used to determine whether sub-groups or patterns of agreement and disagreement exist across different issues or judgements made in the Delphi exercise, e.g. do the people who feel a certain way about an issue feel the same way about another issue? This type of analysis should, in most cases, be provided first to the facilitator, who should in turn decide which relationships need to be passed back to the group. Many Delphi exercises have identified sub-groups of participants from different disciplines, leading to the question of whether the administrators, researchers, lawyers, insurers and practitioners have differing views based upon their perspective on a new medical treatment. The facilitator must evaluate the utility of these insights in the context of the application. With groups that work together over a long period, it might be desirable to provide such an analysis in terms of direct feedback without facilitator intervention.

Scaling methods span a wide range of techniques, from fairly simple and straightforward to fairly sophisticated. An example of a sophisticated approach is Multi-Dimensional Scaling (Carroll and Wish 1975). MDS allows subjective estimates of similarity between any two objects to be translated into a relative position in a Euclidean space. It provides, in essence, n-dimensional interval scaling of similarity estimates. The number of meaningful dimensions found suggests the number of independent dimensional factors underlying the way both the individuals and the group view the similarity among objects. By looking at the alternative two-dimensional projections, it is possible to arrive at an understanding of the dimensional factors.

The process for using MDS in a Delphi exercise would be to ask for the similarities and then provide graphic layouts of the alternative dimensions. Participants would then be asked to try to determine what these dimensions mean or represent. The result is a very powerful technique for potentially exposing the hidden factors a group is

using to make judgements about similarities. The question of similarity is, one that can be applied to a very wide range of items, e.g.
goals, products, countries, relationships, jobs and criteria. MDS may
also be viewed as a form of Cluster Analysis, and many methods in
Cluster Analysis (Anderberg 1973) can also be usefully applied to
analysing the subjective comparison judgements made by Delphi
respondents.

When a group uses voting and estimation structures over a long
period so that they make judgements about a growing number of
similar situations, it is possible to introduce 'scoring' methods
(Dalkey 1977) into the Delphi process. Given later feedback upon the
accuracy of estimates or the quality or success of a given judgement,
feedback can be provided to estimators on degrees of 'accuracy' or
on possible biases due to factors such as conservatism. At the point
where individuals are utilising Delphi techniques on a continuous
basis, it will be possible to conduct the sort of investigation needed
to develop this particular area as a decision aid.

Designing a Delphi process, whether carried out via paper-and-
pencil or on the computer, includes the process of designing a survey.
In this task, all guidelines for survey design and all analysis methods
are potentially applicable. There is, however, a fundamental difference in objectives, which determines how one employs a given
method, and whether it is applicable in a given situation.

Most scaling methods were evolved to aid in assessing human
judgement on the premise that this is a stable and constant quantity.
One's intelligence or personality would not be affected or changed as
a part of the measurement process. The goal is to discover biases and
inconsistencies and to produce more accurate measurements. In the
Delphi process, however, we are interested in informing the respondents about what they are really saying, and how it compares to the
group as a whole. We are also interested in promoting changes in
viewpoints and the other items we measure, if it will promote a
superior group view of the situation. We also want to detect and
expose hidden factors or relationships of which the group may not
be completely aware. With this in mind, one has to take special care
that the use of these methods of analysis does not convey a false
impression of finalisation in a group view.

Related to scaling is the area of Social Choice Theory, which
provides alternative methods for the summarising of voting processes (Hogarth 1977). The use of multiple methods of viewing the
summarising of a given voting process can be useful in preventing a
group from over-emphasising a single voting result.

Probably the most important single consideration that has in the
past prevented the incorporation of many of the approaches

discussed here is the difficulty of educating participants in the interpretation of the method when they are involved in only one short-term Delphi process. With the potential that Computer-Mediated Communications offers for long-term continuous use by groups, it is now possible to consider incremental training for individuals to gain an understanding of more sophisticated methods.

With the appropriate use of scaling methods it becomes possible to establish that individuals will mean the same thing when they use terms such as: desirable, very desirable, likely, unlikely, agree, strongly agree, etc. It becomes possible to determine which alternatives are truly similar and which are distinctly different. Scaling methods, in essence, serve the objective of eliminating ambiguity in the judgmental and estimation process of a group.

Structural Modelling

The term 'Structural Modelling' (Lendaris 1980; Geoffrion 1987) has come to represent a host of specific methods that have the objective of allowing an individual to express a large set of independent relationships and judgements which the given method utilises to produce a 'whole' model of the 'system' being described. In computer terms, these are methods that allow a user to build a model of a situation without having to program or go through the use of experts in modelling and simulation. These methods vary from ones that provide a simple static relationship model (e.g. Interpretive Structural Modelling, Warfield 1974), to more dynamic probabilistic and time-varying models (e.g. Cross Impact and Time Series Regression). Just about any technique that organises data into some sort of framework is a candidate for Structural Modelling, including Decision Trees and Payoff Matrices.

The objective of these approaches is to allow participants, as individuals or as part of a group, to contribute pieces of a complex solution and to be provided with a composite model. For example, in Interpretive Structural Modelling the individual is asked only to make a series of judgements about each two components of a model (such as two goals) with respect to whether they are related. The resulting complex network of relations is analysed to collapse the network to a hierarchy of levels utilising the existence of cycles within the network to make that simplification. The result for the individual or group is a set of levels or clusters of objects which infer a relationship of higher to lower levels. This provides a graphical representation of the binary judgements made about each set of objects, taken two at a time. This technique takes into account the fact that individuals are good at estimating individual relationships, but they are not always able to maintain consistency in developing complex models. The problem is compounded for group efforts.

The Cross Impact model allows individuals to express probabilities of occurrence for a series of events, and conditional probabilities based upon assumptions as to which events will or will not occur. This is used to construct a quasi-causal model that allows participants to vary the original estimates of individual events and see the consequences on the whole event set.

An excellent example of structural modelling to determine the important relationships and impacts on changes in medical care policies may be found in an article by Vennix *et al.* (1990) where the example is based upon the specification of negative and positive feedback loops. The model was developed through the joint use of a paper-and-pencil Delphi exercise and follow up face-to-face meetings.

All these techniques may be used in a Delphi process to help a group develop a collaborative model of a complex situation. This is one area where the merger of the Delphi process and the computer presents a unique opportunity for dealing with situations of unusual complexity. More often than not, the individual experts who can contribute to building a complex model are geographically dispersed, and the effort to derive and improve such models must take place over time. In other words, improvement of the model has to be based upon feedback from its performance and incremental refinement.

One experiment (Hopkins 1987) produced the very significant finding that it was possible to distinguish the degree of expertise an individual had about a complex situation by the measured richness of the models specified by each individual. This finding suggests the possibility of incorporating automated procedures for rating potential quality or inferred confidence in the contributions made by various individuals. This possibility deserves further investigation, as it would obviously reduce the communication load of future models.

Developing all the structural relationships in models of symptoms, tests, diagnosis and treatment is an obvious area for the application of structural modelling. Appropriate techniques can be utilised on the computer to allow individuals to visualise the structure resulting from their individual inputs and to examine that structure for consistency. At the group level, the same methods can be used to examine composite models for consistency and feedback inconsistencies for further refinement.

A group can improve the nature of a model only by first seeing the results and consequences of the current design. Model building is a long-term, incremental process. The proper integration of Delphi methods, Computer-Mediated Communications and Structural Modelling methods makes possible effective large-scale modelling efforts not otherwise currently achievable.

Delphi, Expert Systems, GDSS and Collaborative Systems

The objective of an Expert System is to capture the knowledge of a group of experts and store it in a computer for utilisation by non-experts. The incorporation of the Delphi Method in computer environments makes possible a number of significant refinements of this objective and some fundamental possible changes to the nature of Expert Systems.

The common approach to the development of an expert system is to achieve agreement among all involved experts before actually coding the knowledge base. At present, this is usually accomplished by a 'knowledge engineer' or team of knowledge engineers, who must link with a team of 'domain experts'. Beside being time-consuming, the fundamental flaw in this approach is that even within scientific and/or engineering fields, there is incomplete agreement among experts. Furthermore, agreement and disagreement are evolving properties that change dynamically over time. The Delphi Method may be viewed as an alternative approach to collecting and synthesising expert knowledge. Within the current terminology, the design of a Delphi exercise is in fact the design of a knowledge base or structure for the collected information. It has also been an important objective of Delphi design to capture disagreements as well as agreements.

Another potential problem area is that experts concerned with a common problem can be in conflict. For example, design, production, and marketing professionals can have severe conflicts about the properties of a potential new product. Different medical researchers have different views about the most promising directions for research. Some of the problems addressed here have been investigated in the work on Multi Expert Knowledge Systems (MKS) (LeClair 1985, 1989). LeClair's work represents one of the few in-depth approaches to incorporating the knowledge of disagreeing experts into the same system. However, this work still assumes the final system no longer incorporates humans, but only their knowledge.

On the other hand, the view that we believe is the most promising is an objective for Collaborative Expert Systems, where the experts are provided with a knowledge structure (a Delphi design) that allows them dynamically to contribute their knowledge to the system and to modify and evolve the system over time. Clearly, such a system is one which the experts must desire to use for themselves as well as a tool for others who need their knowledge. In this situation, the experts are both the creators and the users of the resulting expert system.

Without the above form of expert systems, the only feasible systems are those that restrict themselves to well-established rules and agreements. In our view, the future of expert systems lies in their ultimate ability to be utilised by working groups of experts as a tool for gathering and assessing their collective knowledge about their work.

The current approach to expert systems through the use of knowledge engineers has been recognised as the chief bottleneck to the creation of these systems (Welbank 1983; Waterman 1986) for four main reasons:

1. Human expertise is usually complex, undocumented and consists of many different types and levels of knowledge (e.g. casual knowledge, common sense, meta knowledge).

2. Different experts may solve the problem differently and therefore may argue with or even criticise one another on the method used.

3. There often exists a communication barrier between the knowledge engineer and the domain experts. Often, the knowledge engineer is not an expert on the area under investigation and many domain experts do not understand their own problem solving process. As a result, many details and complications of the reasoning process may be ignored or obscured.

4. Motivation for the expert is often lacking because the results are often delayed or are not intended to benefit him or her.

Many of these problems can be overcome if one can develop collaborative design systems that focus on allowing a group of experts to develop their own expert system in an evolutionary manner and as an aid to their own work. The evolving system could also be tapped by non-experts for use. In that mode it would be considered by the experts as an aid to disseminating needed information to a wider circle of users and freeing the time of the experts for more difficult problems.

A collaborative expert system has to deal with at least four types of knowledge:

1. deductive reasoning as represented by rule-based models;

2. inductive and intuitive reasoning representing experience on the part of experts;
3. objectives, goals, and vested interests which are viewpoints of experts in given circumstances;
4. values and beliefs which often underlie judgements about viewpoints.

The first two types have been typical of current expert systems. The other two areas have largely been the domain of Group Decision Support Systems (GCSS), Delphi and Nominal Group Techniques (NGT), decision and utility theory, and psychological measurement methods. All four of these types of knowledge in a collaborative expert system must handle disagreement among the participants.

The deductive level of disagreement

At the predicate logic level, experts may disagree about both the predicates to use and the rules that are valid in the real world. A well-designed knowledge acquisition and expert environment should permit experts to 'speak their mind' without limiting them to a preconceived vocabulary. It is therefore necessary that the accumulation of the vocabulary for specification of the rules be an integral part of the collaborative process.

Even if experts agree on a basic vocabulary, they often disagree about subtle details of representation. This problem occurs whenever there are several possible reference frames, a situation well documented in the literature (e.g. Sondheimer 1976). Unfortunately, in the current state of the art, two relations with different numbers of arguments are treated by logic programming environments as being two completely different entities.

One approach to this problem is to allow each member of a collaborative group to construct and tailor his or her own knowledge base and then to superimpose a system of analysis for determining various types of agreement and disagreement. Various weighted voting procedures (Shapley and Grofman 1984) and scaling methods (Torgenson 1958; Merkhofer 1987) are promising for analysing this situation. Weights have been used in some expert systems (e.g. Reboh 1983). When such information is being accumulated over time then there are various 'scoring' approaches (Dalkey 1977) that may also be employed and coupled with 'explanation-based learning' approaches (Pazzani 1988). Early work with the Delphi method indicated that even experts in a given area differ in expertise in various sub-domains and that the greatest improvement in accuracy of estimates was obtained by weighting estimates by this type of difference (Dalkey 1970).

The inductive level of disagreement

One of the major problems in designing knowledge representations that reflect common sense models of the world is that the world is not a discrete and well-specified place but is, in fact, quite vague and ambiguous. Ambiguity is the key property that most people have to deal with in reaching conclusions and decisions (Daft and Lengel 1986). Ambiguity results from differences in concepts (e.g. 'expensive') among different people and, in this context, from the collaborative process itself. In many cases the problem of ambiguity can be structured in terms of the degree to which an object 'more or less belongs' to a class. Fuzzy sets (Zadeh 1965; Klir and Folger 1988) are a generalisation of standard sets that allows for degrees of membership. One approach to this problem is to utilise fuzzy set theory to represent the types of ambiguity that result from intuitive thinking.

The major research issue in this area is to develop methods for accurately combining multiple judgements and resolving disagreements about estimates of degrees of membership in fuzzy set relations (Stephanous and Sage 1987). In this instance, scaling methods seem particularly appropriate. Humans are good at ranking (object 'A' scores more than object 'B') but not good at direct estimates of correlation factors needed for fuzzy set relationships. However, various scaling methods can be used to convert a collaborative set of ranking measures to interval or ratio scales.

Another approach is to incorporate multivalent and fuzzy logic (Dubois and Prade 1980) into any model framework where the expert group is building the relationships. An example of degrees of truth and the resulting treatment of logical inference from a fuzzy perspective may be found in Baldwin (1981).

In essence, the problem is the recognition that models that capture intuition have to capture the structure of disagreements. A result is no longer true or false, but possibly a little of both. Rather than a group process being dedicated to eliminating disagreement, the objective is to capture it, quantify it, and integrate it into the collective model. There has always been a bias against disagreement as a part of the result of a scientific process. Because of this we can become blind to the forcing of unwarranted consensus. It would be a far more realistic view of the world to recognise the necessity for disagreements and 'fuzzy' relationships as a fundamental part of any model meant to reflect the collective intuitions of a group of experts.

Goal and value disagreements

This is the area that is typically included in applications of Group Decision Support Systems. While there are certain specific approaches (e.g. stakeholder analysis) for eliciting this type of information, the current state of the art is largely the use of human facilitators to guide the group process for the treatment of this type of knowledge. The fundamental issue of how far one can go in the process of substituting computer facilitation for human facilitation is very much an open issue. Earlier experiments in this area (Turoff and Hiltz 1982; Hiltz *et al.* 1986) showed that under some circumstances computer facilitation can degrade the performance of the group.

The approach that seems to be the most promising is to evolve a collaborative expert system that would be used to guide the meta-group process. This would suggest to the group at what points in the activity they should shift the nature of what they are doing. However, such a facility could also be tailored by the group so that it can gradually adapt to the preferred group process. Such a system would have to employ 'default reasoning' approaches (Post and Sage 1990).

As can be seen, there is no fixed dividing line between such areas as Delphi, Computer-Mediated Communications, Group Decision Support Systems, and Expert Systems. The concept of 'collaborative expert systems' is really based upon the foundations established in each of these other areas. Subjective estimation, collaborative judgement formulation, and voting are strongly related support areas that also contribute to the potential for design in this area.

Conclusions

The Delphi Method has reached a stage of maturity in that it is used fairly extensively in organisational settings in either the paper-and-pencil mode or in combination with face-to-face meetings and Nominal Group Techniques. Since most of these exercises are proprietary in nature not many of the results are reported in the open literature. The one exception to this are applications in the medical field which are in fact actively reported and documented (Fink, Kosecoff, Chassin, and Brook 1984). This clearly is a result of the growing need to formulate collaborative judgements about complex issues that are associated with the production of guidelines on medical practice and decisions.

Computer-Mediated Communications (CMC) has also seen some very significant applications in the medical field with respect to the formulation of collaborative judgements. One of the most significant to be reported in the literature was the use of leading researchers in Viral Hepatitis to review the research literature and update guidelines for practitioners (Siegel 1980). While this was not run in an anonymous mode, it had all the other aspects of structure necessary for a dozen experts to deal with some five thousand documents and reach complete consensus on the resulting guidelines.

Another CMC application with Delphi-like structuring (including anonymity) was a group therapy process to aid individuals in the cessation of smoking (Schneider 1986; Schneider and Tooley 1986). A general review of CMC applications in the medical field can be found in Lerch (1988).

Despite the advances, however, a true merger of Delphi with Computer-Mediated Communications has yet to come. It is only recently that the technology has become generally available to support the high degree of tailoring necessary to structure communications dynamically within a single conferencing system (Turoff 1991). Most conference systems to date have only represented single design structures with very little control available to facilitators and moderators. Also, the general lack of graphics has considerably limited which Delphi techniques can be adapted to the computer environment. The merger of Delphi techniques and Computer-Mediated Communications potentially offers far more than the sum of the two methods.

Long before the concept of Expert Systems it was known that statistical factor models (Dalkey 1977) applied to a large sample of expert judgements could produce performance that was consistently in the upper quarter of the performance distribution curve. Such models did not suffer from 'regression to the mean' and could result in matching the best decisions by the best experts in the group. Expert Systems involving the emergence of tools to allow this to be done on a fairly wide scale. However, the results of Expert System approaches, as currently practised, are never going to do better than the best experts.

The merger of the Delphi Method, Computer-Mediated Communications and the tools that we have discussed opens the possibility for performance of human groups that exceeds the composite performance curve. We have termed this phenomenon 'collective intelligence' (Hiltz and Turoff 1978). This is the ability of a group to produce a result that is of better quality than any single individual in the group could achieve acting alone. This rarely occurs in face-to-face groups.

A recent experiment in utilising human judgement in conjunction with the types of models used in Expert Systems confirms that this is in fact possible (Blattenberg and Hoch 1990). In recent years too much attention has been focused on utilising computer technology to replace humans and far too little effort devoted to the potential for directly improving the performance of human groups. This can be achieved through integration of computer-based methods and the concept of structured communications at the heart of the Delphi method.

References

Anderberg, M.R. (1973) *Cluster Analysis for Applications*. New York: Academic Press.

Baldwin, J. F. (1981) 'Fuzzy logic and fuzzy reasoning.' In *Fuzzy Reasoning and its Applications*. E.H. Mamdani and B.R. Gaines (eds). New York: Academic Press.

Benbasat, I. and Taylor, H.N. (1982) 'Behavioural aspects of information processing for the design of management information systems.' *IEEE Transactions on Systems, Man and Cybernetics, SMC 12*, 4, July/August, 439–450.

Blattenberg, R.C. and Hoch, S.J. (1990) 'Database models and managerial intuition: 50% model + 50% manager.' *Management Science 36*, 8, August, 887–889.

Carroll, D. and Wish, M. (1975) 'Multi-dimensional scaling.' In H. Linstone and M. Turoff (eds) (1975) *The Delphi Method: Techniques and Applications*. Reading, MA: Addison-Wesley.

Conklin, J. (1987) 'Hypertext: an introduction and survey.' *IEEE Computer*, September, 17–41.

Conklin, J. and Begeman, M.L. (1987) 'IBIS: a hypertext tool for team design deliberation'. *Proceedings of Hypertext Conference*. New York: ACM Press, 247–251.

Daft, R.L. and Lengel, R.H. (1986) 'Organizational information requirements, media richness and structural design.' *Management Science 32*, 5, May, 554–571.

Dalkey, N.C. (1977) 'Group Decision Theory Report to ARPA.' *UCLA Engineering Report 7749*, July.

Dalkey, N.C. (1970) 'Use of self-ratings to improve group estimates.' *Journal of Technological Forecasting and Social Change 1*, 3.

Delbecq, A.L., Van de Ven, A.H. and Gustafson, D.H. (1975) *Group Techniques for Program Planning: A Guide to Nominal Group and Delphi Processes*. Glenview, IL: Scott-Foreman & Co.

DeSanctis, G. and Gallupe, B. (1987) 'A foundation for the study of group decision support systems.' *Management Science 33*, 5, May, 589–609.

Dubois, D. and Prade, H. (1980) *Fuzzy Sets and Systems*. New York: Academic Press.

Fink, A., Kosecoff, J., Chassin, M. and Brook, R.H. (1984) 'Consensus methods: characteristics and guidelines for use.' *American Journal of Public Health 74*, 9, September, 979–983.

Geoffrion, A.M. (1987) 'An introduction to structured modelling.' *Management Science 33*, 5, May, 547–588.

Hiltz, S.R. (1984) *On-line Communities: A Case Study of the Office of the Future.* Norwood (NJ): Ablex Press.

Hiltz, S.R. (1986) 'The virtual classroom: using CMC for university teaching.' *Journal of Communications 36*, 2, Spring, 95–104.

Hiltz, S.R. (1988) 'Productivity enancement from computer mediated communications.' *Communications ofthe ACM 31*, 12, December 1438–1454.

Hiltz, S.R. (1990) 'Collaborative learning: the virtual classroom approach.' *T.H.E. Journal 17*, 10, June, 59–65.

Hiltz, S.R., Johnson K. and Turoff, M. (1986) 'Experiments in group decision-making, 1: communication, process and outcome in face-to-face vs. computerized conferences.' *Human Communication Research 13*, 2, Winter, 225–253.

Hiltz, S.R. and Turoff, M. (1978) *The Network Nation: Human Communication via Computer.* Reading, MA: Addison-Wesley.

Hiltz, S.R. and Turoff, M. (1985) 'Structuring computer-mediated communications to avoid information overload.' *Communications of the ACM 28*, 7, July, 680–689.

Hiltz, S.R., Turoff, M. and Johnson, K. (1986) 'Experiments in group decision-making, 3: disinhibition, deindividuation, and group process in pen name and real name computer conferences.' *Journal of Decision Support Systems 5*, 217–232.

Hogarth, R.M. (1977) 'Methods for aggregating opinions.' In H. Jungermann and G. de Zeeuw *Decision-making and Change in Human Affairs.* Dordrecht: Reidel.

Hopkins, R.H., Cambell, K.B. and Peterson, N.S. (1987) 'Representations of perceived relations among the properties and variables of a complex system.' *IEEE Transactions on Systems, Man and Cybernetics, SMC 17*, 1, January/February, 52–60.

Hsu, E. (1989) 'Role-event gaming simulation in management education: a conceptual framework and review.' *Simulation and Games 20*, 4, December, 409–438.

Kiesler, S., Siegel, J. and McGuire, T.W. (1984) 'Social-psychological aspects of computer-mediated communication.' *American Psychologist 39*, 1123–1134.

Klir, G.J., and Folger, T.A. (1988) *Fuzzy Sets, Uncertainty, and Information.* Englewood Cliffs, NJ: Prentice Hall.

LeClair, S.R. (1985) *A Multiexpert Knowledge System Architecture for Manufacturing Decision Analysis.* Unpublished PhD Dissertation. Arizona State University.

LeClair, S.R. (1989) 'Interactive learning: a multiexpert paradigm for acquiring new knowledge,' *SIGART Newsletter 108,* 34–44.

Lendaris, G. (1980) 'Structural modelling: a tutorial guide.' *IEEE Transactions on Systems, Man and Cybernetics, SMC 10,* 12, December, 807–840.

Lerch, I.A. (1988) 'Electronic communications and collaboration: the emerging model for computer aided communications in science and medicine.' *Telematics and Informatics 5,* 4, 397–414.

Linstone, H.A. (1984) *Multiple Perspectives for Decision-Making.* New York: North Holland/ Elsevier.

Linstone, H.A. and Turoff, M. (eds) (1975) *The Delphi Method: Techniques and Applications.* Reading, MA: Addison-Wesley.

Lowe, D. (1985) 'Cooperative structuring of information: the representation of reasoning and debate.' *Journal of Man-Machine Studies 23,* 1, July, 97–111.

Merkhofer, M.W. (1987) 'Quantifying judgmental uncertainty: methodology, experiences and insights.' *IEEE Transactions on Systems, Man and Cybernetics, SMC 17,* 5, Sept./Oct., 741–752.

Nelson, T. (1965) 'A file structure for the complex, the changing and the indeterminate.' *ACM 20th National Conference Proceedings* 84–99.

Pazzani, M.J.(1988) 'Explanation-based learning for knowledge-based systems.' In B.R. Gaines and J.H. Boose (eds) *Knowledge Acquisition for Knowledge-Based Systems.* New York: Academic Press.

Post, S. and Sage, A.P. (1990) 'An overview of automated reasoning.' *IEEE Transactions on Systems, Man and Cybernetics 20,* 1, Jan./Feb., 202–224.

Rao, U. and Turoff, M. (1990) 'Hypertext functionality: a theoretical framework.' *International Journal of Human-Computer Interaction 2,* 4, 333–358.

Reboh, R. (1983) 'Extracting useful advice from conflicting expertise.' *Proceedings of the 8th International Joint Conference on Artificial Intelligence.* Los Altos, CA: William Kaufmann Inc., 145–150.

Rice, R.E. and Associates (1984) *The New Media: Communication, Research, and Technology.* Beverly Hills, CA: Sage Publications.

Rohrbaugh, J. (1981) 'Improving the quality of group judgement: social judgement analysis and the nominal group technique.' *Organizational Behaviour and Human Performance 28,* 272–288.

Schneider, S.J. (1986) 'Trial of an on-line behavioural smoking cessation program.' *Computers in Human Behaviour 2,* 277–296.

Schneider, S.J. and Tooley, J. (1986) 'Self-help computer conference.' *Computers and Biomedical Research 19,* 274–281.

Shapley, L. and Grofman, B. (1984) 'Optimising group judgemental accuracy in the presence of interdependencies.' *Public Choice, 43*, 3, 329–343.

Siegel, E.R. (1980) 'The use of computer conferencing to validate and update NLMs hepatitis data base.' In H. Henderson and J. MacNaughton (eds) *Electronic Communications: Technology and Impact*, AAAS Selected Symposium 52. Boulder, CO: Westview Press.

Sondheimer, N.K. (1976) 'Spatial reference and natural-language machine control.' *Journal of Man-Machine Studies 8*, 3, 329–336.

Stephanous, H. and Sage, A.P. (1987) 'Perspectives on imperfect information processing.' *IEEE Transactions on Systems, Man and Cybernetics, SMC 17*, 5 September/October, 780–798.

Streitz, N.A. (1987) 'Cognitive compatibility as a central issue in human-computer interaction: theoretical framework and empirical findings.' In G. Salvendy (ed) *Cognitive Engineering in the Design of Human-Computer Interaction and Expert Systems*. Amsterdam: North Holland/Elsevier.

Torgenson, W.S. (1958) *Theory and Methods of Scaling*. New York: Wiley.

Turoff, M. (1989) 'The anatomy of a computer application innovation: computer mediated communications (CMC).' *Journal of Technological Forecasting and Social Change 36*, 107–122.

Turoff, M. (1991) 'Computer mediated communication requirements for group support.' *Organizational Computing 1*, 1, 85–113.

Turoff, M. (1970) 'The Policy Delphi.' *Journal of Technological Forecasting and Social Change 2*, 2, 149–172.

Turoff, M., (1972) 'Delphi Conferencing: computer based conferencing with anonymity.' *Journal of Technological Forecasting and Social Change 3*, 2 159–204.

Turoff, M. (1974) 'Computerised conferencing and real time Delphis: unique communication forms.' *Proceedings 2nd International Conference on Computer Communications*, 135–142.

Turoff, M. and Hiltz, S.R. (1982) 'Computer support for group versus individual decisions.' *IEEE Transactions on Communications, Com 30*, 1, January, 82–90.

Turoff, M., Rao, U. and Hiltz, S.R. (1991) 'Collaborative hypertext and computer mediated communications'. *Proceedings of the 24th Hawaii International Conference on Systems Science IV*. Washington DC: IEEE Computer Society Press, 357–366.

Vennix, J.A.M., Gubbels, J.W., Post, D. and Poppen, H.J. (1990) 'A structured approach to knowledge elicitation in conceptual model building.' *System Dynamics Review 6*, 2, Summer, 31–45.

Warfield, J.N., (1974) 'Toward interpretation of complex structural models'. *IEEE Transactions on Systems, Man and Cybernetics, SMC 4*, 405–417.

Waterman, D.A. (1986) *A Guide to Expert Systems*. Reading, MA: Addison-Wesley.

Welbank, M. (1983) *A Review of Knowledge Acquisition Techniques for Expert Systems*. British Telecom Research Laboratory Report.

Zadeh, L.A. (1965) 'Fuzzy Sets.' *Information and Control 8*, 338–353.

Part 2

Applications

Chapter 4

A Comprehensive Study of the Ethical, Legal and Social Implications of Advances in Biomedical and Behavioural Research and Technology[1]

Peter Goldschmidt

Introduction

Context of the study

Individuals' actions shape policy; policies shape individuals' actions. Nowhere is this inter-relationship seen more clearly than in health care, particularly with regard to such matters as life and death, reproduction, and responsibility for individuals' behaviour. Actions and policies depend on both politics and ideology, often with marked differences in preferences and predilections among various groups. Ultimately, such decisions as to whether or not parents should be free to choose the sex of their offspring, and, if so, with what encouragement or constraints, are political. However, politics, unless determined solely by ideology, can be informed by rational analysis.

Surveys to determine who holds what opinions and why are widely accepted and straightforward. Analysis of the implications of

---

1 The study was conducted by Policy Research Incorporated (Bethesda, Maryland) and the New Jersey Institute of Technology (Newark, New Jersey) for the National Commission for the Protection of Human Subjects of Biomedical and Behavioural Research, under contract No.1-HU-6–2105 (administered by the US National Institutes of Health). Material on methods and findings presented in this chapter is based on that in the study's final report.

The author thanks Dr Miriam Kelty (who was the Commission's project monitor for the special study) for reviewing the manuscript, and Ms Yosephine Allies for wordprocessing it.

decisions is far more complex. People may differ in their views about the consequences of an action or its absence. They may differ about the probability of an event's occurrence; its consequences were it to occur; when they are likely to occur; who is likely to be affected; whether the event's occurrence and its consequences would represent a net benefit or net cost; and the implications of actions that should be taken, to promote or to prevent or ameliorate the anticipated consequences were they to occur. The complexity is magnified when the decisions presented are unclear or uncertain, as is the case, for example, with yet-to-be-developed technologies. Science fiction is often closer to science fantasy than science fact. The fantastic does not materialise and technologies may not have the hoped for or feared consequences. Yet, we can be surprised. Only recently have we become aware that human inventions and activities can change the world in which we live, perhaps to the point of threatening all of human existence.

An example of things not turning out as expected – or scientific boon becoming technological bane – is the optimistic view of using atomic technology for peaceful purposes that arose in the aftermath of World War II giving way to the realisation that the technology could have unintended and negative consequences. The perceived need to assess technologies resulted in the establishment, in 1972, of the Office of Technology Assessment, an investigative arm of the United States Congress. In 1974, the US Congress mandated a comprehensive study of the ethical, legal and social implications of advances in biomedical and behavioural research and technology. This became known as 'the special study.' To fulfil this challenging mandate, the Commission established by the same Congressional Act that mandated the special study issued a request for proposals. The winning design proposed a structured inquiry based on the Policy Delphi (Turoff 1970). The resultant method serves as a model for assessing technologies and for informing complex policy debates. This chapter describes the study's methods, summarises its results, discusses its findings and the method that produced them, and offers some conclusions about the method's applicability.

Background to the study

In 1974, the US Congress enacted the National Research Act, Public Law 93–348. Part of this Act established the National Commission for the Protection of Human Subjects of Biomedical and Behavioural Research. Section 203 of the Act mandated the special study described here. It states that the study should include:

- an analysis and evaluation of scientific and technological advances in past, present, and projected biomedical and behavioural research and services;
- an analysis and evaluation of the implications of such advances, both for individuals and for society;
- an analysis and evaluation of laws and moral and ethical principles governing the use of technology in medical practice;
- an analysis and evaluation of public understanding of and attitudes toward such implications and laws and principles; and
- an analysis and evaluation of implications for public policy of such findings as are made by the Commission with respect to advances in biomedical and behavioural research and technology.

The Commission issued a Request for Proposals (RFP) to undertake the special study. It noted that responses should be particularly cognisant of the 'implications of biomedical and behavioural scientific and technological advances for ethnic, racial, and economic minorities.' The Commission selected the proposal submitted by Policy Research Incorporated (PRI) and the Center for Technology Assessment of the New Jersey Institute of Technology (Center) to respond to the special study mandate. The study began in September, 1975, and was completed in January, 1977.

The objectives of the special study were:

- to identify a limited number of subject areas and advances in biomedical and behavioural research and services within each subject area that will probably take place in the next 20 years; that is, quintessential examples, to serve as foci of inquiry;
- to identify foreseen implications of these quintessential advances in biomedical and behavioural research and services, and appropriate policies to respond to them;
- to examine the implications of policies that might be implemented with respect to selected quintessential advances in biomedical and behavioural research;
- to evaluate certain general policies that may be used to control or direct certain aspects of biomedical and behavioural research and the implications of resultant technologies;

- to examine the consequences of a possible national policy that might be adopted with respect to biomedical and behavioural research and the implementation of resultant technologies;

- to analyse and evaluate public understanding of and attitudes towards advances in biomedical and behavioural research, technology, services and their effects, the use of technology in medical practice, and policies pertinent to the entire subject of study.

Study management

An eight-member Study Design and Management Group, representing experts in the fields of medicine, law, ethics and social sciences, designed and implemented the special study.[2] The designers formulated the initial design; monitored its implementation; revised the design and guided the development of the project to meet the objectives of the study; and reviewed all reports issued. The designers retained five consultants to assist them. These consultants functioned as independent reviewers of the various instruments and reports that the designers produced. They were chosen for their diverse expertise to add scope to project management, and to enhance the quality of study products. A number of additional consultants participated in the study. Their roles included supplying specific technical assistance and pre-testing instruments. Implementation of the study design flowed from the designers through a project coordinator to the other seven members of the study coordinating staff (staff), who were employees of PRI. The staff implemented the study's functional aspects, including processing, reviewing, synthesising, and summarising the responses of panellists to PEIs; preparing drafts of the final report, and maintaining contact with members of the panel.

The designers met 14 times during the course of the study to monitor its progress and guide its development. The Commission's

---

2   Members of the Study Design and Management Group were: Peter G. Goldschmidt, Principal Investigator, and Irene Jillson-Boostrom, Assistant Investigator, (Policy Research Incorporated); Sanford Bordman and Murray Turoff, Assistant Investigators (New Jersey Institute of Technology); John Williamson (then Professor, The Johns Hopkins University, School of Hygiene and Public Health), William Duerk (then partner, Perito, Duerk, and Carlson, Washington, DC); Ian Mitroff (then Professor, Department of Information Science, University of Pittsburgh, Pittsburgh, Pennsylvania), and Prakash Grover (then Senior Epidemiologist, Fox Chase Cancer Center, Philadelphia, Pennsylvania).

representative, who served as the project monitor, attended these meetings on a regular basis to maintain communication between the project and the Commission. The designers sent all study materials to the Commission as they were produced. In addition, the designers made four presentations to the Commission during the course of the study. The first presentation, in October 1975, related to the design of the study and initial progress, including development of the issues for inclusion in the study, the selection of panellists, and the first Policy Evaluation Instrument. Interim reports were presented to the Commission in April 1976, and September 1976. A final presentation to the Commission was made in 1977 after submission of the study final report.

Methods

About study methods

The special study consisted of two components: a policy study involving a national panel of 121 experts; and a national opinion survey, an adjunct to the policy study suggested by the study's designers as necessary to meet the Congressional mandate. Expert panellists completed three Policy Evaluation Instruments (PEIs). Consultants and panellists were offered honoraria for participating in the study; the magnitude of this financial payment was not commensurate with the experts' considerable effort. The national opinion survey questionnaire was based, in part, on material generated by the first and second PEIs. It was administered to a probability sample of 1679 Americans in individual face-to-face interviews. In order to provide a basis for evaluating public understanding and attitudes a parallel version of the questionnaire was included in the third PEI sent to consultant panellists. This chapter describes only the policy study.

The policy study design assumed that normative plans for the future are idealised plans for extending what is known in the present. Inherent in the policies which people recommend is an implicit view of the future that is predicated on their view of the past and of the present. Consequently, the most fruitful way of understanding the ethical, legal and social implications of advances in biomedical and behavioural technology is to engage in a realistic discussion of the policy alternatives available to influence these advances, and the problems inherent in the means used to produce them. The projections of as many diverse disciplines, professions, and types of personality as are feasible should enter this discussion. Moreover, it should encompass ethical as well as technical considerations, thereby following a system of inquiry suggested by Churchman (Churchman 1971).

The method elaborated to conduct this study represents a new way of systematically analysing complex, value-laden, policy-related subjects. Essentially, it is a dynamic communications process in which information generated by a group at one point in time is elaborated on in the next. This dynamic communications process incorporated a dialectic between contrasting views, about as many relevant considerations as possible. This dialectic is designed to produce the best underlying *pro* and *contra* arguments which form the basis of various policy or resource allocation alternatives, or outcomes, impacts and effects.

The study involved a discussion of the implications of advances, and policy alternatives available to control and regulate the conduct of research and the distribution of technology. This discussion focused on five quintessential subject areas in research and technology which confront the various facets of the health system. Participants in the discussion included 121 eminent individuals (the panel) who represented different perspectives on the problem. The panel consisted of persons drawn from the following five broad categories, with about 25 in each category: ethicists; lawyers; medical scientists; representatives of public interest; and social scientists.

The discussion was conducted through three Policy Evaluation Instruments (PEIs) that were mailed to panellists (in February, May and August, 1976). Each PEI subsequent to the first built upon panellists' responses to previous PEIs, and was designed to permit a dialectic between competing views. Individual respondents remained anonymous to permit points of view to be expressed without the obligation to adhere to past positions, or to be fixed in one's position. Moreover, since panellists could independently and freely assess the material presented, interpersonal considerations and group dynamics were minimised. During the course of completing PEIs, panellists were able to make known their views, arguments, and assumptions about advances; policies unfolded from the flow of information from one PEI to the next. The progress of the discussion was from the general to the specific; from general implications of a number of quintessential advances, to specific implications of stated policies with respect to advances, to specific positions with respect to selected advances; and from general policies to address biomedical and behavioural research and the implementation of the resultant technology, to specific policies governing many aspects of research and the implementation of resultant technology.

Selection of consultant panels

To provide a broad variety of views and perspectives pertinent to the subject of the study, panellists consisted of persons drawn from the following five broad categories:

- ethicists, philosophers and religious leaders;
- lawyers and members of the judiciary;
- medical scientists and persons in related fields, including medical doctors from various specialised areas; biochemists, biophysicists and biologists; experimental psychologists; pharmacologists; and representatives of the drug, health appliance, research apparatus, and hospital industries;
- representatives of the public interest, including members of the US Congress and other legislative bodies; members of the executive branch of government; and members of special interest groups including minority groups, consumer interest groups, and organisations who maintain a particular moral/ethical position vis-a-vis the practice of medicine;
- social scientists, including sociologists; psychologists; economists; urbanologists; planners in various disciplines; and managers and administrators.

The panel was selected in a number of discrete waves to ensure balance. Nominations were generated from project staff and consultants, the staff of the Commission, the chairpersons and ranking minority members of seven Congressional committees and sub-committees relevant to the study, and from panellists. Biographical data on each nominated panellist were collected from over 30 different reference works. The data were transcribed on to panellist nominating forms which were distributed for evaluation to a panel selection task force consisting of four persons drawn from among the study designers and staff. Each member made an independent assessment of the suitability of a nominee. The principal criteria for selection were qualifications and experience relevant to the study. Final selection of panellists was made from the pool of those nominees that reviewers felt were appropriately qualified. Qualified persons were selected to the panel so as to ensure that minorities, including women, were represented and that panellists were drawn from all regions of the country.

Letters of invitation to selected potential panellists were mailed at various times during the study. Each person approached received a letter inviting him/her to join the panel, a copy of the study design and a consultant panellist information survey form. This form requested administrative data, and asked the panellist to place him/herself in the most appropriate of the five panel categories. Analysis of returned survey forms produced the data necessary to balance the panel to the greatest extent possible. Persons selected in later waves of the selection process were no less qualified than those selected earlier.

The panel selection process resulted in the nomination and review of 680 people, of whom 281 were invited to serve as panellists at some point in the study. A total of 149 people consented to serve (Table 4.1).

Table 4.1 Selection of the consultant panel: persons nominated, invited, accepting and completing PEIs (by category of panellist)

Selection step	Category of Panellist					
	Ethicists	Lawyers	Medical Scientists	Reps. of Public Interest	Social Scientists	Total panel
Nominated to consultant panel	83	96	204	131	166	680
Invited to join consultant panel	35	68	61	61	56	281
Accepting invitation	28	34	29	26	32	149
Completing at least one PEI	25	23	26	22	25	121

Panellists who were unable to continue with the study at any time were replaced from the pool of qualified persons within their own category so as to maintain an appropriately balanced panel. Such replacement permitted the panel to consist of a least 125 people at each PEI mailing. The final panel represents the 121 people who completed one or more PEIs.

Selection of issues

The issues to be addressed by the policy study were selected at the issues clarification meeting held in October 1975, in Baltimore. Its purpose was to develop:

- a limited number of quintessential subject areas in which advances in biomedical and behavioural research and technology might be expected to take place;
- the important societal concerns that these advances would challenge;

- some of the potential problems that might be produced through the impact of particular subjects on specific concerns.

Ten panellists, two from each of the five panellist categories, participated in the issues clarification meeting. Each of these ten participants completed a pre-meeting assignment that included recommending subject areas for inclusion in the study, and indicating relevant concerns related to each subject area. The results of this assignment were the starting point for the meeting. At the opening of the meeting, participants were divided into two groups of five persons (one from each panellist category).

Each group was provided with a copy of the subject areas and societal concerns identified by members of that group in the pre-meeting assignment. Participants added to the subject areas and social concerns listed. Separate votes were taken on the importance of the subject areas and societal concerns identified. Subject areas were ranked according to socio-political importance and the potential for revealing differences of opinion among the five panellist categories. Additionally, the eight top-ranked subject areas were rated for their impact on the societal concerns considered most important. Subsequently, the two groups met in plenary session to compare and discuss the items that had been identified. A final vote on the socio-political importance and potential for revealing differences of opinion among panellist categories was taken on a combined list of subject areas produced from the eight most important subject areas identified by each small group.

The designers reviewed the results of the meeting and analysed the subject areas' ratings and the relative importance of the societal concerns. In the final analysis, the subject areas that were selected represented the minimum number that would reflect the maximum number of important societal concerns. Following several meetings with the Commission's staff, the following five subjects were chosen as foci of inquiry for the study: Data Banks, Computer Technology; Genetic Screening; Extension of Life; Reproductive Engineering; and Systematic Control of Behaviour.

First policy evaluation instrument

Purpose and scope

The first Policy Evaluation Instrument (PEI) was designed to identify foreseen implications of technological advances in biomedical and behavioural research and technology and to suggest policies to respond to these implications. It consisted of 206 pages. Two designers independently developed skeletons of the material to be addressed by panellists. One design skeleton emphasised the development of policies based on the implications of specified advances in biomedical and behavioural research and technology. The other emphasised the elaboration of general policies related to scenarios which were based on advances in biomedical and behavioural research. The final design incorporated aspects of both skeletons.

To identify three likely advances in each subject area, the authors of background papers (described below) and at least two other recognised experts in the particular subject area, were each asked to suggest and describe from three to five advances that were expected to occur in the next 20 years, and to rank them in order of importance with regard to the impact that the advance would have on society. The three most often mentioned advances in each subject area were selected for inclusion in the first PEI, yielding a total of 15 advances for the five subject areas. Designers wrote individually a total of 48 scenarios, which were reviewed by other designers and consultants. The six scenarios receiving the most votes in a poll of the designers and consultants were included in the first PEI. A scenario pertinent to each subject area was included, and one scenario cut across all subject areas.

Pre-test

Ten pre-testers, two from each of the study's five panellist categories, were asked to complete a pre-test version of the first PEI along with a pre-testers' evaluation workbook that accompanied the instrument. Pre-testers were selected to be representative of panellists insofar as possible, except that all resided in the Baltimore/Washington area. Two Center students also pre-tested the first PEI. Nine of the twelve pre-testers completed the task. On the basis of these pre-tests and reviews, the designers developed a second pre-test version of the first PEI. Two additional consultants pre-tested this version of the first PEI and completed the pre-testers' evaluation workbook. The major concerns at this juncture were the time it would take for a panellist to complete the PEI and the comprehensibility of items. The final version of the first PEI was mailed to panellists in February 1976. It consisted of three sections: introductory materials, background papers, and evaluation workbook.

Introductory materials

The introductory materials consisted of three documents: introduction, definitions, and completed example. The introduction's principal purpose was to acquaint panellists with the study process. It also defined certain terms for study purposes. These definitions were drawn from a variety of sources: dictionaries and other reference works, designers, consultants and panellists. The completed example was designed to assist panellists to complete the evaluation workbook. Responses given in the completed example were based on those obtained in pre-tests of the instrument for an advance and a scenario not included in the final version of the PEI.

Background papers

For each of the study's five subject areas, designers recruited a panellist who had demonstrated expertise in that area to write a background paper. Background paper writers were provided with a standard outline, so that the papers would include a comparable degree of information. Designers reviewed and edited papers, and, when appropriate, supplemented them with material from other experts.

Evaluation workbook

The evaluation workbook consisted of two parts: five subject areas (arranged alphabetically) and six scenarios (ordered by subject). For each subject area under consideration, panellists were asked to review the three selected advances included and to choose from those listed (or from the one they were allowed to add) the one advance that was most important, that is, the one having the most significant implications for society. For this most important advance, panellists were asked to identify and rank up to three significant types of implication of the advance, and to elaborate on these implications. Finally, panellists were asked to choose among separate policies with respect to research that gave rise to the advance; and implementation of the advance itself, and, if appropriate, to elaborate on these policies. The six scenarios followed the five subject areas. In the scenarios, panellists were provided with two options, asked to decide which they favoured, and then asked to elaborate on the basis for their decision. Finally, they were asked to select which groups and agencies should participate in the resolution of the issue, and to describe a policy that would be helpful in resolving issues of the type depicted in the scenario.

Second policy evaluation instrument

Purpose and scope

The second PEI was designed to examine the implications of policies that might be implemented with respect to selected technological advances in biomedical and behavioural research, and to evaluate policies pertinent to the subject of the study, taken as a whole. It consisted of 250 pages. Of the fifteen advances and six scenarios included in the first PEI, five were brought forward to the second PEI to serve as models in this respect. They were:

- computerised medical records in use;
- environmental causes of disease and trauma further controlled;
- amniocentesis becomes routine;
- . select-a-boy, select-a-girl marketable kits; and
- actions of psychopharmacological agents further understood.

These five items were chosen because of the importance designers attached to them; because of the wide range of opinions panellists held regarding research and implementation of the advance; and to ensure that they encompassed the study's five subject areas.

Pre-test

A draft version of the second PEI was pre-tested by six people, at least one from each of the study's five panellist categories. As with the first PEI, each pre-tester completed a draft version of the instrument and a pre-tester's evaluation workbook. Designers prepared the final version of the second PEI based on pre-test results. It was mailed to panellists in May 1976. The second PEI consisted of three sections: introductory materials, synthesis papers, and an evaluation workbook.

Introductory materials

Introductory materials included with the second PEI consisted of an introduction and a completed example. The introduction contained a brief statistical summary of the results of the first PEI, a discussion of the development and intent of the second PEI, and instructions for completing the PEI. The completed example included a discussion of the implications of both policies and general policy statements. The implications of the policies part were drawn from material contained in the first PEI which had not been carried over, to avoid any potential bias induced by using issues considered in the PEI. Similarly, the general policy statement part was drawn from policy statements which the designers had not selected for inclusion in the second PEI. As in the first PEI, final drafts of these documents were prepared after the evaluation workbook had been finished.

Synthesis papers

Panellists were provided with a synthesis paper for each advance or scenario brought forward from the first PEI. Each synthesis paper consisted of three parts: a pro-position statement advocating the promotion of research and implementation of the advance; a contra-position statement advocating control or limitation of research and implementation of the advance; and general summaries of the policies and implications. Each position statement was written by a panellist who selected the particular policy for the advance in the first PEI. Position statement writers were provided with and drew on the anonymous responses of all panellists who also selected the same overall policy to respond to the advance. The authors of position statements were allowed considerable latitude in presenting the best possible argument for the policy they advocated, and in developing the implications of the advance. Project staff developed the general summaries of policies and implications, and described the results of the first PEI. In addition, project staff reviewed and, if necessary, edited all position statements to ensure their clarity.

Evaluation workbook

In the second PEI, as in the first, the evaluation workbook consisted of two sections: one on the implications of specific policies; the other on general policy statements. The implications of the policies part of the workbook built upon the synthesis papers, and particularly on the position statements advocating either promotion of or control of research and implementation. In this part of the PEI, panellists were asked to identify which of the two opposite policies they would least like to see implemented. After selecting the policy liked least, panellists were asked to think about the implications of this (antithetical) policy not only in terms of benefits or harms intrinsic to the technology, but also in terms of the additional harms or benefits that might stem from implementing the policy itself. Panellists were asked to identify and describe briefly the three most significant negative consequences (undesirable effects, disbenefits) that would occur if the least-liked policy were to be implemented. They were also asked to identify what group or groups, if any, would be particularly affected by these negative consequences. Finally, panellists were asked to describe what specific policy could be adopted, or what other steps could be taken, to ameliorate the most significant negative consequence of implementing the least-liked policy, thereby making it more tolerable. Such policies could be aimed at preventing or minimising the occurrence of the negative consequence or at compensating for it were it to occur.

The general policy statements part of the workbook contained 23 major policy statements that were compiled from: the results of the first PEI; a review of the legislative intent in setting up the Commission, the mandate for the study; and various documents produced by the Commission itself. Designers reviewed an initial list of policy statements and selected those to be included in the second PEI. Panellists were asked to decide whether or not they agreed with the policy statement and whether or not it was urgent to implement the policy. Other general policies that panellists considered should be implemented urgently could be added in space provided for this purpose. Panellists were then asked to choose the five most urgent policies (from among those listed and any they may have added), and to rank them in order of urgency. Finally, they were asked to elaborate on the three policies selected as most urgent to implement.

Third policy evaluation instrument

Purpose and scope

The purpose of the third and final PEI was to examine the consequences of a possible national policy that might be adopted with respect to biomedical and behavioural research and the implementation of the technologies that result from such research. It consisted of 288 pages. The material brought forward from the second PEI consisted of the results of the responses to the general policy statements and the panellists' own descriptions of the most urgent policies. In addition, panellists were asked to establish priorities for health research, to complete the same general opinion questions asked of the public, and to describe, in the form of two newspaper stories, what might happen if the specified national policies were implemented and if they were not implemented.

Pre-test

Five persons completed copies of a draft version of the third PEI and the pre-tester's evaluation workbook which accompanied the instrument. As in earlier iterations of the study, designers prepared the final version of the third PEI based on pre-test results. It was mailed to panellists in August 1976. It consisted of three sections: introductory materials, a synthesis paper, and an evaluation workbook.

Introductory materials

The introductory materials for the third PEI included an introduction and a completed example. The introduction contained a summary of the statistical results from the second PEI, some background on the intent of the instrument, and instructions for its completion. The completed example used material on health care delivery as the basis for policy questions and resource allocation decisions. Examples of general opinion questions were drawn from items deleted from earlier versions of the national opinion survey.

Synthesis paper

The synthesis paper contained an overview of responses to the general policy statements from the second PEI, and a general summary of panellists' responses to each separate policy statement, prepared by project staff. The overview identified, interpreted, and summarised the salient dimensions underlying panellists' responses to the general policy statements. Each general summary of a policy statement followed a common outline, reporting as faithfully as possible panellists' elaborations of the policy.

To ensure that staff summaries reported accurately what panellists had said, the general summaries and verbatim transcripts of panellists' responses were sent to two panellists for review. The two panellists, each reviewing one-half of the general summaries, were asked to examine each general summary in conjunction with the verbatim transcripts to identify and correct any significant biases or deficiencies in the summary. Reviewers' comments were taken into account in preparing the final synthesis paper. Reviewers were also asked to identify, interpret, and summarise the salient dimensions underlying panellists' responses for those general policy statements reviewed, and to provide a summary of their findings. Staff combined and edited the separate summaries. This composite review was sent to each reviewer for comment to ensure that it met the intent of the original review.

Finally, these two panellists were asked to review four policy scenarios which the designers had developed, on the basis of the results of the general policy statements part of the second PEI, to serve as the principal focus of the third PEI. The purpose of this review was to ensure that the policy scenarios reflected the content of panellists' elaborations to the general policy statements.

Evaluation workbook

The focus of the third PEI was on general policies with respect to research and implementation rather than on specific research projects or the implementation of specific technologies. Since it was impossible to identify all the advances that might result from biomedical and behavioural research and technology, the most meaningful approach would be to identify and discuss mechanisms to evaluate, regulate, control, and direct research and implementation. In this way, it would be feasible to examine the likely impact of the policies on society, and on the research and implementation process itself.

This PEI drew together the policies that panellists had described previously to deal with biomedical and behavioural research advances, the resultant technologies, and the implications of implementing the policies themselves. In the third PEI, panellists were asked:

- to examine four policy scenarios that collectively described a possible national policy with respect to biomedical and behavioural research and technology, each scenario dealing with one aspect of the national policy. The four policy scenarios were:

  - a permanent national commission;
  - public involvement in policy decision-making;
  - biomedical and behavioural research;
  - implementation of biomedical and behavioural technologies;

- to review past trends in resource allocation policy and in expenditures on health related research, and to establish priorities;

- to respond to a number of general opinion questions (asked also of the general public);

- to describe what they thought might occur if the national policy described in the four scenarios was implemented, and what might occur if the policy was not implemented.

For each policy scenario, panellists were asked to consider the implications of the national policy the scenario described. First they were asked to identify and describe up to two positive consequences (desirable effects, benefits) and up to two negative consequences (undesirable effects, disbenefits) anticipated if the policy described in the scenario were implemented. Next, panellists were asked to identify and describe up to two barriers to implementing the policy described in the scenario, and the ways in which these barriers might be overcome. Finally, panellists were asked to indicate the degree to which they supported or opposed the particular policies that comprised the national policy described in the scenario, and to offer any specific amendments.

In the resource allocation part of the evaluation workbook, panellists were provided with a brief overview of national resources devoted to health and health research. They were asked to indicate their preferred allocations for health and health research vis-a-vis other activities, and the relative priorities that should be afforded to the different types of health research activities described. In the general opinion questions part of the evaluation workbook, panellists were asked to respond to the same series of questions that was put to the general public in the national opinion survey (which is not described here). Finally, panellists were asked to write two brief newspaper stories that might be filed by a science reporter in 1999: one if existing policies with respect to biomedical and behavioural research and technology continued to operate unchanged until that time; and the other if the policies described in the third PEI's four policy scenarios were implemented in the late 1970s.

Analysis and summary of PEI data

At each PEI mailing, the consultant panel consisted of at least 125 people. The response rates for the three PEIs were 76%, 86%, and 88%, respectively (Table 4.2). A total of 121 panellists completed at least one PEI and 87 panellists (72% of those completing PEIs) completed all three instruments; an additional 20% completed two PEIs. Each PEI took approximately six to eight hours to complete. The intake period for each PEI was 40 days from the date it was mailed. Staff carried out each step of the analysis systematically and made every effort to ensure that panellists' views were reported accurately. Each summary represented, as completely as possible, the ideas expressed

Table 4.2 Panellists completing PEIs, by category

	Category of panellist					
	Ethicists	Lawyers	Medical Scientists	Reps. of Public Interest	Social Scientists	Total
First policy evaluation instrument						
No. of panellists at time of PEI mailing	26	23	26	26	28	129
No. completing PEI	22	14	21	21	20	98
Per cent completing PEI	85	61	81	81	71	76
Second policy evaluation instrument						
No. of panellists at time of PEI mailing	25	25	27	25	26	128
No. completing PEI	25	19	25	20	20	110
Per cent completing PEI	100	76	93	80	81	86

by panellists who responded to an item. Where appropriate, staff prepared overviews of responses. A panellist reviewed critically each staff summary. The objectives of this review were to evaluate the summaries for accuracy in reporting panellists' responses (and to correct any biases or deficiencies identified), and to identify, interpret, and summarise the salient dimensions in panellists' responses. To accomplish these objectives, panellist reviewers were provided with printouts of verbatim responses, in addition to staff summaries, and a set of instructions. Another panellist was asked to review independently staff summaries pertaining to an entire part of a PEI. The objective of this review was to identify, interpret, and summarise the salient dimensions common to all the items, summarise those that cut across several items, and those unique to a particular item. Staff compared and synthesised the findings of these independent reviews that formed the basis for drafting the study report.

Preparation of final report

Findings from the three PEIs that comprised the policy study and from the national opinion survey were combined in the final report of the study. Designers and staff prepared the first draft of the final report and submitted it for review by other designers, consultants, and Commission staff. Based on findings presented in the report, each reviewer identified what he/she considered to be the principal study conclusions. In addition, to ensure that study findings were reported accurately, the principal investigator and another designer independently compared reported findings with those identified by panellist reviewers and those contained in the survey tabulations. Based on their findings and reviewers' comments, designers prepared a second draft of the report. The second draft contained reviewers' conclusions drawn from reading the findings reported in the first draft. The same groups who reviewed the first draft also reviewed the second draft of the report. In addition, the principal investigator and another designer compared independently conclusions to findings to ensure their supportability. Based on their findings and reviewers' comments, designers prepared a final draft of the study final report, and edited it for publication.

Selected Findings of the Special Study

Key findings

The special study produced findings of an extent and richness that cannot be done justice in the short summary that space permits here.[3] These findings are remarkably fresh today, even though the study was completed 18 years ago. At the study's completion in 1977, a press release summarised its findings and conclusions as follows:

- The equitable distribution of health care, particularly scarce new technologies, will be one of the greatest problems facing society in the next 20 years.

- Although the advances that are expected to occur until the turn of the century are likely to be extensions of those we already know, they may sharpen existing conflicts and cause old problems to be viewed in new ways.

- Most, but not all panellists thought that a new national agency should be established to formulate and coordinate national policy on biomedical and behavioural research and technology. The agency would not make detailed rules, but it would evaluate the results of research in sensitive biomedical and behavioural fields. One of its functions would be to help people make informed choices about the advances that will soon be available.

- The expert panel also agreed, though by no means unanimously, that there is a need for a thorough assessment of new technologies, for increased public participation in setting policies on medical advances, and for educating not only the public but also researchers themselves about the implications of startling advances in behaviour control, genetic screening and reproductive engineering, among others.

- The national opinion survey found the American public quite optimistic about past advances in medicine but cautious about the effects of some new technologies on society and the family. For example, indications are that select-a-boy, select-a-girl kits will find slow acceptance. By contrast, the expert panellists were more concerned than the

---

3   There are ten volumes (see Appendix) available from Policy Research Incorporated, 4715 Cordell Avenue, 5th floor, Bethesda(MD) 20814, USA.

public over how advances in bioscience might abridge
individual rights and freedoms. Both groups listed the cure
for cancer as the most desirable advance in the next 20 years.

* The means by which health benefits are to be attained may
  come to be seen as harmful or dangerous either to people
  directly or to their rights. For example, if the prevention or
  treatment of cancer could be accomplished only through
  rigid specification and control of individual behaviour, it is
  doubtful that the public would regard it as the most
  desirable advance. There is a need for national mediation of
  these potential conflicts. Many of the implications of
  advances foreseen by panellists do or will pose considerable
  problems for society. Many issues will have to be resolved,
  many trade-offs examined, and many decisions made.
  Draconian measures are not necessary, and hasty,
  ill-conceived action may be counterproductive.

* At least for the present, there is time to improve inadequate
  systems of control and to construct new ones where
  necessary. However, panellists did warn against inaction.
  They expressed a sense of urgency; action is required.

The remainder of this section presents the study's principal findings
about advances (for each subject area, individual, social and moral
issues, and some conclusions based on them) and about policies (for
each scenario and resource allocation policy, their implications, and
some conclusions based on them).

Findings about advances

Data banks and computer technology

The major implications of data banks and computer technology relate
to the invasion of privacy. Even proponents of the technologies
admitted the potential for the invasion of privacy and for negative
effects on the poor and minorities, many of whom would be unwill-
ing or unable to use the technology. While proponents of computer
technology felt the potential benefits outweighed the risk of a slight
loss of personal autonomy, opponents feared that even the willingness to accept such a trade-off would erode present values relating to
privacy and confidentiality.

Panellists saw both positive and negative effects for the quality of
health care. Claims by proponents included predictions of reductions
in the cost of care, increased accuracy, speed and ease of access to
medical records, and improvements in the quality control of health
care. Opponents countered these claims with predictions of higher

costs for computer equipment and support, loss of intimacy and trust in the physician-patient relationship, and actual harm perpetrated through errors in programming or input. Similar arguments took place over benefits to research and planning as some felt computer technology would lead to great strides in research and planning while others considered these claims at least overblown, if not unfounded.

Extension of life

Panellists saw issues related to extension of life more as trade-offs than as pros and cons. The question was not whether there were costs on one side and no costs on the other, but rather which costs should be borne by whom. Extending life complicates the allocation or redistribution of scarce resources. For example, investment in these technologies may force the taxing of the many for the support of the few maintained by expensive life-sustaining equipment. Life-extending technologies will increase the proportion of older people in the population, raising a potential resource allocation conflict between generations. Advances in life-extending technologies may also cause us to choose between support for medical intervention and for prevention. Panellists showed little interest in providing extensive funding for developing these technologies.

Genetic screening

The principal concerns in genetic screening were the trade-offs between individual rights and the public good and, to a lesser extent, the need to resolve the problems of long-term genetic change and equity in distributing the technology. Some panellists thought that individuals had 'rights' to the kind of information provided by screening programmes, and associated these rights with the exercise of personal responsibility for decision-making. Other panellists suggested there should be a right not to seek the information which would be provided by a screening programme, and that this personal choice could be perverted or denied by governmental or commercial coercion or through social pressures.

The relationship between screening technologies and abortion as a consequent therapeutic intervention lies at the base of many concerns about the social aspects of screening. Abortion of defective foetuses was viewed favourably by some panellists in that it could decrease the cost of custodial care or treatment. Some argued that it was imperative to avoid these costs, which were generally seen as rebounding on to society when they exceeded a family's ability to sustain them. Other panellists were concerned that the identification of defective foetuses could only bolster a growing notion that abortion is a responsible and acceptable course of action, which would intensify pressures on those morally or religiously opposed to it. These panellists argued that society should support options which would allow those not in favour of abortion to avoid it without social stigma.

Concern was also apparent for the existing population of 'defectives' and for those who might 'slip through the net' of screening technologies. Some panellists feared that the fewer defectives, the greater the stigma for those who remained. Finally, there was substantial agreement that implementation of screening programmes would require equity in the distribution of the technology in order to prevent the development of a differential birth rate for children with defects among particular ethnic or economic minorities.

Reproductive engineering

Panellists saw such advances in reproductive engineering as select-a-boy, select-a-girl kits, as producing tension between individual rights and freedoms and the 'good of society'. Some panellists felt that individuals had the right to use reproductive technologies. People could be free to choose whether or not to have children, to determine family size or composition, and to sever the link between sexuality and reproduction. However, others felt that the absolute exercise of such 'rights' as the ability to select the sex of one's children must be restrained to avoid social disruption (manifested in predictions of changes in the sex ratio) or family conflicts where the views of one individual clashed with another. Equity was also at issue. Some panellists feared that restricted access to scarce and expensive technologies, such as *in vitro* fertilisation, would discriminate against the poor. Others feared that the availability of inexpensive technologies such as medical sterilisation might result in their differential promotion to selected groups, such as the poor or minorities.

Systematic control of behaviour

Panellists were divided over whether advances in systematic control of behaviour would enhance or detract from individual freedom. There was particular apprehension about the possibility of government intervention going too far. Such benefits as increased productivity, lowered cost of curbing social deviance, and profits for private enterprise, must be balanced against the cost of compromising individual rights and the notion that behavioural treatments might become the only acceptable option for controlling social problems.

Implications and issues

Implications for individuals

The panel generally upheld individual rights and values where these conflicted with the needs of society. The central question about individual rights related to whether or not they were freely relinquished. The panel generally objected to aspects of advances or policies which tended to curtail individual rights when individual consent was not solicited or received.

Panellists generally favoured aspects of advances which tended to enhance individual choice and the exercise of personal responsibility. Some panellists were unequivocally in favour of the absolute operation of concepts of individual freedom and autonomy while others viewed them within a social context. While advances themselves tended to be seen as increasing individual choice and responsibility, the interaction of technology with the individual, society, the government, and various agencies, was sometimes seen as limiting choice.

Questions of individual health centred largely on the relative risks and benefits of research and technology. Where the potential existed for technologies to result in physical harm, or where there was a possibility that inequities in the distribution of the technology would differentially affect individuals of differing backgrounds or classes, panellists were divided over whether the risk of harm or inequity was acceptable.

Implications for society

Technological effects such as new knowledge and improvements in health care were often mentioned as social benefits, and a number of panellists appeared to hold the implicit assumption that a freewheeling approach to technological development would produce the greatest good for the greatest number. This viewpoint was challenged by others who felt that all-out promotion of technology was likely to prove harmful in the long run. Similarly, economic issues produced disagreement over whether the added costs of bureaucratic supervision, believed necessary to control some technologies, would overwhelm the economic benefits which they might produce. Some panellists noted that advances could lead to major changes in the national or world economic picture, such as the amelioration of the world population problem, and redistribution of population away from areas of pollution or polluting industries.

Some technologies were seen as promoting changes in social patterns. In particular, some panellists considered developments in reproductive engineering as capable of producing changes in the sex ratio of the population, patterns of marriage and family life; that behaviour control technologies could influence the relationship between governing and governed; and that screening technologies could lead to notions of genetic equality as an obtainable social end. Finally, some panellists suggested that minorities and the disadvantaged would suffer from the implementation of technologies, while others suggested that minorities and the disadvantaged would suffer from the failure to implement them.

Moral and ethical issues

The broad moral and ethical issues identified by the study related to potential changes in human biology and behaviour and to the question of equity or social justice. Advances in reproductive engineering and genetic screening raised questions about the potential for changing the biology of the human species, but produced substantial disagreement over whether changes would actually occur. Developments in the systematic control of behaviour might result in certain fundamental Western values of free-will and personal responsibility being altered. Panellists tended to accept behaviour control technologies if their use were confined to the rehabilitation of individuals, but to decry their application to classes of people, or their use to avoid the exercise of personal responsibility.

Some conclusions about advances

Advances and their implications

During the last century, we have made great strides in our understanding of and ability to influence our health and behaviour; seemingly these advances are occurring at an ever increasing rate. The benefits to be derived from new knowledge and new technology to promote health, to prevent disease, and to treat sickness when it does occur, are apparent. No less important, but perhaps less obvious, are the flaws in our knowledge, and the unintended consequences of applying the technologies that result from research. We have become increasingly aware that new technologies can directly or indirectly affect present and future individuals in society in unsuspected and perhaps deleterious ways. The more technology we apply the more opportunities there are for unintended negative consequences to occur. Technology may also serve to raise new conflicts or sharpen old ones.

Ends and means

When people are asked about desirable advances in biomedical and behavioural research, they tend to think of things which have major health implications or effects. Moreover, they seem to assume that the means by which these health benefits will be attained are themselves good, or at least do not conflict with other equally important values. However, when advances are focused, and the means of their attainment delineated, value conflicts begin to arise. Careful analysis may show that the health benefits may not be as great as once imagined; there may even be the potential for iatrogenic impairment of health. More importantly, the means by which the health benefits are to be attained may come to be seen as harmful or dangerous either to people directly or to their rights. When examined in detail, advances may no longer look so attractive.

Need to mediate value conflicts

The study illustrated the need to mediate potential conflicts among values, particularly between individual rights and societal needs. All of the subject areas raised questions about this particular trade-off, and it was very clearly illustrated in the application of technologies to control behaviour, particularly violent behaviour. This idea appeared extremely attractive to many. Yet the application of behaviour control technologies raises questions about individual rights. Who will decide what behaviours to control? Who will administer the controls? Who will watch the watchers? Will any resultant limitation of rights ultimately affect society more adversely than if the controls were not applied? Sometimes, apparently good ideas can have counter-intuitive consequences that ultimately require trading-off one good with another. For example, providing information about physician performance may allow people to make more informed choices among practitioners, promoting individual freedom of choice. However, given practitioners of unequal skill, there is likely to be competition for the skill of highly rated physicians, thus creating potential problems in the equity of health care distribution. Are the highly prized to be highly priced? If not, how are their services to be distributed?

Findings about policies

Some panellists contended that the costs of research and care justified the establishment of a permanent national commission, while others contended that the commission itself would create staggering bureaucratic costs. Some panellists contended that a permanent regulatory agency would create efficiency and enhance quality of research while others contended that red tape and politicisation of research would cause a deterioration in research quality. Finally, some panellists contended that present abuses of power in the health industry justified the creation of an independent regulatory agency; others suggested the agency itself would become abusive in its use of power.

In considering public involvement in policy-making, panellists debated three views of the public: as interested, informed and helpful; as disinterested and likely to be led by demagogues; and as self-selected individuals and groups whose impact could be either positive or negative.

Two major themes emerged from the discussion of the scope of the proposed commission's authority and control over biomedical and behavioural research. One was the freedom of research and inquiry, maintained by some as inviolable but considered by others to be necessarily secondary to the public need. The other was the quality of research. Some panellists felt that rationalisation of the review process and the development of standards for its conduct would improve research quality. Others contended the review process would be encumbered by bureaucratic inefficiency and would result in a decline in the quality of research.

The principal focus regarding the implementation of biomedical and behavioural technologies was health status. Many felt the policies described would improve the health of individuals and society. However, others were concerned that the policies would result in limiting choices among treatment options, and contribute to lowering population health status. Panellists also foresaw differing impacts of the policy on the market place, with some suggesting benefits in the reduction of dangerous or useless products, and others fearing that the reviews and evaluations would be so expensive and time-consuming that only large companies could provide the capital for development, thus driving individual or small-group development efforts from the field and abetting the growth of monopolies.

With respect to resource allocation policy, the majority of panellists favoured future resource allocations which would: increase the percentages of the nation's allocation of Gross National Product to health; increase the percentage of the health dollar that goes to health research and development; increase generally total federal outlays to research and development; and increase the percentage of federal research and development dollars going to health. Panellists were unanimous in favouring greater allocations to biomedical research than to behavioural research. There was also general agreement that a greater proportion of resources should be allocated to health services and quality assurance research and a lesser proportion to basic research than existed at the time of the study.

Some implications and issues

Need for controls and the role of government

Panellists were split over the need for the control of biomedical and behavioural research and technology. Some panellists were strongly in support of a comprehensive national policy which would control and regulate all research and implementation, public or private, at all stages. These panellists tended to see the existing system as uncontrolled and indifferent to social need. Opposing this view were panellists who favoured continuation of a loosely-knit system of control, supplemented where necessary by the strengthening of existing agencies, or the use of *ad hoc* measures. These panellists tended to consider peer controls as sufficient to guide research. Those in favour of regulation tended to see the role of government as beneficial, providing coordination, planning, and representation. Panellists opposed to the regulatory approach were certain that the attendant bureaucracy itself would be restrictive, unresponsive, and inefficient. Additionally, they feared that research quality would suffer as the bureaucracy favoured those who could manipulate red tape over those who were truly creative.

Panellists favouring a comprehensive national policy for research hoped that economies would result from the coordination of research and the delivery of health care. They suggested that duplication would be avoided, available funds would be distributed equitably, and insurance premiums or malpractice awards might be reduced. Countering these favourable views was the fear that a massive regulatory bureaucracy would drive the costs of research and health care delivery even higher. In addition to costs in federal dollars, some feared that regulation would create higher prices to consumers as providers of goods and services passed on the regulatory overhead.

Justice and freedom

There was considerable agreement among panellists regarding the desirability of such things as equality of opportunity, the provision of safeguards for special groups, and the need to compensate subjects of research for any harm. The major differences which appeared in this area related to questions of the freedom of individual researchers or the research community to pursue their own course. Some panellists felt that a comprehensive regulatory policy would violate the individual rights of researchers; others saw the curtailment of individual rights as a legitimate subordination of the individual to society, rather than as an infringement on personal liberty.

Public participation

The active involvement of the public in the biomedical and behavioural research and development enterprise was lauded by some panellists who felt that research could be made more responsive to social need and that a dialogue between producing researcher and consuming public would prove beneficial to research and to society. Some panellists saw it restoring public confidence in research, decreasing polarisation on important issues, and producing an anticipatory rather than a reactive approach to technological development. These views were directly contradicted by others who felt public confidence in research would be undermined by the emphasis on rules and regulations, dogma would be substituted for dialogue in public debate, and the public would be lulled into a false sense of security that 'something was being done'.

Some conclusions about policies

Coordinated national policy

Most, but not all, panellists rejected the existing piecemeal approach to developing policy with regard to biomedical and behavioural research and technology. Also rejected by the majority of panellists was the notion that enhancing the mandate of existing agencies and institutions would suffice as a way of dealing with the problems that are likely to be faced in research and in the implementation of new technologies. These panellists believed a new independent national agency was needed. They saw a central policy-making agency not simply as a way of avoiding abuse, but also as a means of doing good. For the most part, however, it was recognised that the new national agency would not solve many problems – because they cannot be solved. In the end, for every gain there is a loss, and the trade-offs must be made clear to all concerned. Moreover, the purpose of such an agency was not seen simply to prevent all risks to all people on all occasions, but to assess risks and benefits and to strike the appropriate balance.

In establishing a new national agency, cognisance would need to be taken of the need to develop the appropriate linkages with existing agencies, to prevent duplication of effort (particularly with regard to regulations), to prevent inter-agency rivalry, and to establish clear lines of authority and responsibility. Care should be taken to avoid simply producing an added layer of bureaucracy (resulting in loss of productivity), politicising research (resulting in unproductive conflict), or overly centralising control (resulting in tyranny). It is not sufficient to add or duplicate agencies or functions; one must subtract or integrate them as well.

While there was considerable disagreement among panellists about the scope and power which ought to be accorded to a national policy-making body, there were some areas of general agreement. Agreement was widespread for policies which involved regulating the conduct of research, including the protection of human subjects and the assessment of the risks and benefits of research to both individuals and society. Panellists also widely supported policies involving the enforcement of appropriate conduct of research and use of technologies, including penalties for abuse or misuse.

The autonomy of researchers and providers

Panellists were deeply divided over the extent to which researchers and providers should be autonomous or operate within a publicly defined context. On the whole, the scales were tipped toward the latter view, and for most panellists the benefits outweighed the costs. Some panellists mistrusted researchers and providers, others mistrusted the governmental bureaucracy which might be erected to deal with researchers and providers, and still others mistrusted both entities. Two opposing views regarding researchers underlay many policy choices. To some people the researcher is an individualist pursuing his/her own intellectual interests – something of a hero contributing to society. They see management structures which tend to direct or control research as stultifying the development of new knowledge and harming society in the long-run. To other people the same individualistic researcher is an egoist, pursuing his/her own interests at public expense. They see management structures as necessary to make the development of new knowledge responsive to the public need and to protect research subjects, and as benefiting society in the long run. Mediation of these conflicting viewpoints will decide the nature, extent, and productivity of tomorrow's research system.

There was substantial agreement for some level of direction of research through a national strategy, though panellists varied on exactly how much direction. There was disagreement about the extent to which a national strategy would increase research productivity. Medical scientists, particularly, were inclined to be wary of highly directed research, believing instead that essentially non-directed research was the most productive in the long-run. There was agreement from all panellists, however, that more resources should be spent on health, particularly on health research. A smaller than existing proportion of research funds, however, should be spent on research to develop technology and a larger proportion on health services and quality-assurance research.

Public participation

The public should be encouraged to participate in policy-making to the greatest extent possible. Panellists gave high marks to the dissemination of information (particularly through established channels of communication), open meetings, and publication of evaluations. To make informed decisions, the public must be provided with valid information. Panellists called for closer monitoring of research, studies of the implications of research, the evaluation of technologies for safety and efficacy, and better information about the possible implications of advances or courses of action. In addition, the government should encourage (or, if necessary, mandate) that sufficient information be disclosed to the public, for example, through appropriate product labelling, or through the disclosure of physicians' performance records. In the same vein, explicitness of policies was seen to be essential. People should know what is being done, how it is being done, who is doing it, etc. To foster this end, policies should be written in lay language; implementation of policies should be monitored; and evaluations should be conducted by independent third parties to eliminate collusion between regulator and regulated.

Individual responsibility and freedom

The individual should be responsible for his/her own actions and should be free to decide what is best, provided society has no compelling interest in the outcome. Of course, there were substantial differences of opinion as to when society's interests become compelling. Panellists generally tended to support notions of individual freedom, and to dislike excessive governmental intervention in private affairs. Where individual responsibility was involved, as in the relationship between smoking and lung cancer, or in the decision to undergo genetic screening, the panel frequently suggested individual solutions. The tendency was to prefer public education to promote informed choice, rather than to enforce regulations to satisfy social need. The public was inclined to allow the operation of individual responsibility in such cases as the decision to participate in a risky experimental treatment, but inclined to endorse conformity to social need where an individual's behaviour or choice adversely affects others. Panellists who commented on the subject indicated generally that minority or disadvantaged groups (economic, ethnic, religious, etc.) would be adversely affected under any set of circumstances.

There was substantial resistance to extending the hegemony of the federal government over the private sector (industry, universities, or individual practitioners), except to control the conduct of research, where society's interest in protecting research subjects and its own integrity was generally seen to be over-riding. Concern for the social good can overwhelm and erode individual freedom of choice. To some degree, people should be left alone, even if they choose to be unhealthy, in the interests of preventing the development of a health-oriented totalitarianism. In short, individual freedom of choice is more important than research progress or the pursuit of health.

Discussion

Central questions

The special study was completed 18 years ago. With this perspective, one might well ask a number of questions about its findings and methods. This final section examines two such questions: How have the findings stood up over time? What was learned about the method?

Findings about advances

The study's principal conclusion regarding the equitable distribution of health care still holds today. In the US, 30–40 million people have no health care insurance to speak of; the coverage afforded countless others is inadequate. Medical technology continues to proliferate; costs to increase. Paradoxically, concerns about the appropriateness and quality of care continue to increase as resource consumption grows. Generally, US health care is believed to be the best in the world, with instant access to the latest technology, for those who can afford it. Yet, in common with all health care systems, little research is done to find better treatments, and what research is done is mostly inadequate. We have little idea about the extent to which care improves patients' health status or conforms to accepted standards. Little or no money is spent on effectiveness or outcomes research, or on assessing or improving the quality of care.

Data banks and computer technology

The last 15–20 years have seen remarkable progress in computing power and its widespread distribution, to which everyone with a personal computer (PC), which first appeared circa 1977, can attest. The PC has facilitated word-processing, database management, and data analysis. However, its application to clinical medicine is almost non-existent, and, despite some promising activities, seems likely to remain a distant possibility. In health care, even administrative systems are relatively primitive compared to what could be envisaged. The computerised medical record, the principal advance considered in the special study, remains as elusive as ever, even though some aspects of records and their management are increasingly computerised. In health care, the computer's greatest impact so far may have been on paying for care. Computers have facilitated sophisticated billing and payment systems, such as those based on DRGs (Diagnosis Related Groups), introduced in the USA in 1983; programs to maximise payments (for providers); and those to screen claims (for payers).

Extension of life

Since the special study was conducted, in industrialised countries, increases in life-expectancy at birth have slowed down, and in some countries and for some groups, life-expectancy has actually declined. The extent to which life-expectancy can be increased by any means, let alone traditional medical care, which is seen increasingly to play a relatively small role despite soaring costs, is uncertain. Recognition of AIDS (Acquired Immune Deficiency Syndrome), circa 1981, and increasing deaths from violence, have complicated the picture. The principal advance considered in the special study was 'environmental causes of disease and trauma further controlled'. Certainly, consumer protection and environmental movements have flourished in all industrialised countries, spawning the so-called 'greens', and have doubtless contributed to health improvement. Life-style changes, including diet and exercise and smoke-free environments, will also improve health, at least for some individuals, while creating new social pressures on the fat, the slothful, and smokers. Humankind's relationship with the environment and its social consequences are both complex and potentially catastrophic, as Chernobyl has demonstrated. Fears of global warming and ozone depletion, and their believed consequences, may evoke greater changes than the phenomena themselves, which may or may not be real, and if real, may or may not be irreversible or have negative consequences.

Genetic screening

Advances in molecular biology have been rapid in the last 15 years. Almost daily, claims are made about the discovery of genes for this or for that. The human genome project and related activities have advanced our knowledge, our ability to test for, and, ultimately, to manipulate human and other species' genetic material – the basis of life. Yet, few medical practitioners have been trained to interpret the results of newly available tests. Fears of runaway recombinant organisms seem to have been exaggerated, although the effects of genetic manipulation remain largely unknown since the technology is still in

its infancy. The benefits of biotechnology seem to require more resources and take longer to realise than was hoped originally. Amniocentesis, the principal advance considered in the special study, is now
routine, in the sense that it is an accepted medical practice (although
it may be replaced or supplemented by chorionvillus sampling), and,
in the USA, the abortion debate rages with increased ferocity. If
amniocentesis finds an impaired foetus, induced abortion is virtually
the only therapeutic choice. Up to now, the only stimulus for the test
was the woman's interest in knowing whether or not her foetus was
impaired. Most people believe in the woman's choice to abort an
impaired foetus. However, some people believe it is wrong to destroy
any human conceptus, while others believe that the woman has a
duty to prevent the birth of a deformed infant on moral or economic
grounds because of the burdens its birth would place on society.

Reproductive engineering

The world's population continues its seemingly inexorable increase.
An individual's freedom to reproduce remains paramount. In the last
15–20 years, advances in contraceptive technology have consolidated
older ones, rather than ploughing new ground. The recent introduction of a long-acting implanted contraceptive may harbour the possibility, for example, of metering out lenient punishments to
wayward female drug abusers who agree to have the drug implanted.
The so-called sexual revolution, which occurred in the 1960s, and was
supported, if not initiated, by the widespread availability of extremely reliable contraceptives in women's hands (the 'pill'), is now
the prevailing normality. Knowledge about AIDS and other sexually
transmitted diseases may again change behaviour, although the extent and nature of such changes remains to be determined. Advances
continue to be made in treating infertility. The birth of the world's
first 'test-tube' baby, in 1978, caused a sensation, but *in vitro* fertilisation is now routine. The controversy has shifted to surrogacy, with
wombs for rent and donations of sperm and/or eggs. The selection
of the sex of one's offspring is now a practical reality, although the
technology is not yet available in the form of the widely marketed
'select-a-boy, select-a-girl kits' considered in the special study.

Systematic control of behaviour

Use of biomedical and behavioural technology to regulate individuals' behaviour is a relatively new possibility that might put frightening powers in the hands of rulers who often seem all-too-ready to
exercise them. Recent world events, most notably those that have
taken place in Eastern Europe and the former Soviet Union, seem to

portray a movement toward more democratic, participative societies. Yet within these societies, violence against individuals is increasing. Mass-murders seem everyday realities, and body counts are reported daily on television news broadcasts. Effective technologies to control such behaviour seem elusive. Technologies which have existed for millennia, such as prison, seem increasingly inadequate. Certainly, were effective technologies to exist, societies would face agonising choices about their use to prevent individuals who have committed violent acts from repeating them, let alone 'treating' individuals 'prone to violence' in an attempt to prevent violence from occurring. Violence, of course, is only one, if perhaps the most salient, of the behaviours that society may be interested in controlling. Use of psycho-active substances is wide-spread. Tranquillisers and other psycho-pharmaceutical substances have helped many mentally disturbed individuals to lead more normal lives. Drug abuse, the use of illicit or misuse of licit psycho-active substances, has increased measurably. It has serious deleterious effects on individuals and the trade in such substances, and its accompanying violence, is a major social problem. No area harbours more consequences for individuals or society than policies designed to regulate use of mind-altering or behaviour-controlling technologies. Such policies stem from individual desires to enhance capabilities or to avoid pain, beliefs about what works and what does not, and notions of right and wrong.

Findings about policies

Today, in the US, there is no commission or national regulatory body of the type most panellists favoured. The public can participate generally in the political process and comment on federal regulations. However, none of the grander schemes for public participation that panellists favoured have materialised. The sun set, in 1978, on the original Commission that oversaw the special study. That same year, Public Law 95–622 created a Presidential Commission, which became active in 1980 and continued until 1983. Between 1978 and 1980 an Ethics Advisory Board existed in the US Department of Health and Human Services (part of the federal executive branch of government). In 1985, Public Law 98–158 created a Congressional Biomedical Ethics Board comprising members of the US Senate and House of Representatives, with an attendant advisory committee of experts and lay people. The committee met first in September 1988, just days before the Board's authorisation was to expire. Although re-authorised for two additional years, the effort folded in September 1989, without having completed any of its mandated activities. Today, in 1992, interest in and responsibility for the topics that the special study encompassed are spread out over at least 16 federal departments and agencies. There is a Federal Co-ordinating Council for Science and Technology, and one of its sub-committees is concerned with human subjects. The NIH plans to establish a centre for the development of public policy, including the analysis of ethical, legal, and social issues. Although NIH is not a regulatory agency, it has taken the lead in matters concerning the protection of human subjects of research, and, in 1991, its guidelines on this subject were adopted by all federal agencies.[4]

There are few discernible ways in which the funding and conduct of research have changed in the past 15–20 years. The one notable exception is the degree of formality accorded to the protection of human subjects of research. The National Commission for the Protection of Human Subjects of Biomedical and Behavioural Research established the basic ethical principles and guidelines in 1979 which the NIH codified in 1983 and 1989 (Protection of Human Subjects: Code of Federal Regulations, 45 CFR 46 1989). Public Law 99–158, the Health Research Extension Act of 1985 required that all applicants for grants conform to NIH guidelines for the protection of human subjects. However, the system that NIH set up has yet to be evaluated, although it says that such a study is being planned. Concerns about the welfare of animals used in research also increased during this period and regulations for their use and protection are now much more stringent. Another exception is the extensive regulatory activity that has developed in response to genetic engineering.

In 1975, at the Asilomar Conference, scientists discussed guidelines for recombinant DNA experiments, after having imposed an informal moratorium because of concerns about their safety. In 1976, NIH published its guidelines for research involving recombinant DNA molecules, which it updates periodically.[5] In 1986, the federal government published the 'Coordinated framework for regulation of biotechnology' (Coordinated Framework for Regulation of Biotechnology. Federal Register 1986). Different agencies are responsible for different types of experiments, e.g. the US Department of Agriculture (USDA) for field test of transgenic cotton (Purchase and MacKenzie 1989). A permit is required to introduce an organism that has been

---

4   Part II. Federal Policy for the Protection of Human Subjects; Notices and Rules. Federal Register 1991; 56 (117) 28001–28032 (Tuesday, June 18).

5   Part III. Guidelines for Research Involving Recombinant DNA Molecules; Notice. Federal Register (1986) 51 (88) 16958–16985 (Wednesday, 7 May, 1986), plus eight amendments through 15 October, 1991).

genetically engineered (via recombinant DNA techniques) from a donor organism, vector or vector agent that is a plant pest or contains plant pest components,[6] and USDA has issued guidelines for their introduction (User's Guide for Introducing Genetically Engineered Plants and Micro-Organisms 1991). Funding for the human genome project covers both work intended to characterise the form and content of the human genome, and:

> work aimed at anticipating the social consequences of the project's research and developing policies to guide the use of the knowledge it will produce... (This project) will quietly become the vehicle for the largest US investment in biomedical, ethical, legal and social analysis to date... Three sets of questions have been identified as particularly important: the integration of new genetic tests into health care; education and counsel of individuals about genetic test results; and access to and use of genetic test results by third parties. (Juengst and Watson 1991)

The implementation of biomedical and behavioural technologies has also remained largely unchanged. The introduction in 1983 of DRGs (Diagnosis Related Groups) and prospective payments for hospitalised Medicare patients (beneficiaries of the US federal government health insurance scheme), did affect the incentives governing the introduction of new technologies, and, in theory at least, enhanced the value of cost-saving technologies. Hospital cost increases did moderate somewhat during the 1980s, but the US is now experiencing another cost explosion, at a time when health care already consumes over 14% of the nation's Gross National Product – by far the highest ratio in the world – and the economy is dogged by no or slow growth. The time it takes, and the cost of introducing new drugs, reached a new high. As a result of this pressure, the demands of AIDS (Acquired Immune Deficiency Syndrome) activists, and a de-regulatory climate, steps were taken at the end of 1991 to streamline the approval process, to mixed reviews. The creation of the Agency of Health Care Policy and Research (AHCPR) at the end of 1989, on a level with NIH, has renewed interest in such matters as the effectiveness and outcomes of medical care, practice guidelines, and health systems research. However, only small amounts of money are being allocated to health systems and quality assurance research.

---

6   Part II. Animal and Plant Inspection Service: Plant Pests; Introduction of Genetically Engineered Organisms or Products; Final Rule. Federal Register (1986) 52 (115) 22891–22915 (16 June, 1987).

Responding, in 1976, special study panellists wanted to alter resource allocations in a number of ways. They are listed below (with a comment on what has happened to date). The panel wanted to:

- see an increase in the percentage of GNP allocated to health (it has increased 69%, from 8.3% to 14.0% of GNP in 1992 (Sawyer 1991));

- increase the percentage of the health dollar spend on R&D (it has remained constant at about 3.5% (National Center for Health Statistics 1991));

- increase federal outlays for R&D and the percentage for health (total federal research outlays, in real terms, increased by 51%, from 1975 to 1991 (US Bureau of the Census 1991); the percentage for health is about the same, 13.4% for 1992 (*The Washington Post* 1991), even though federal health research expenditures have remained essentially flat, not withstanding a huge increase in AIDS research, which at $2.3 billion amounted to 25% of the total in 1989 (National Center for Health Statistics 1991);

- redress an imbalance in allocations to basic research vis-à-vis health systems and quality of care research (the imbalance remains, and may have worsened).

The method

The study described in this chapter was probably the largest, most complex Policy Delphi study ever conducted. It was designed to answer a specific set of questions posed by the US Congress, and worked as designed. The study produced a rich source of information on the implications of advances in biomedical and behavioural research and technology and policies that might be implemented to respond to them. Its greatest effect may have been to educate participants, since none possessed the fullness of experience that emerged. Today, the same approach might be applied fruitfully to reform of the US health care system, for example. The study design and implementation was so successful that if asked to repeat the study today, I would essentially follow the same blue-print. Why was the study so successful? What could be done differently?

The Delphi Method involves a structured, iterative inquiry among experts with statistical feedback. Delphi design involves selecting the participants, structuring the inquiry, and conducting the study in a number of iterations with feedback between each one. The first, and most central issue, that designers face is whether or not the Delphi is the most appropriate method of inquiry to answer whatever question is posed. Given that Delphi is the inquiry of choice, designers must address each of its characteristics.

Selecting the participants

Who should take part in the Delphi process? How many participants should there be? How should they be selected? The Delphi Method aims to identify and explore issues. Thus, there is no intention of extrapolating from participants to any population from which they might be considered to have been drawn. Notions of probability sampling are therefore irrelevant. Instead, the goal must be to identify as many relevant viewpoints as possible, in the attempt to ensure that all relevant issues are identified and explored. Consequently, the number of participants can be relatively modest. The key question relates to the marginal utility of each additional participant in terms of the probability that a significant issue would be added to those identified by the existing number of participants. Conceptually, designers may want to set this probability as one in 100 or one in 1000, although we have little information on the relationship between the number of participants and the number of important issues they identify, which, of course, must depend in part on participants' knowledge. Every participant must be considered qualified to contribute to the inquiry, and designers must establish explicit criteria for qualifying potential participants and for selecting participants from among the pool of those who are eligible. Selection from the pool will depend on such factors as known viewpoint, background, and geographic location.

Essentially, one must decide how many distinct perspectives exist on the subject of inquiry. In the special study there were five: ethicists, lawyers, medical scientists, representatives of the public interest, and social scientists. For each perspective 20–30 participants are usually sufficient. With that number of participants per perspective, one can compare responses among perspectives. The study could have been completed with a total of 30 participants, the equivalent of six per perspective. However, it is unlikely that six medical scientists, for example, could be sufficiently knowledgeable about the breadth of subject matter that the study encompassed, and cross-perspective comparisons would not have been meaningful.

Response rates are important for two reasons. First, if one went to the trouble of making sure that potential participants encompassed all relevant views, one would want those views to be among the responses. Second, a high response rate indicates that participants believed the study was worthwhile. Clearly, in only the most unusual of circumstances can one expect everyone contacted to participate or all of those who agree to participate to complete questionnaires. To allow for this contingency, the original panel must be about one third larger than the minimum acceptable number of responses. Ideally, there should be two participants for every essential viewpoint. Given that one wants to end up with 100 competed questionnaires, the original panel should number 150 individuals if one expects a two-thirds response rate, the minimum that one should consider acceptable. From the pool of eligible individuals, one would draw 150 to form a balanced panel. If a potential panellist declines to participate, he/she should be replaced from the pool with a person as similar as possible to the one who has declined. Panellists who fail to complete the first questionnaires should be asked about their intention to complete subsequent questionnaires. This procedure should be repeated after the closing date for return of each questionnaire, except that any panellist who fails to complete two consecutive questionnaires should be replaced automatically. Panellists who replace those who decline to serve or who drop out for any reason should be no less qualified than those selected originally from among the pool of eligible people.

Panellists, who are, by definition, experts in the subject of the inquiry, are in an excellent position to judge the study's value. If less than two-thirds of them complete questionnaires, the study, as designed, has little value. High response rates depend on the study's importance and its relevance to participants, the quality of the design, the work load and mental and emotional stimulation involved, and the incentives to participate. The high response rate achieved in the special study was due to the study's importance, its relevance to participants, the quality of the design and the mental and emotional stimulation it engendered, and the fact that participants were offered an honorarium to participate. Payments to participants are important because they recognise the value of their contributions. Rarely is it possible to compensate eminent professionals commensurate with the full value of their time. However, if possible, participants should be paid fully to ensure their full attention to the study task.

Structuring the inquiry

The structure of the inquiry determines its outcome. No amount of compensation to participants nor use of technology can overcome ambiguity of purpose or poorly constructed questionnaires. The special study design was appropriate to its purpose and it was elaborated by a skilled team of relevant, experienced professionals. The design of the entire study was decided at the outset, although details of the next round depended on the results of the preceding one. Each round built on the last one, and information from one round was elaborated in the next.

Conducting the study

A Delphi exercise consists of several rounds, or iterations, of an inquiry with statistical feedback. In forecasting Delphi applications, for example, this feedback consists of statistical summaries of estimates. Classically, participants have been asked to revise their estimates based on this information and to rate their certainty. In Policy Delphis of the type described here designers summarise information from one round for participants to elaborate in the next.

In the special study, a main-frame computer was used to accomplish this task. Today, personal computers (PCs) could do the same task more quickly and efficiently. In fact, the entire study could have been done electronically. Although today it is technologically feasible to conduct the study electronically, I would still repeat the study using mailed questionnaires for a number of reasons. First, many senior policy-makers are not comfortable with PCs and prefer to complete paper-and-pencil questionnaires. Also, it is difficult to achieve the same design standards electronically. For example, participants can leaf through a summary of responses, and refer to a completed example, while completing a questionnaire. While this effect can be duplicated or improved electronically, with context searches and pop-up-windows, for example, the cost of doing so is often prohibitive. Today, PCs would be reserved for those participants who wanted to respond electronically or to wordprocess narrative responses. In the future, use of Delphi expert systems may permit such studies to be done entirely electronically.

Discrete 'rounds' are a product of paper-and-pencil Delphi questionnaires, because that is the only way such studies can be iterated. In electronic media, feedback can be continuous. Nevertheless, it is important to preserve the 'round' structure of the inquiry. Without structure the Delphi exercise can degenerate into amorphous communication or game playing. However, the free flow of communications permitted by message exchange systems allows participants to clarify questions with designers or swap ideas with fellow participants before completing the round's 'official' questionnaire. Designers should close rounds before providing statistical feedback. Good designs provide participants with ample opportunity to change their positions and explain why they did so without recourse to continuous voting. In the Policy Delphi, issues are elaborated rather than iterated in the sense used in classical forecasting Delphi exercises.

The special study consisted of three rounds, the maximum number that could be accomplished in the time available and the minimum number necessary to achieve the study's purpose. Each iteration was completed in three months, no mean feat given the complexity of the design, the number and extent of responses, and the primitive means of automated processing available at the time. Adding more rounds would permit greater elaboration, of course, but would also add to the study's duration, making it difficult to hold participants' interest; it would also cost more.

Conclusions

The method described in this chapter provides a structure to elicit a wide range of views about a topic, policy responses, and their implications. In societies that are increasingly democratic, participative, and technological, policy making becomes inherently more complicated and contentious. The method permits explication of positions and allows modelling of the complexities inherent in reality, avoiding the need to simplify issues into insignificance. Final choices are still influenced by the ideologies of policy-makers, of course, but are better informed. The method may result in no action, because issues or policies are too contentious or their consequences too uncertain, for example. On the other hand, policy-makers may charge ahead, no matter what the evidence, risking chaos (e.g., politicisation and polarisation) in the face or order (e.g., live-and-let-live dynamic stability). The method merely informs decisions; it does not constrain them (beyond the power of rational information).

The advent of personal computers and their attendant software has greatly facilitated implementing the method (see Chapter 3 above). Indeed, the entire inquiry could now be conducted on-line with experts distributed over the entire world. These breakthroughs in telecommunications and information processing in no way diminish the importance of specifying clearly the inquiry's purpose, its end products, and the methods necessary to produce them. No amount of technology can overcome ambiguity of purpose. The method of inquiry emphasises the dynamics of alternative policies, people's possible responses to them, and their consequences. The resultant interplay produces a rich source of information to inform policy-making.

References

Churchman, C.W. (1971) *The Design of Inquiring Systems*. New York: Basic Books.

Coordinated Framework for Regulation of Biotechnology. Federal Register (1986) 51:23303 (26 June).

Juengst, E.T. and Watson, J.D. (1991) 'Human genome research and the responsible use of new genetic knowledge.' *International Journal of Bioethics 2*, 2, 99–102.

National Center for Health Statistics (1991) *Health United States 1990*. Hyattsville, MD: US Department of Health and Human Services (DHHS Pub. No PHS–91–1232).

The National Commission for the Protection of Human Subjects of Biomedical and Behavioural Research (1979) *The Belmont Report: Ethical Principles and Guidelines for the Protection of Human Subjects of Research*. Bethesda, MD: US National Institutes of Health.

Protection of Human Subjects: Code of Federal Regulations (1989) 45 CFR 46. Bethesda, MD: US National Institutes of Health.

Purchase, H.G. and MacKenzie, D.R. (eds) (1989) *Agricultural Biotechnology: Introduction to Field Testing*. Washington, DC: US Department of Agriculture.

Sawyer, K. (1991) 'Health-care spending may reach 14% of GNP.' In *The Washington Post*, Monday, 30 December, p.A6.

Turoff, M. (1970) 'The design of a Policy Delphi.' *Technological Forecasting and Social Change 2*, 2, 141–171.

US Bureau of the Census (1992) *Statistical Abstract of the United States: 1991*. Washington, DC: US Government Printing Office.

User's Guide for Introducing Genetically Engineered Plants and Micro-Organisms (1991) Washington, DC: US Department of Agriculture (Technical Bulletin No.1783).

The Washington Post, Tuesday, 10 December, 1991, p.A12.

Appendix

The following ten volumes are available from Policy Research Incorporated, 4715 Cordell Avenue, 5th floor, Bethesda(MD) 20814, USA.

Summary of the Final Report. This volume is a concise summary of the study purpose, methods, principal findings, and conclusions (48 pages).

The Final Report. This volume describes the need for the study, the study purpose, methods, findings, and conclusions. The implications of advances and of policies that might be adopted with respect to biomedical and behavioural research and the use of resultant technologies are described, analysed, and evaluated. The report also describes, analyses, and evaluates public understanding of and attitudes toward advances in biomedical and behavioural research, technology and services and their effects, the use of technology in practice, and policies pertinent to the entire subject of study. Appendices to the report describe study methods, provide lists of consultant panellists and other study participants, and give descriptions of the advances and scenarios examined as part of the study (298 pages).

Policy Evaluation Instrument – 1. The first PEI sent to consultant panellists for completion (206 pages).

Summary of responses to the first Policy Evaluation Instrument. This volume summarises: the implications of the 15 advances examined (three in each of the five subject areas), and the appropriate policies to respond to them; the advances added by panellists; the implications underlying resolution of the six scenarios considered; and the policies that would be helpful in resolving issues of the type depicted (402 pages).

Policy Evaluation Instrument –2. The second PEI sent to consultant panellists for completion (250 pages).

Summary of responses to the second Policy Evaluation Instrument. This volume summarises: the negative consequences of implementing the research and implementation policy least liked by panellists with respect to five advances carried forward from the first PEI, and the ameliorative policies suggested if the least liked policy were implemented; panellists' elaborations of 23 general policy statements listed; and a summary of those urgent policies added by panellists (272 pages).

Policy Evaluation Instrument – 3. The third PEI sent to consultant panellists for completion (288 pages).

Summary of responses to the third Policy Evaluation Instrument. This volume summarises: the positive and negative consequences of implementing the possible national policy described in four policy scenarios, the barriers to the implementation and ways of overcoming them, and amendments offered to the particular policies that comprise the scenarios; appropriate resource allocations to health, health R&D, and types of health R&D; and panellists' responses to the national opinion survey questions (414 pages).

Dateline 1999. This volume provides alternative futures depicted in the form of newspaper stories written by panellists who responded to the third PEI. Panellists were asked to write two brief newspaper stories that might be filed by a science reporter in 1999: (1) if existing policies with respect to biomedical and behavioural research and technology continued to operate unchanged until that time; and (2) if the policies described in the third PEI's four policy scenarios were implemented in the late 1970s (90 pages).

National Opinion Survey. This volume contains the schedule of questions administered to a probability sample of 1,679 Americans in individual face-to-face interviews – the national opinion survey. It also contains the report of survey results prepared especially on behalf of those respondents who requested a copy of the survey results (20 pages).

Chapter 5

The Use of the Delphi Method in Construing Scenarios on the Future of Mental Health and Mental Health Care

Rob Bijl

Introduction

Between 1987 and 1990, a future scenario study on mental health and mental health care in the Netherlands in the next two decades was carried out (Idenburg *et al.* 1990; Bijl 1991). The questions to be answered were: what might be the developments in the field of mental health and the associated need for care over the next two decades; what are their implications and to what extent can these developments be influenced?

An inquiry based on the Delphi Method formed an essential part of this study. This chapter focuses on the design of the Delphi study and some major methodological issues in connection with this specific public health sector and this type of research.

For some years, the Dutch government has encouraged scientific research on the future of public health and health care. The special interest of the Dutch government in future studies can be explained by the unique organisation of health care in the Netherlands (Bauduin 1988). The organisation of the health care system in the Netherlands is almost entirely private; however, the functioning of health institutions is publicly controlled by means of staff allocation regulations, through the health inspectorate, by means of public standards for medical training, and so on. Health care is also partly publicly financed by the social security system. So the government is directly involved in the health care system.

Forecasting is common in fields such as economics or demography, but in the health sector, looking ahead for more than five years has not been done systematically. In 1983, as a result of Dutch participation in the Health for All by the Year 2000 strategy of the

World Health Organisation (WHO 1982), a Steering Committee on Future Health Scenarios (STG) was established. The STG acts as an independent advisory board to the Minister of Health.

The committee's main task is to create alternative scenarios of possible and desirable futures in the field of public health and health care. The aim of these efforts is to improve long-term public health and health care planning and to enhance the ability of policy makers to anticipate developments in the next decades (Brouwer and Schreuder 1986). The STG determines the subjects to be studied. The priorities are set on the basis of social relevance and the feasibility of the research project in a particular field. For each subject, an independent scenario committee is set up. Each committee cooperates with a research team of experts in the relevant field as well as with experts in scenario research.

Scenarios

Futures research has nothing to do with utopias, prophecies, predictions, witchcraft or crystal balls. It is, rather, a prosaic activity and its prime objective is to stimulate discussion among those concerned in the health care sector. The idea of providing multiple forecasts has become a cornerstone of scenario analysis. It is an explicit recognition of the frailty of forecasting, and suggests that the accuracy of a forecast is largely dependent on its underlying assumptions (Schnaars 1987). The construction of several future scenarios, based on a number of plausible assumptions, should make policy makers, medical staff, nursing staff, hospital managers and patient organisations aware of the sensitivity of the field to future developments. Showing what might happen if business goes on as usual, or what the future would be if health policy is changed, or unexpected events occur such as the discovery of new drugs or the appearance of new modes of treatment, are examples of what can be done.

A scenario is defined as a description of the present situation in society and of a desirable or possible situation in the future, as well as a description of the events that can lead to that future. A scenario study, in other words, involves delineating possible alternatives to the present. It is not simply concerned with prediction but is an interesting mixture of scientific efforts and creative thinking.

In the Netherlands, in addition to the mental health scenario project, scenario studies have already been carried out on a great number of topics: ageing (Hollander and Becker 1985), cardiovascular diseases (Dunning and Wils, 1987), cancer (Cleton and Coebergh 1988), accidents and traumatology (Lapré and Mackenbach 1989) diabetes mellitus (Casparie and Verkleij, 1990), health and working conditions (Van Wely *et al*. 1991), the social impact of AIDS, primary health care (Wennink *et al*. 1991), dentistry (Bronkhorst *et al*. 1992) and the future of medicines (Leufkens *et al*. 1993). Most of the Dutch scenario studies concentrate on one disease or one clearly defined category of diseases. However, the study of mental health and mental health care covered a broad and diverse field, epidemiologically as well as institutionally.

Mental health and mental health care are of great importance within the health sector. On an annual basis, psychiatric and severe psychosocial problems affect about 25 per cent of the Dutch population. Also, professional mental health care is not exactly a minor activity compared with somatic care: 15 per cent of the national health care budget is spent on mental hospitals, psychogeriatric nursing homes, sheltered housing, psychiatric day care, outpatient services and so on. On top of that, substantial mental health care is provided outside the above-mentioned specialised institutions, e.g. psychosocial guidance of former psychiatric patients; crisis intervention and psychotherapy supplied by general practitioners, social workers and self-employed psychiatrists and psychologists.

Future Scenarios on Four Mental Health Themes

From a wide range of possible themes within the field of mental health and mental health care, four rather divergent themes were studied in detail. The following selection criteria were used:

- The diversity of mental health problems and care should be reflected. Mental health problems vary widely from psychiatric disorders, such as schizophrenia and depression, to psycho-social problems, such as stress and drug abuse. The diversity of mental health problems can be studied along many dimensions. Mental health problems differ as regards causes and onset, subjective suffering, duration and course, possibilities for recovery, in their socially invalidating character, social (in)tolerance, etc. Mental health care also covers a wide range of possibilities including many different institutions, therapeutic methods and forms of care concentrating on specific psychopathology or population categories.

- The themes should represent major mental health (care) problems. The social and political relevance of the study required themes that could be seen as exemplary for more general future developments in the mental health sector.

Gazing into the Oracle

- Sufficient empirical data should be available. It is not possible to design future scenarios without an adequate empirical foundation.

Two of the themes studied in detail were psychiatric disorders – dementia and schizophrenia – both of which have rather stable age-specific incidence and prevalence rates. The third theme was not a simple disease or disorder, but rather a broad category of problems in a specific target population – emotional and behavioural problems in children and adolescents. This subject is of considerable socio-cultural importance and depends strongly on social and cultural factors. It has direct connections with many adjoining areas of care, e.g. schools, child welfare and the criminal justice system.

The last theme was occupational incapacity due to mental disorders. In economic and social terms, this is currently an immense problem in the Netherlands. It focuses primarily on one of the most far-reaching social consequences of mental problems – the loss of a job – and the problems associated with a return to employment. It highlights the economic and political aspects of the relationship between mental health and disability pensions and the opportunities for misusing psychiatric labels for non-medical economic reasons.

All four themes show a considerable variation in relation to biological versus social causes, the intensity of care required, the possibilities for primary and secondary prevention, the burden on the family, the possibilities for in-patient and out-patient care, the extent of social concern and the influence of government policy.

Steps in the Scenario Study

For each of these themes, several future scenarios were constructed. Despite the differences among the themes, we succeeded in using one methodological approach in constructing the scenarios. Three main steps can be distinguished. First, the 'state of the art' was studied by means of a baseline analysis. Second, an analytical scenario model was developed. Finally, scenarios were constructed on the basis of quantitative data and the opinions of mental health experts.

Baseline analysis

First, a so-called baseline analysis was carried out on each of the four themes. This is a description and interpretation of the most recent scientific findings and insights on prevalence, incidence, aetiology, the possibility of prevention, treatment and care and trends in the utilisation of mental health care in recent years. This baseline analysis involved reviewing relevant literature and gathering epidemiological data from population surveys, mental health case registers and medical records. These analyses also gave an idea of relevant developments, risk factors and possible breakthroughs in the near future.

Scenario model

The second step involved the construction of a scenario model, the purpose of which was to visualise the relationships between the two main variables: morbidity and the utilisation of mental health care on the one hand, and the relevant determinants of these two variables on the other. The model shows at which points in the field of mental health and mental health care interesting or radical developments might take place or be brought about.

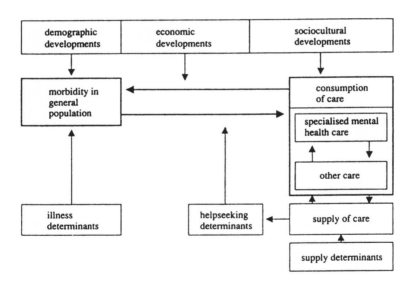

Figure 5.1 Scenario model

This simple model (see Figure 5.1) was used for all four themes. It was deliberately chosen since a scenario model is a theory-based abstraction and not an attempt to reflect all the complexities of reality. One can recognise the well-known filter model of pathways to psychiatric care, originally designed by Goldberg and Huxley (1980). The morbidity of mental health problems of the population is shown on the left-hand side of the Figure, and the utilisation of mental health services on the right-hand side. The other variables in the model are the so-called determinants influencing either morbidity or the consumption of mental health care.

It is well-known that only a small proportion of people with mental health problems seek help from mental health services. In the Netherlands, only one out of every five persons with severe mental health problems attends a mental health institution. Even for disorders requiring intensive care, like schizophrenia or dementia, less than 50 per cent of the people with those disorders receive specialised services, despite the fact that the services are freely available and well distributed throughout the country.

For future studies these findings are extremely important. The relationship between mental health problems and the utilisation of professional health care is not as tight as it is for cancer, accidents or cardiovascular diseases. Socio-cultural developments can change this relationship. For example, altering society's tolerance of deviant behaviour, diminishing the willingness of relatives to provide care, and increasing awareness of patients' rights can lead to a different proportion of mentally ill people attending professional care institutions.

So-called autonomous factors that are not supposed to be affected by policy measures are presented at the top of the model. The central system of mental health and mental health care functions within the context of economic, demographic and socio-cultural developments.

In spite of being a simple and elegant model, it is very difficult to find sufficient and appropriate epidemiological data. For the two unorthodox subjects, occupational incapacity and children's disorders, the available epidemiological data were very limited, and for the two psychiatric illnesses (dementia and schizophrenia), we had to deal with many estimates since the available data was very unreliable.

Scenario construction: exploratory and target-setting scenarios

The third step, the construction of the future scenarios, was the core of the study. As will be shown later, the contribution of the Delphi process was of paramount importance in this phase of the study. Both exploratory and target-setting scenarios were constructed. A sharp distinction must be made between these two types of scenarios (Brenner 1986). Exploratory scenarios can be described as objective or neutral future studies, while target-setting scenarios are essentially normative, ideological or political. Despite these essential differences, both scenarios dealt with the same topics mentioned in the model.

The exploratory scenarios, also called anticipatory scenarios, started with the present situation and looked ahead to the year 2010, indicating which autonomous and influenceable events could happen in the meantime. The reference scenario was a special kind of exploratory scenario. It included the most likely set of developments according to statistical projections and expert opinion. Each theme had its own reference scenario. Interesting future developments that were considered less likely, but nevertheless possible, were laid out in two alternative scenarios. For instance, three scenarios on dementia were developed. The first was a reference scenario that identified the most likely trends in the prevalence and incidence of dementia and in the size and nature of care to be delivered to the elderly in the near future. In addition to this scenario, two alternatives were constructed reflecting minority viewpoints. One described a development towards intensive professional care of elderly dementia patients and the other described one in which relatives, neighbours and other non-professionals were heavily involved, with mental health care professionals playing a more modest role.

The target-setting scenarios had a fundamentally different character. They started with a target to be realised in the future and then looked back to the present situation to indicate which specific measures, strategies or policies would be either desirable or necessary to achieve this aim. These targets were of course political in nature. For each of the four themes, targets were set which were to be realised by the year 2010. The targets were formulated in terms of diminishing incidence and prevalence and improving the quality of care that would be delivered. The exact formulation of the targets was undertaken by the research team and the scenario committee, while the expert Delphi panels gave critical feedback on the desirability and feasibility of the targets. The targets were rather provocative but were realistic according to the experts. For example, in the field of occupational incapacity resulting from mental problems, a target was set that the number of persons affected should diminish from 185,000 in 1990 to 145,000 in the year 2010, in spite of the growth of the working population during that period.

The formulation of future targets in the field of mental health and mental health care was a successful attempt to add to the health targets WHO-Europe has formulated in the Health for All by the Year 2000 programme, which emphasises quantitative targets on somatic health care and includes only a few mental health targets. In our scenario study it proved possible to formulate concrete mental health targets. It also proved possible to secure agreement and the acceptable operation of qualitative targets such as improvements in the quality of care.

Applying the Delphi Method

Quantitative forecasting can be applied when the following conditions exist (Makridakis and Wheelwright 1978; Godet 1987):

- there is information about the past;
- this information can be quantified as data;
- it can be assumed that the pattern of the past will continue into the future.

This last condition is known as the assumption of constancy and is an underlying premise of all quantitative methods.

The most uncomplicated quantitative procedure for constructing health scenarios is to project past trends in morbidity and the consumption of mental health care into the future. The idiosyncrasy of the concepts of mental health and mental health care, however, makes this simple approach impracticable in the mental health sector. Furthermore, empirical data are scarce.

The first impediment to a quantitative approach in the mental health field is the lack of valid epidemiological data over a sufficiently long period. Data on the incidence and prevalence of mental health problems in the Dutch population are scarce. The same applies to the quantification of help-seeking behaviour and to the strength of the relationship between morbidity and the consumption of care for different populations. Data on the utilisation of mental health care are available only for recent years. Furthermore, since the mental health sector has been transformed considerably, recent data are not really comparable with data collected a decade ago.

A second obstacle is that the mental health care sector in the Netherlands is clearly a field of conflicting political, social and institutional interests. Projecting trends from the past to the future is therefore unrealistic, since it would neglect future developments and shifts in the balance of power that cannot be deduced from the past. The Dutch mental health care system is heavily influenced by economic and political decisions and only slightly by autonomous changes in the morbidity of mental disorders in the population.

The conclusion was that epidemiological data were of limited relevance to the construction of scenarios. Quantitative methods of forecasting could only be used in a very limited way and more sophisticated techniques, like time-series and regression analysis, could not be performed. The Delphi Method, as a predominantly qualitative method for data collection, was chosen as the main additional source of information about future developments.

The selection of the Delphi Method should not be considered a second-best choice, however, despite the fact that it was driven by the weakness of quantitative data. Other considerations strongly favoured the use of the Delphi Method as well. For instance, the Dutch mental health sector is a complex system reflecting a diversity of interests among patients, professionals, institutions, hospitals, health insurance companies and local and national governments. Competition and cooperation, attraction and rejection are characteristic features of this sector. To evaluate shifts in this balance of power and to assess future interventions and policies, the subjective opinions of well-informed people were indispensable. The Policy Delphi (Chapter 3, see also Turoff 1975), a special application of the Delphi technique, seemed appropriate for tackling this problem.

In addition, anonymity – one of the key characteristics of the Delphi Method – was essential to reduce as much as possible the response bias which results from defending financial or political positions. Finally, the processes of iteration and feedback were other positive reasons for choosing the Delphi Method. Since each of the four mental health themes had several key aspects, experts with different backgrounds and specialised knowledge were invited to act as Delphi panellists. For instance, scientists familiar with the functions of neurotransmitters in the human brain joined a panel with psychiatric nurses and former psychiatric patients. To prevent ambiguous responses and to advance a common language for discussion, the systematic feedback of information and responses that characterise a Delphi exercise seemed desirable.

Designing the Delphi exercise

The selection of four different mental health themes required four separate Delphi inquiries. The Delphi procedure consisted of four stages and was established in advance for reasons of time-planning, budget-planning and engaging potential panellists. This pragmatic procedure, forced upon us by the reality of contractual research, differs from the ideal Delphi exercise, where the pace at which a specified level of consensus is reached determines the number of rounds to be performed.

In the first preparatory stage, fundamental choices were made about the extent of consensus that should be achieved, the use of the scenario model as a frame of reference for the Delphi exercise, and the selection of mental health experts. In the second stage, draft questionnaires were tested. The Delphi panellists received their first questionnaire containing questions which were intended to gather information for the exploratory scenarios. Draft versions of the reference scenario and the alternative scenarios were then constructed. In the third stage, the panellists had to comment on these draft scenarios and to answer questions specifically aimed at constructing target-setting scenarios. In the last round, panellists were invited to a final conference with the research team to discuss – no longer anonymously but in full view – drafts of all scenarios.

Stage one: preparatory activities

In the preparatory phase of the Delphi exercise, some basic orientations and choices were formulated. This phase is basic to every Delphi inquiry and thus a decisive factor in the success or failure of a scenario study. The first choice concerned whether or not the Delphi experts should be allowed or encouraged to re-define the central problem of the scenario study and to change the analytical scenario model that had been designed by the research team. Answering this question required some reflection on the functions the Delphi inquiry was expected to fulfil in the scenario study.

The functions a Delphi exercise can be expected to fulfil in a future scenario study are:

- Increasing knowledge about the subject or field under study. This function is especially important when the subject is still unexplored or information about it is not easily accessible to the research team. In this case, the Delphi exercise serves to add new or more detailed information to the present stock.

- Confirming or correcting information. A Delphi panel can be used to verify information the research team has gathered elsewhere. Unlike the previous situation, this 'second opinion' could be important when the quality of the information derived from other sources may be in doubt.

- Establishing priorities. In many studies, the main objective is not to make forecasts but to set out all the options with their respective pros and cons. The function of a Delphi application could involve weighing the advantages and disadvantages of possible futures and ranking the measures to be taken. This function fits in with target-setting scenarios.

- Stressing the validity of results and disseminating the findings to society, political decision-makers and others concerned. The composition of the Delphi panel might contribute to or interfere with the spread of the research findings and their implementation in legislation or government policy. A factor which should not be underestimated is that the credibility and plausibility of scenarios depends not only on what they contain but also on who is associated with them.

Since the mental health field was not *terra incognita* for the research team, the first function – adding new information to that already collected – was relatively unimportant. It followed from this that the theoretical framework which had been developed in advance, and which was represented by the scenario model, should constitute the frame of reference in the Delphi exercise. By implication, the variables and relationships between them should be respected by the Delphi panellists. The fundamentals of the scenario model should not be commented on or altered by the experts. The Delphi panels had only to indicate the probabilities of changing relationships between the variables in the model, the strength and direction of change, and finally, the consequences for both morbidity and consumption of care.

Since all four themes in the scenario study were rather broad and complex, it was first decided that the panellists had only to comment on topics on which they considered themselves to be experts. For example, an expert on psychotherapy had only to comment on the likely effects of therapy on schizophrenia and was not expected to forecast the future scope of family guidance for schizophrenics. Similarly, a nurse was expected to express views on nursing and not on psychopharmacological breakthroughs. In general, since the Delphi panellists were not all-round experts, they did not have to express their views on all the variables and relationships in the model. The changes over time in the background variables, i.e. economic and demographic developments, were considered autonomous processes. None of the experts had to comment on them, because their development between 1990 and 2010 was postulated as the frame of reference for all experts.

In the scenario construction, the last phase of the study, not all the panellists' answers were incorporated. For each topic, only the answers of the self-designated experts were processed.

A second decision to be made concerned consensus. In a conventional Delphi group, generating consensus is a major objective. As Sackman (1974) has persuasively argued, the consensus obtained in a conventional Delphi application is often specious since it results from pressure to conform to group opinions. As indicated above, in the mental health sector a Policy Delphi project was seen as more appropriate. The prime objective of a Policy Delphi is to serve as a forum for ideas (Turoff 1975). Its function is not so much to obtain a consensus as to expose all the positions advocated and the principal arguments for and against those positions. For the scenario study this implied that a Delphi design should stimulate the expression of conflicting views about the future of mental health and mental health care in the Netherlands rather than obscuring them through the use of sophisticated procedures. This approach has important consequences for the scenarios that could be composed. The points of view where the Delphi exercises succeeded in obtaining consensus could be transformed into the reference scenario. The disagreements and differing opinions, provided they were well-founded, could form the basis for alternate scenarios.

The third important decision taken in this phase was the selection of experts – an important condition for success. Important selection criteria were:

- Diversity of expertise. For every theme in the scenario study, the most relevant aspects were distinguished and experts were chosen accordingly. For instance, for dementia, some of the important topics were considered to be neurobiological aspects, the provision of out-patient care and the burden on the family, etc. Each aspect was represented by one or more experts.

- Diversity of experience. Many different professional and non-professional groups are involved in the mental health field, e.g. scientific researchers, medical personnel, psychiatrists, nurses, patient organisations, etc., all of whom have a unique perspective on future developments. Relevant types of experience were selected for all four scenario panels.

- Diversity of interests. This refers to the balance of power and the existence of conflicting interests in the Dutch mental health sector. For two reasons, several interest groups should be represented in the Delphi panels. First, since the scenario study focused both on expectations (to construct exploratory scenarios) as well as prerequisites and assumptions (to compose target-setting scenarios), a balanced composition of panels without over- or under-representation was needed to obtain unbiased results. Second, a more strategic consideration was that the panels which contained the important interests in the mental health sector might enhance the impact and facilitate the dissemination of the results of the study.

'Snowballing' and consultation with non-participating mental health experts were the methods used to find appropriate members of the Delphi panels. Besides the general criteria for selection, some individual judgements were made, for example concerning the status of a potential panellist, and verbal or written evidence that the person had an opinion and the capacity to express it. The procedure resulted in four Delphi panels ranging from 25 to 27 experts on each.

Stage two: the first questioning round

In the first round of questioning, the collection of information was exclusively directed at the construction of exploratory scenarios. It followed that the experts were explicitly asked to express only their future expectations. This was in sharp contrast with the second round of questioning. Questions about necessary policy measures and desirable changes in the mental health field were deliberately left until this round. A questionnaire was constructed with a structure analogous to the scenario model. Draft versions were tested by the research team on colleagues and other mental health experts.

Two types of questions – open-ended and multiple-choice – were asked. The open-ended questions were meant to emphasise and to stimulate the brainstorming character of the first round. For instance, the very first question asked of the Delphi panellists required them to name spontaneously five developments of major importance in the field of dementia in the next 20 years. The panels were asked to write down their arguments and explain their lines of reasoning at some length.

The multiple-choice questions focused on relevant developments – partly expressed by the panels and partly formulated beforehand by the research team – and asked about:

- the probability that the development would occur;
- the direction of its consequences, expressed in terms of an increase or decrease in morbidity or consumption of care;
- the strength of its consequence, expressed in terms of the amount of change in morbidity or consumption of care.

The respondents were limited to a choice among specific alternatives. For example, the answers to questions relating to the strength of the consequences range from 'very strong increase' to 'very strong decrease', with three fixed alternatives between them. The next questions about dementia provide some illustration.

The scenario model served as a guideline for the questionnaires. They were designed so that the respondents could be systematically questioned about the individual determinants in the scenario model. The questionnaires ended by asking the panellists their overall view on morbidity and the consumption of care in the future, taking into account all opposing or reinforcing factors.

The first questionnaire was accompanied by a paper containing information about the project and an explanation of the question-naire. The aims of this paper were first, to motivate the panellists to participate in the study; second, to ensure that respondents started with the same basic knowledge about the two dependent variables, morbidity and consumption of care, and about projected trends in

Table 5.1 Probablity and consequence

Possible development	Probability (score %)			Consequences in 2010 for the prevalence of dementia, supposing this will occur (score %)				
				++	+	0	-	--
a) primary prevention of Alzheimer dementia will be possible	0 (56	1 44	2 0)	(0	5	21	53	21)
b) recovery from vascular dementia will be possible	0 (50	1 39	2 11)	(0	5	37	47	11)

Probability: 0 = not possible, 1 = not inconceivable, 2 = probable

Consequences:

  ++ = strong increase of percentage of demented elderly (to more than 7.5%)

  + = increase (to 5.5-7.5%)

  0 = no or little change (constant: 4.5-5.5%)

  - = decrease (to 2.5–4.5%)

  -- = strong decrease of percentage demented elderly (to less than 2.5%)

the two autonomous variables, economy and demography. The paper was also used to define a number of key concepts. It must be stressed that providing the participants of the Delphi exercise with this kind of information is an absolute precondition for obtaining reliable and valid results. Creating a common understanding is particularly important when the composition of the panels is diverse.

Stage three: the second questioning round

Despite the fact that the first round of questioning was quite time consuming, requiring an average of one-and-a-half hours per respondent to complete, there was a high response rate in the second round of questioning (ranging from 73% to 92%). With only slight variations amongst the four themes, about 90% of the first round respondents participated in round two.

The second round of questioning had a two-fold purpose:

- to elicit comments on the reference scenario which had been composed from first-round responses;
- to generate those policy measures which were necessary to realise targets for the year 2010, resulting in the target-setting scenario.

Commenting on the reference scenario

On the basis of the first-round answers, the research team composed draft versions of the reference scenario on all four themes. It would be beyond the scope of this chapter to discuss this procedure of scenario construction in detail. In brief, a weighting procedure was carried out on the answers to the multiple-choice questions, using some simple descriptive statistical techniques (e.g. the proportional distribution of scores per item), supplemented by comments from the open questions. This procedure resulted in a reference scenario with developments which were seen as the most probable, and two alternative scenarios based on opinions differing from the reference scenario.

Unlike the method commonly applied in a conventional Delphi project, respondents were given a complete scenario as feedback, rather than simply the original questions and accompanying answers. The reasons for choosing this approach were time saving, the good quality of the first round answers (which made scenario construction possible), and the conviction that feedback at a higher level of aggregation would be more stimulating for participants and would enhance attention in the third round.

The experts were asked to comment on the following aspects of the reference scenario:

- Consistency: did it have a plausible and balanced structure, free from internal contradictions?
- Probability: could the scenario, viewed in its entirety, be considered probable?
- Desirability: panellists were asked to repudiate up to two developments in the scenario in order to indicate what actions and policies would need to be taken to bring about a change of direction.

The first two questions were aimed at testing and improving the quality of the reference scenarios. The aim of the third question was to generate ideas and arguments that could be implemented later on in the construction of the final versions of the exploratory scenarios and target-setting scenarios. The necessary and feasible policy measures were structured in advance around six topics. The experts were invited to express their views and recommendations on: prevention; the system of funding the health care sector; cohesion and collaboration within the mental health field; quality of care; scientific research; and, finally, inter-governmental mental health policy. Since the first Delphi round had yielded satisfactory data, no more questions were asked for the future construction of exploratory scenarios.

Generating policy measures to realise targets

The generation of policy measures was the essence of the second round of questioning. The panellists had to express their opinions on two mental health and mental health care targets formulated by the research team. To ensure the comparability of the scenarios, the targets should have been formulated in terms of the two central variables of the scenario study – morbidity and consumption of care. However, since the four themes studied in detail were rather divergent in character, the targets had to be worded accordingly. This implied, for example, that the dementia targets mentioned only health care topics, since morbidity targets were rather meaningless considering the two decades the study covered. Conversely, for the occupational incapacity theme, targets were formulated for the reduction of mental health problems as well as for the quantity and quality of care to be supplied.

For example, the threefold target for the theme 'occupational incapacity due to mental disorders' was:

- a structural decline in mental health problems in the working populations between 1990 and 2010, particularly in the categories of employees and occupations currently seen as high-risk;
- a fall in the number of disability benefits claimants with a 'mental disorder' diagnosis to 2% of the work force (a decline in absolute terms from 185,000 in 1990 to 145,000 in 2010);
- the gradual creation, over 20 years, of a situation in which 90% of disability-benefit claimants with a mental disorder diagnosis (i.e. over 20,000 people per year) can return to employment, possibly of a modified nature, within two years of becoming entitled to benefits.

The Delphi panellists had to assess the feasibility of these targets. Furthermore, they had to state the actions and policies which would need to be taken to ensure the realisation of the targets by the year 2010. Finally, the respondents had to establish priorities for their proposed interventions.

Stage four: the panel meeting

On the basis of the second-round answers, the revised target-setting scenarios were constructed and the exploratory scenarios were revised and refined. All panellists were invited to a meeting with the research team to discuss the semi-final versions of all the scenarios on their specific themes. About 40% of the respondents actually took part in these three-hour sessions. The purposes of this round were to check again the quality of the scenarios in the ways mentioned above, and to make a start with one of the scenario project's prime objectives, namely encouraging a discourse on the future of mental health and mental health care in the Netherlands.

At this stage of the study, lifting the anonymity of the participants was no longer considered an obstacle to the open exchange of ideas and opinions. On the contrary, the panellists who had found the time and made the effort to attend the conference showed a sense of collective responsibility, or even 'togetherness', concerning the results of the Delphi inquiry. The discussions in these meetings about the future that should be striven for (as worded in the original target-setting scenarios) produced a number of new insights and approaches and some more precise statements of possible interventions in the mental health field. For the research team, this phase served as a valuable check on the validity of the procedures of scenario construction.

It would not be appropriate in the context of this chapter to describe the future scenarios of all four themes which resulted from the Delphi exercise. However, to give some idea of what a scenario actually looks like, the reference scenario on dementia is presented as an Appendix.

Conclusions

The Delphi Method has been used as a tool in the process of scenario construction on the future of mental health and mental health care in the Netherlands in the next two decades. Since prediction was not an aim of the scenario project, the quality of the research outcomes (the scenarios) cannot be judged in terms of their precision in describing future events. In any case, 20 years would have to pass until the accuracy of the scenarios' assessments of morbidity and consumption of mental health care could be evaluated. Thus, the quality of the Delphi inquiry should not be equated with the assessments of the experts. Perhaps the word 'expert' is ambiguous and misleading in this context, and should be replaced by 'advocate' or 'spokesperson'. The panellists were selected as representatives of different professional and non-professional groups or interests involved in mental health and mental health care, and in that capacity they were expected to possess explicit opinions on the contemporary mental health field, not to possess expertise in prognosis. As Veatch (1991) has put it: 'One cannot presume that one is an expert in evaluating matters in an area simply because one is an expert in the science of the area'. In this respect the experiences in our study make us share the scepticism expressed by several authors (Godet 1987; Caws 1991; Ascher 1978) about the value and the status of consensus as well as the accuracy of future judgements that emerge from panels and committees.

To pass judgement on the quality of the Delphi inquiry, it must be evaluated against the aims of the study that it was part of. The explicit aim of scenario construction was to reveal to people involved in the mental health field and to political decision-makers some of the most important events and developments that could happen between now and 2010. Based on a number of plausible assumptions, a number of logical lines of thought were elaborated, resulting in two types of scenarios – exploratory and target-setting ones.

The scenarios that were created are neither true nor false. Of course, it might turn out that one of them will correctly describe the morbidity rate for schizophrenia or the number of psychiatric hospital admissions in the year 2010. This, however, would be a mere statistical coincidence, since, in a way, many scenarios have a self-defeating character. As mentioned before, the mental health sector is very policy-sensitive and this means that most developments are the outcome of deliberate interventions. Autonomous changes are rare. The publication of scenarios might promote activities or policy measures and, by doing so, undermine their own projections. For example, a future situation described by an exploratory scenario (a highly likely reference scenario) could be generally perceived to be so frightening or unacceptable (e.g. homelessness of abused children because of a shortage of crisis centres) that people would take action to prevent this future from materialising.

In addition to self-defeating prophecies, one can imagine self-fulfilling prophecies related to less likely scenarios. For example, the implementation of one appealing idea from a 'minority' scenario on improving the quality of care for the demented elderly could trigger a chain of events and interventions resulting in a realisation of a scenario on the treatment of the elderly which had not been considered likely.

Taking into account these phenomena, it is clear that the strength of scenarios and, likewise, the strength of the Delphi exercise, must be found in their capacity to generate new, surprising and plausible ideas and options for policy interventions, and for enhancing a new consciousness of the future in order to reinforce the rationality of decision-making processes. However, some important conclusions can be drawn from the mental health scenario study.

The Delphi panellists proved to be eager to express their aspirations. Even in the first round of questioning, which was only meant to generate expectations, the replies had to be carefully sifted to distinguish expectations from aspirations. Researchers must be alert to this potential confusion of answers. However, it is clear that the Delphi Method is pre-eminently suitable as a means of obtaining information for target-setting scenarios. This type of scenario focuses on concrete interventions and policies that should be adopted to realise a target, so it is clearly a value-laden or 'normative' type of scenario. This appealed very much to the participating experts and to those involved in the mental health field, including policy makers. Clarifying *dis*sensus on the issues under study proved to be as interesting and relevant to the scenario users as was the elucidation of *con*sensus. In a highly policy-sensitive field, the classical consensus-striving aim of the Delphi Method is surpassed by the quest for alternative options for managing the future.

Another conclusion is that questionnaires with many open-ended questions stimulate the experts' expression of their point of view. Since the lines of reasoning are as important as future expectations for scenario construction, questions with fixed alternatives may be inadequate since they discourage panellists from elaborating their thoughts. On the other hand, the interpretation and analysis of qualitative data resulting from open-ended questions requires special methods and is usually more time-consuming. It turned out to be very useful to employ some simple descriptive statistical procedures to analyse the quantitative data and to get a first impression of the major results. The additional value of the Delphi Method, however, lies in the qualitative responses which promote an abundance of detail and contribute to the construction of life-like and forceful scenarios.

A rather intriguing finding was the difference between the way that social and medical professionals answered questions. In general, social scientists, social workers and the like were more eloquent and comprehensive, while medical scientists and practitioners were more restricted and indicated more often that they did not feel able to give judgement on specific topics. Connected to this finding is the observation that a key issue in using the Delphi Method is to create a common understanding in situations where many experts are engaged with complicated subjects. In our study, considerable effort was put into providing the panellists with information. That did not alter the fact that in some cases the answers were ambiguous or could be interpreted in multiple ways, albeit only for a minority of responses.

In their enthusiasm for spreading their opinions, the Delphi panellists sometimes overlooked the projected trends in the two autonomous variables (economy and demography) and the findings in the reference scenario which served as a frame of reference for the target-setting scenarios. Consequently, they expressed their 'lay' views about developments in these autonomous factors and their consequences for future mental health and mental health care, and it turned out to be an important task to keep them in line to prevent the emergence of incommensurable expert answers.

The final conclusion is that a well-considered selection of experts not only improves the quality of the responses, but also increases the impact of the Delphi results (i.e., the scenarios) on society. Arousing interest about the future, from policy makers, the press, the mental health workers and, last but not least, the consumers, will be assisted by an influential Delphi panel which can inspire confidence in its results.

References

Ascher, W. (1978) *Forecasting, an Appraisal for Policy-Makers and Planners.* Baltimore, MD: Johns Hopkins University Press.

Bauduin, D. (ed) (1988) *A Guide to Mental Health Care in the Netherlands.* Utrecht: The Netherlands Institute of Mental Health (NcGv).

Bijl, R.V. (1991) *Construction of future scenarios. Policy-oriented scenario research, applied to the field of mental health and mental health care* (Dutch only). Utrecht (thesis): NCGV.

Brenner, M.H. (1986) 'Scenario decision-making and strategic planning: a framework.' In J.J. Brouwer and R.F. Schreuder (eds) *STG* 21–34.

Bronkhorst, E.M. *et al.* (1992) *Toekomstscenarios Tandheelkunde (Future Scenarios Dentistry).* Houten/Antwerp: Bohn Stafleu van Loghum.

Brouwer, J.J. and Schreuder, R.F. (eds) (1986) (Steering Committee on Future Health Scenarios, STG) 'Scenarios and other methods to support long term health planning.' In *Proceedings and Outcome of an STG/WHO Workshop*, Noordwijk, the Netherlands, 14–16 October.

Casparie, A.F. and Verkleij, H. (1990) (under the authority of the Steering Committee on Future Health Scenarios, STG). '*Chronische ziekten in het jaar 2005. (Scenarios over diabetes mellitus 1990–2005).* Utrecht/Antwerp: Bohn, Scheltema & Holkema.

Caws, P. (1991) 'Committees and consensus: how many heads are better than one?' *Journal of Medicine and Philosophy 16*, 4, 375–392.

Cleton, F.J. and Coebergh, J.W.W.(eds) (1988) (under the authority of the Steering Committee on Future Health Scenarios, STG) *Cancer in the Netherlands 1 and 2.* Dordrecht/Boston/London: Kluwer Academic Press.

Dunning, A.J. and Wils, W.I.M. (eds) (1987) (under the authority of the Steering Committee on Future Health Scenarios, STG). *The Heart of the Future/The Future of the Heart 1 and 2.* Dordrecht/Boston/London: Kluwer Academic Press.

Godet, M. (1987) *Scenarios and Strategic Management*. London: Butterworth.

Goldberg, D. and Huxley, P. (1980) *Mental Illness in the Community: The Pathway to Psychiatric Care*. London/New York: Tavistock.

Hollander, C.F. and Becker, H.A.(eds) (1985) (under the authority of the Steering Committee on Future Health Scenarios, STG) *Growing Old in the Future*. Dordrecht/Boston/London: Nijhoff.

Idenburg, P., Ketting, E., Bijl, R.V., Janssen, M.A. and Kroon, J.D. (1990) (under the authority of the Steering Committee on Future Health Scenarios, STG). *Zorgen voor Geestelijke in de toekomst. Toekomst Scenario's Geestelijke Volksgezondheid en Geestelijke Gezondheidszorg 1990 – 2010. (Caring for Mental Health in the Future Scenarios on Mental Health and Mental Health Care 1900–2010)*. Utrecht/Antwerpen: Bohn, Scheltema & Holkema. (English edition: Dordrecht/Boston/London: Kluwer Academic Press, 1991).

Lapré, R.M. and Mackenbach, J.P. (1989) (under the authority of the Steering Committee on Future Health Scenarios, STG) *Accidents in the Year 2000*. Dordrecht/Boston/London: Kluwer Academic Press.

Leufkens, H.G.M. *et al.* (1993) (under the authority of the STG) *De toekomst van het geneesmiddel in de gezondheidszorg (The future of medicines in health care)*. Houten/Antwerp: Bohn Stafleu van Loghum.

Makridakis, S. and Wheelwright, S.C. (1978) *Forecasting: Methods and Applications*. Santa Barbara, CA: Wiley.

Sackman, H. (1974) *Delphi Critique: Expert Opinion, Forecasting and Group Process*. Lexington, MA: D.C. Heath.

Schnaars, S.P. (1987) 'How to develop and use scenarios.' *Long Range Planning 20*, 1, 105–114.

Turoff, M. (1975) 'The Policy Delphi.' In H.A. Linstone and M. Turoff (eds) *The Delphi Method: Techniques and Applications*. Reading (Mass): Addison-Wesley, 84–101.

Van Wely, P.A. *et al.* (1991) (under the authority of the STG). *Arbeid, gezondheid en welzijn in de toekomst (Working conditions and health in the future)*. Houten/Antwerp: Bohn Stafleu van Loghum.

Veatch, R.M. (1991) 'Consensus of expertise: the role of consensus of experts in formulating public policy and estimating facts.' *Journal of Medicine and Philosphy 16*, 4, 427–446.

Wennink, H.J. *et al.* (1991) (under the authority of the STG). *Toekomstscenario's voor eerstelijkszorg en thuiszorg (Future scenarios primary health care)*. Houten/Antwerp: Bohn Stafleu van Loghum.

World Health Organisation Regional Office for Europe (1982) *Regional Strategy for Attaining Health for All by the Year 2000*. Copenhagen: WHO Regional Office for Europe.

Appendix
Reference Scenario Dementia 1990–2010

Incidence and prevalence

The reference scenario envisages a rise from 5.3% to 6% in the proportion of over-65s with severe dementia and related syndromes over the next 20 years, giving around 150,000 sufferers in 2010 as against around 100,000 in 1990. Almost 60% of these demented elderly will be over 80.

By far the most important factor in the increase is the ageing of the population. Life expectancy will continue to grow, thanks partly to technological advances in the area of somatic medicine, and in the absence of any breakthrough in the prevention or treatment of the main forms of dementia (particularly the Alzheimer type), the chance of contracting the condition in old age will be considerable. Some progress will be made in slowing the dementing process in old people by medication, adding to the rise in the numbers of very elderly sufferers.

Dementia will continue to be seen as a primarily biological condition whose genesis and course does not normally depend on and cannot be influenced by other factors. In the long run, ecological factors such as air, ground and water pollution may lead to an increase in the number of dementia cases.

While improvements in early diagnosis (and particularly in differential diagnosis) will give some scope for cutting the incidence of certain relatively rare reversible forms of dementia over the next 20 years, the impact on the total number of cases will be negligible. Preventive measures will allow some slight further reduction in the incidence of dementia due to cerebrovascular disease but this will be offset by the growth in the number of cases due to alcohol abuse.

Both the range of diagnostic facilities and the demand from a more knowledgeable and articulate public for early diagnosis will grow, producing an increase in the number of elderly patients with recognised dementia. In other words, more cases will be identified but the scope for treatment and cure will not expand proportionally.

While measures to reduce the number of dementia cases (through prevention and information campaigns concerned with alcohol abuse and through the promotion of multidisciplinary research into the causes and ways of dealing with dementia syndromes) will have some slight impact, their effects will become visible only in the very long term. Moreover, although the number of new patients will be cut, the standing patient population will not.

Services and their utilisation

Over the next 20 years, the intensity of care provided per patient will increase. The growing focus on dementia in the media and among carers and the resulting 'protoprofessionalisation' of the relatives of demented patients will lead to a sharp increase in the demand for both intra-mural and extra-mural care.

The public will increasingly demand screening tests for dementia and fear of dementia will put growing pressure on general practitioners to offer such tests. Given their inadequate specialist knowledge and limited diagnostic resources, GPs will refer individuals for such screening to more specialised facilities such as memory clinics and the geriatric departments of Regional Institutes for Ambulatory Mental Health Care (RIAGG) and general and psychiatric hospitals.

Patients in whom dementia has been diagnosed will also make greater use than at present of intra-mural and extra-mural services. This has various causes.

When they become sick or otherwise infirm, a growing number of elderly people will need and want to be nursed at home as far as possible and for as long as possible, but such home care will increasingly be provided by (or at least with support from) professional care-givers such as the community nursing service. The main reason for this is that, while people's willingness to care for demented relatives will neither decline nor grow, family and friends will not be in a position to take on the long-term care of sick relatives, perhaps because they are too old themselves (as the average age of demented patients rises) or live too far away due to the fact that in the future relatives will more often be spread throughout the country.

A further complication is that many demented elderly will be widows with no partner to look after them. Moreover, people now have fewer children, on average, who might care for them in old age. Finally, the higher standards increasingly demanded will mean that care can often only be provided by professionals.

The confidence of the majority of elderly people and their carers in the professional services will not decline and old inhibitions about seeking help with one's own or a relative's mental problems will weaken. This will cause difficulties. The 50% rise in the number of demented elderly over the next 20 years will be accompanied by an increase in the number of cases where nursing home admission is indicated. Under the existing norm for numbers of nursing home beds, however, intra-mural capacity will be inadequate to accommodate the growing number of patients and admissions will be blocked. The pressure on other intra-mural institutions (notably old-people's homes) and extra-mural care (out-patient clinics and the RIAGGs) will rise as a result.

Among the extra-mural facilities, sheltered accommodation and the institutions and departments providing day care will have to deal with large numbers of demented elderly. However, these will be only the milder cases. Little experimentation is likely in the new forms of accommodation for psychogeriatric patients and the nursing home will remain the final destination of many.

Despite this considerable increase in the utilisation of professional services of all types, the majority of the demented elderly will continue to be cared for by relatives in their own or their relatives' homes, albeit often for lack of any alternatives and under far-from-ideal conditions. The continuing low social status of old people and the lack of tolerance in society for deviant behaviours will remain significant factors in this connection over the next two decades.

Chapter 6

Delphi Techniques and the Planning of Social Services
The Prevention of Dependency Among the Old

Giovanni Bertin

Introduction

The research presented here deals with the problem of using the Delphi Method in support of decision-making in a situation in which it is necessary to secure the involvement of professionals with different types of knowledge and experience, and who are not used to working together.

The chapter is divided into five sections. The first provides a preliminary account of the usefulness of the Delphi Method in organisational contexts where relations among the personnel are characterised by conflict. In the second section an account is given of the approach used in specifying appropriate preventive policies and of the role played by the Delphi Method in the decision-making process. The third section describes the strategy used to involve and motivate the judges. In the fourth section, the Delphi exercise is described in terms of both the methodological choices made and the results obtained. The last two sections offer some reflections: first, on the capacity of the Delphi Method to play a part in choosing amongst priorities when policy decisions have to be taken in contexts where only inadequate information is available and where relations amongst the various professional groups are marked by conflict; second, on the possibility of motivating the personnel concerned by involving them in the decision-making process.

Reasons for Using the Delphi Method

The research presented here tackles one particular field of application of the Delphi Method. The aim of the project was to find a way of involving in the decision-making process members of professional categories in the health services who are not accustomed to working with each other and who tend to have little faith in the knowledge and information possessed by the other personnel involved in the sector (Kahnemann, Slovic and Tversky 1982). This is in fact the situation that characterises the relations between the areas of curative and preventive intervention within the health services in Italy. Curative activities are, generally speaking, undertaken within the hospital system, while preventive measures are left to the local health services. In this way, two distinct organisations are formed, each with its own characteristic forms of knowledge, its own perception of the relative importance of the phenomena in question, and with differing operating procedures that, at times, come into conflict with each other. Prevention and cure are not, however, distinct spheres that can afford to ignore each other. Rather, there is a need for those involved in the two areas, and the organisations in which they work, to be brought into direct contact with each other, despite the fact that they are unaccustomed to collaboration and each of them is sceptical about the other's activities.

On the other hand, responding to this situation by bringing directly face-to-face the separate knowledge and opinions of those involved, carries the risk of provoking 'perverse' effects for the following causes:

- the subjects who carry out managerial functions are those who have least contact with the day-to-day reality of the operations and who therefore finish up perceiving changes in the environment with some delay. Basing decisions on their points of view alone would have involved a risk of increasing the distance between environment and organisation (Bertin 1989).

- in the eyes of the subjects involved in the process of actually implementing the project, the management of the organisation has a poor reputation. There would certainly have been resistance on their part if they had not been involved in the process of choosing. This consideration is all the more pertinent in that the subjects involved in supplying the services were from different institutions, not all answerable to the same management, and in any case their relation to the system was that of 'freelance' professionals.

For these reasons it was decided to use a Delphi approach, making it possible for a high level of agreement to be reached among the subjects involved in the decision-making process and allowing the models the individual subjects have for interpreting reality to be recovered and taken up in a way unconnected with the role and functions they carry out in the organisation. In particular, the research presented here was intended to single out appropriate preventive measures which could be taken to combat the loss of autonomy in the population of old people.

The objectives that guided our work in designing the model of analysis, and that orientated the methodological choices underlying the Delphi research, can be summarised as follows:

- to involve the subjects with a significant role in the
  · decision-making process so as to avoid resistance arising at the moment decisions are implemented;
- to arrange for evaluations to be made within a rational model of analysis;
- to re-establish the principle of legitimation of the individual professional groups, identifying their specific areas of competence;
- to make up for the lack of information by recovering the assessments of the various experts present in the system of the services;
- to find a style and mode of communication with some initial connection with the logic normally used by the separate agents involved as they fulfil their professional roles.

The Analytical Model

The literature dealing with the process of ageing demonstrates quite clearly that a global approach needs to be taken when analysing the phenomenon in question, using measures capable of describing the old person's ability to 'function' in general rather than the state of his or her bodily organs. The degree of autonomy they have as regards mobility and the running of their own everyday life are undoubtedly the elements that best indicate the condition of subjects in this age group. But this approach is not yet sufficiently established among those who are called upon to deal with the phenomenon of ageing in their work.

These considerations led us to take as a starting point for the analysis of the phenomenon of ageing the interpretative frameworks guiding the procedures of the professional groups involved in the process of administering services. Regarding the functional ability of the old person, our approach would take advantage of the presence of precise clinical records. This involved the risk of not taking into account conditions of suffering linked, not so much to a single pathological condition, but to the 'synergy' of several medical syndromes or to the natural physiological deterioration connected with the process of ageing. Such conditions are, however, of less importance when it comes to constructing preventive strategies in that they are unlikely either to be avoided or counteracted.

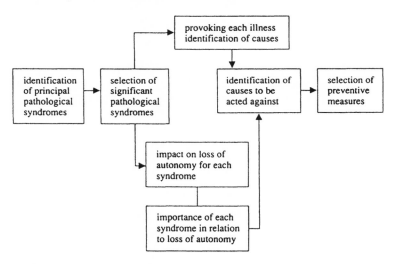

Figure 6.1 The analytical model

The analytical model is based on the identification of the pathological syndromes held to be most significant in determining the state of health of the population of the old. Among the pathologies considered to be of importance, an attempt is made to identify those that bear upon self-sufficiency in the management of daily life. The estimates of the degree of dependency produced by the occurrence of any given medical complaint, and of the probability that such illnesses will in fact give rise to some degree of invalidity, mean that the analysis can be re-connected with the concept of functional ability, this time not in an abstract way but in a way that relates directly to the thinking and the approaches that typically guide actual operating procedures. At the same time it is possible to investigate the causes underlying each separate medical complaint and so to determine the range of possible preventive measures. The choice of the medical complaint to which preventive activity is to be directed also depends on the real chances of acting upon the causal factors. By bringing estimates of the importance of each pathological syndrome alongside others concerning the concrete possibilities of implementing preventive strategies, an informed choice can be made of the areas in which to concentrate the activity of prevention.

The transition from the phase of analysis to that of planning is then less problematic, requiring only a specification of the measures actually capable of combating the processes that compromise the ability of old people autonomously to manage their own daily lives.

Choice of Judges and Strategies for Involving Them

The choice of judges proved to be quite straightforward, given the aims and the logic of the Delphi programme envisaged.

Having taken as our main aim the production of a set of decisions upon which to base planned interventions, we included in the development of the model all the medical staff involved in producing measures that concern the population of the elderly. In particular, since the procedures of the health services directed towards this age group relied on the active participation of general practitioners, we sought to involve all the GPs as well as a group of hospital doctors, who were chosen on the basis of the percentage of old people among their patients.

While it was relatively easy to define the group of judges, the process of involving them in the process of analysis was somewhat complex. These difficulties can be traced back to sets of considerations:

1. those connected with the organisational mechanisms regulating the field of decisions in which the project was to take shape;
2. those relating to the nature and the characteristics of the proposed method of analysis.

Resistance deriving from relations among social and health personnel

The policies that had been adopted by the management of the organisation up to that point had produced a wide gap between the family doctors and the top echelons of the organisation. This soon proved to be a serious obstacle to the implementation of our project, even though it started out from completely opposed premises. Our first contacts with representatives of the professional group made it apparent to us that this group considered themselves to be excluded from the decision-making process. They were also convinced that the management did not have any intention of making serious use of their professional contribution to decision-making.

Another element liable to generate resistance to involvement in the decision-making process was the strong conflict that existed between doctors working within the hospital structure and those who operated outside it. The relationship between these two professional groups very soon showed itself to be grounded in reciprocal mistrust and the absence of any form of collaboration.

Resistance linked to the nature of the Delphi Method

The proposal to base the analysis on a Delphi investigation had provoked sharp resistance from the top management of the organisation. In particular, they resisted the decision to base the analysis on the assessments of those involved in carrying out the work, rather than on direct observation of the real distribution of medical complaints in the area, and to identify causal factors by means of an experiment-based approach. The personnel involved considered such an approach to be insufficiently scientific and suggested that much more complex research projects, which would have called for substantial funding, be started. This would have meant that any decisions would have been pushed into the indefinite future. What was apparent was the difficulty that arises when the verification criteria and methods of analysis that are used differ from those typically found in debate in the medical profession. This situation is a consequence of the fact that there is a tendency in this profession to apply its own specific logical and analytical paradigms to all the other adjacent contexts being investigated. This practice makes it difficult for other analytical paradigms to be accepted and for collaboration to take place with the other professional figures who can contribute to the research and to the development of decision-making procedures in the field of health and social services.

In order to overcome this resistance we adopted three basic strategies:

1. We worked as far as possible in collaboration with representatives of the professional body with delegated responsibilities for coordinating research activity carried out by its members outside the academic framework. This choice proved to have a positive outcome because the body favoured all investigations and research activities that assigned to its members a significant role, thereby allowing them to regain positions of greater power within the organisational hierarchy of the local section of the national health service (USL). The Delphi logic put the knowledge of the doctors at the centre of the decision-making process and

thus implicitly endorsed their professional legitimacy, sanctioning the important role of their contribution in the running of the organisation.

2. A technical-scientific committee was formed within the organisation, and included representatives of the GPs and hospital doctors, top management and members of the research group. This group was assigned the task of coordinating the research and drawing up the old people's project. By doing this we convinced the representatives of the professional groups of our wish to involve them in the decision-making process and motivated them to encourage their colleagues to take part in the research.

3. A training session was organised inside the research group to clarify the methodological aspects of the Delphi Method.

By taking these three steps we were able to 'sell' the proposed strategy of analysis and to initiate a relationship of cooperation between the management of the organisation and the professional group being considered.

The Research Package and Results Obtained

The Delphi Model we applied does not correspond to any of those in the classic typology used in the literature to classify the fields of application of the Delphi Method (Linstone and Turoff 1975). Our research aimed to supply knowledge of the situation but it also had to produce decisions that would be binding on the organisation. The complexity of the project induced us to adopt a multi-dimensional model of analysis which included different stages and instruments of analysis.

The research was broken down into three distinct phases, each employing different instruments and strategies. The phases in question relate to:

1. analysis of the more significant pathologies for each of the different groups considered;

2. comparison between the assessments that emerged from the analysis of the two groups considered and the choice of pathological states;

3. analysis of the relationship between medical complaints, the processes of loss of autonomy and the preventive measures selected.

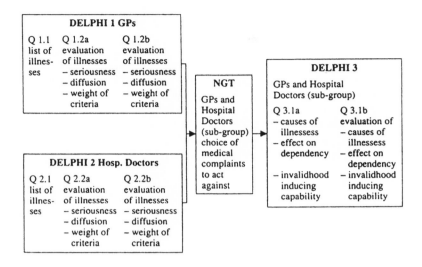

Figure 6.2 Relationship between Delphi questionnaires

The first stage of the research

The two professional groups involved by us are active in the same territorial area, but operate with reference to different clinical cases. Family doctors have to deal with medical conditions present in a stable condition while hospital doctors are called upon to act at critical moments, when the problem is acute. This fundamental difference upsets one of the basic criteria used in defining the group of judges. The subjects involved in the decision-making process observe the same phenomenon but from two quite different standpoints and two complementary rather than coincident positions. Their different perspectives would have made it difficult for us to arrive at a consensus in the evaluations of the judges. It was therefore preferred to keep the evaluations separate at first in order to be able to account later for any differences that might have emerged.

In the first stage of the research, the same type of questionnaire was submitted to the two different groups of judges. The first group included all the family doctors operating in the territory of the local branch of the national health service (USL). Contact was made by sending messages of three different types. In the first place they were sent a letter by their professional body, declaring its sponsorship of the research and inviting the doctors to cooperate and take part in the development of strategic decisions. Subsequently, a meeting was convened with the representatives of the GPs and a plan was agreed for directly contacting all the doctors and asking them if they were willing to participate. Of the 65 family doctors operating in the area, 50 expressed willingness. Those who did not accept were contacted by telephone when the research was over and they justified their position either by informing us that they did not believe in the willingness of the top management of the USL to involve them in strategic decisions, or by stating that they had too few patients to be able to offer useful assessments. Of the hospital doctors, those chosen operated in departments with large numbers of admissions of old people.

**Table 6.1 Participation in and time periods
involved in the first phase of research**

No. of Quest-ionnaire	Number of judges				Reply time
	Family Doctors (GPs)		Hospital Doctors		
	involved	replied	involved	replied	
1.1	60	50	10	10	45 days
1.2	50	45	10	10	35 days
1.3	45	42	10	10	30 days

The questionnaires were sent out and returned by post. This means of information transmission delayed the research somewhat. The time taken for a Delphi research programme to run its course depends on the degree of motivation of the judge least motivated to take part, and on the speed of transmission of the information supplied by the subject who proves to be slowest. The motivation of the judges can be influenced by involving them in the decision process or by paying them for their services. The first type of motivation works if, *and only if*, the judges work within an organisational structure that is required to act on the choices they make and with which they have a pre-existing positive working relationship. For this reason our work initially focused on these features of their work. However, the degree of involvement of the judges is not even, and the researcher carrying out the analysis has to decide when to declare closed any given stage of the survey. This point of closure is determined by the need to have the maximum number of possible replies from the judges, and also by the time necessary to obtain such information. In our case, we decided to begin to follow up the questionnaires by telephoning the judges who had not replied to the questions within a month of their being sent out. This time period was calculated bearing in mind:

1. the fact that the postal service in Italy is rather slow;
2. the time allowed for replying to the questionnaire, set at one week;
3. the average delay accepted, also one week.

We therefore telephoned all those whose questionnaires had not reached us one month after they were sent out. The request was repeated a week later if they had still not sent it back. The decision to do without the questionnaires not returned after two promptings was determined only in part by the need not to let the research drag on interminably. It derived mainly from a methodological concern, namely, that the care and attention with which the questionnaire is filled in by the judges is a function of their degree of motivation, and the time taken in replying is to a large extent a consequence of this.

In view of these factors, it is suggested that there is a threshold of delay in replying connected with possible contingent factors, beyond which such delays can be taken as a lack of motivation in taking part in the research. This observation is particularly pertinent whenever participation in the research is not rewarded by monetary remuneration. In cases in which the contract setting out conditions for taking part in the exercise does not envisage payment for the professional services of the judges, there is a risk of including some subjects who may have felt 'morally' obliged to take part but who in fact turn out not to be very interested in the matter and, as a consequence, do not respect the contract.

The close correlation between the time taken to return questionnaires and the care taken in compiling them led us to decide not to prompt late returners more than twice and to exclude those subjects who did not reply within the permitted time periods from further involvement. This decision allowed us progressively to skim off the least motivated of the doctors, gradually reducing in this way the time taken to complete the survey.

The situation with the hospital doctors was different. Being present at the same time in the same place, it was possible to hand them the questionnaires personally, thereby cutting down considerably on the time needed for the investigation and increasing the likelihood of persuading them to take part.

*Results of the first phase of the research: the importance
of the different medical conditions in the opinion of each
of the professional groups*

The first questionnaire was exploratory in intention and was supposed to define the set of medical conditions that may have some
bearing on the health of the population of old people. For this reason
the first series of questions was very open and was the same for both
groups. The second Delphi questionnaire was composed on the basis
of the results obtained, and was designed to assess considerations
that emerged from the first survey. It proved to be a somewhat
complex business to formulate the second Delphi questionnaire because the definitions used in specifying the various illnesses differed
significantly and related to clinical cases that were not always clearly
separable. Despite the fact that medicine has arrived at a codification
of its scientific terminology, it was immediately apparent that this
systematisation has not been absorbed by all the doctors and that
differing expectations are to be found, reflecting the state of scientific
research at the moment when the particular doctor qualified. The
group, therefore, turned out to be fairly heterogeneous and unable to
communicate directly in a simple, immediate way. This problem was
directly confronted by the doctors who had been co-opted on to the
research group. As a result of their efforts a homogeneous and
one-dimensional set of pathologies was defined.

With the second questionnaire the phase of evaluation was begun
and each doctor was asked to express an opinion with regard to:

- the seriousness of each of the medical conditions;
- the extent to which they were present in the area (their
  prevalence).

They were then asked to give an evaluation concerning the weight to
be assigned to 'seriousness' and 'prevalence' in the choice of medical
conditions on which to focus attention. We opted for these two criteria
on the basis of the conviction that any decision made concerning the
problem areas deserving privileged attention would have to be made
in relation to an assessment of how widespread the medical condition
was and how much of a threat it posed to old people. Since it was
considered unlikely that any medical condition would prove to be
both more serious and, at the same time, more widespread than all
the others, it was decided to make the judges reflect on the relative
importance attributed by them to each of the two criteria considered.
The decisional model employed therefore incorporates a multi-attribute logic to achieve the weighted sum of the values obtained for the
criteria considered.

The doctors involved had to evaluate seriousness and diffusion by means of a free points system, using a scale of values from one to ten. The reliability of the judges' contribution was checked by calculating a measure of dispersion based on the percentage of judgements included in an interval of +/- 1 from the average value. It was decided that the work of the judges could be considered homogeneous and the distribution sufficiently compact as long as two-thirds of the judgements expressed fell within the interval considered. This decision reflected the project's overall objective, which was to do with decision-making. The achievement of consensus was of fundamental importance as the judges would later be called upon to act on the basis of the assessments made. For this reason centrally directed measures were used, and an indicator able to show the degree of consensus achieved among the doctors. We were convinced, both by our analysis of the results and by consultations with some of the doctors, that differences of a single point on the scale would not be considered by the judges to be of significance and, therefore, would be overlooked by them. As a result we felt justified in assuming that if two-thirds of the judges concurred in a certain evaluation it was likely that all of them would agree to it and that, consequently, they would go along with the policies deriving from the evaluations in question. This condition proved to be fulfilled only in the case of the judgements expressed on four medical conditions.

The results that came out of the second questionnaire brought to light considerable variability in the judgements even within single groups of doctors. When preparing the questionnaire we had envisaged that we would find conflicting opinions concerning the evaluation of the diffusion of each medical condition, but we expected to find the evaluations concurring with regard to the seriousness ascribed to each of the pathological syndromes. The results, however, after processing, brought out a marked dispersion in the judgements concerning both evaluation criteria, making it clear that the same professional group, even though it works in environmental and technological conditions that are homogeneous, may have somewhat varied perceptions of the gravity of the effects associated with any particular illness. This situation can be explained as the consequence of the meeting of two variables: one corresponding to the level of scientific explanation provided on any given illness in the course of regular medical study and training, and the other connected with actual experience of dealing with the illness. The same illness can indeed occur in different forms, presenting more or less serious symptoms, and the doctor concerned will tend to consider the illness in relation to the factors at work in the particular case histories with which he or she is familiar. The results that emerged from the hospital

Gazing into the Oracle

doctors' contributions were decidedly more varied over the question of the prevalence of the pathological condition and more cohesive with regard to its seriousness. The level of gravity that this group is called upon to deal with is in effect more homogeneous, their patients having been filtered through the family doctor network. They are more directly involved in the processes of specialised redefining of knowledge in their areas of expertise and their assessment proves to be more readily linked to debates going on in the specialised literature.

The results that emerged from the second evaluation expressed by the judges show a significant degree of reflection on the data.

Pathology of the joints

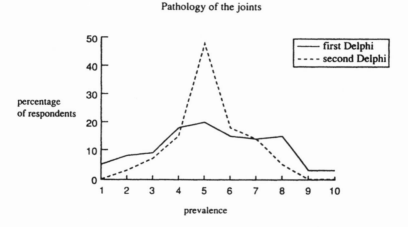

Figure 6.3 Example of the distribution of judgements in the first and second Delphi questionnaires

The two distributions presented in Figure 6.3 are fairly representative of the pattern of judgements expressed in relation to all categories of disease considered. The second distribution can in every case be described by a curve that is much less widely distributed and closer to a normal distribution. The judgements expressed concerning the medical conditions considered all fall within the parameters decided upon for the evaluation to be considered sufficiently reliable.

The process of analysis could therefore be considered to be concluded once the discrepancies internal to each of the professional groups had been reduced, but the problem of the deformities pointed up by a comparison between the assessments made by each of the groups still remained to be resolved.

The characteristics of the second phase of the inquiry

The comparison carried out between the results of the analysis of the judgements expressed by the GPs and those of the hospital doctors, underlined the need to search for a synthesis of the two positions that emerged. It turned out that each of the two different groups of judges had its own opinion of which pathological conditions attention should be directed towards.

Table 6.2 Relative importance assigned to each medical condition

	Average score overall (Score = SxWS + DxWd)			
	Family doctors		Hospital doctors	
Complaint	Score	Rank	Score	Rank
cardiac decompensation	6.70	1	4.00	
disturbances of heart-beat rhythm	6.55	2=	4.40	
chronic obstructive bronchopathy	6.55	2=	6.00	5
arteriosclerosis	6.40	4	5.40	
constipation	6.25	5	5.00	
osteoporosis	6.20	6	5.60	10
ictus	6.10	7=	4.40	
arterial hypertension	6.10	7=	6.80	1=
pulmonary emphysema	6.10	7=	5.00	
hypertensive cardiopathy	6.00	10	5.40	
arthritis	5.00		6.80	1=
anxious-depressive states	5.40		6.80	1=
sleep disturbances	5.70		6.70	4
alcoholism	4.50		6.00	6
lung cancers	5.80		5.80	7
myocardial infarct	5.60		5.60	8
urinary infections	5.20		5.60	9

The scores shown in Table 6.2 were obtained by means of an adjusted sum of the average values assigned by the judges to the two criteria considered. Taking, for example, the score 6.70 attributed to cardiac decompensation, this figure is arrived at by adding the average value attributed to its seriousness (appropriately weighted by a coefficient expressing the relative importance assigned to the criterion of seriousness in the process of choice) to the average value attributed to the prevalence of this particular medical condition (again weighted, this time for the relative importance assigned to its prevalence). That is to say:

$$P = S \times Ws + D \times Wd$$

where P = degree of priority; S = seriousness score; Ws = relative importance assigned to the criterion of seriousness; D = diffusion score; Wd = relative importance assigned to the criterion of diffusion.

The presentation of the data that came out of the first phase of the analysis led the technical-scientific committee to consider as more reliable the evaluations of the family doctors, as far as the frequency of the various medical conditions was concerned, and to pursue the analysis in evaluating the seriousness. The fact of having kept apart the two groups of professionals produced a first significant element for the decision-maker and for the dynamics internal to the different professional groups. The decision that the information supplied by the family doctors concerning the prevalence of the various medical conditions was to be considered more reliable, attributed to them an important role in the ongoing decision-making process. In this way an initial, usable channel of communication was established, linking sectors of the profession not accustomed to pooling their expertise. Building on this base, it was decided to organise a Nominal Group Technique (NGT) (Delbecq, Van de Ven and Gustafson 1975) session with the aim of defining the levels of seriousness to assign to each pathology. The NGT session, involving nine people from both groups, allowed the differences to be reduced so that specifications of the degrees of seriousness to be attributed to the selected medical conditions could be decided upon. The weighted combination of the degrees of seriousness and the estimate of the frequency gave rise to the selection of the five medical conditions generally considered capable of influencing, to a notable extent, the well-being of old people. The pathological conditions in question were:

arthritis

arterial hypertension

sleep disturbances

arteriosclerosis

anxious-depressive states.

The third stage of the research: the relationship between pathological syndromes and autonomy of the population of old people

The third stage of the analysis involved administering and processing two Delphi questionnaires directed at subjects who had been involved in the NGT session. The decision to restrict the group of judges to the participants in the NGT session was made on the basis of the need to get things done without undue delays and the advisability of involving, in a single group, the representatives of both the professional groups who would be concerned with putting into effect the preventative measures chosen. In addition, having taken part in the NGT session, those involved were certainly more motivated, meaning that the two questionnaires could be dealt with more quickly (Alemi, Cats-Baril, Gustafson 1984).

The first Delphi questionnaire used in this part of the analysis concentrated on three different questions. The first question aimed to explore the relationship between pathological conditions and the process of loss of autonomy. In practice this involved bringing the analysis back within the strategies at the centre of the decision-making process. The assumption upon which the prevention programme was to be built had the aim of singling out the illnesses that should be acted on in order to counteract the loss of autonomy in old people. For this reason two further criteria of evaluation were introduced, relating to:

1. the frequency with which these medical conditions generate effects causing invalidity (this criterion was labelled 'correlation'); and

2. the extent to which the condition plays a part in determining the level of dependency present in the population of old people under consideration (the criterion of 'importance').

The evaluations of the judges enable us to establish that in the area we examined there exist two medical conditions that together determine 79.5% of the situations in which an old person comes to lose the ability to manage his or her own life without help. The strong link between the onset of arthritis or arteriosclerosis and the manifestation of effects significant for the autonomy of the elderly population is in any case confirmed by the estimate of the probable correlation with this phenomenon. These are, then, the two medical conditions that, in the opinion of the judges, are most often connected with significant changes in the self-sufficiency of the subjects concerned.

Table 6.3 Correlation and importance measures for selected illnesses

	Correlation	Importance
arthritis	21.0%	26.5%
arterial hypertension	4.5%	6.5%
sleep disturbances	6.0%	3.0%
arteriosclerosis	41.0%	53.0%
anxious-depressive states	13.0%	7.0%
others		4.0%

The second part of the Delphi questionnaire employed was of a directly propositional nature and aimed at identifying the causal factors on which to direct attention in order to reduce the presence of the established illnesses and their capacity to bring on invalidity. With this aim, the judges were asked to list the causal factors they held to be particularly significant and then to put them in descending order, assigning the value 1 to the most important and 10 to the least important. The choice of the evaluation criterion was guided by the need to construct a scale of priorities for tackling the different measures to be taken.

The result brought out various areas and causal factors upon which to concentrate the preventive measures. These areas of action pertain to:

- styles of life (with reference in particular to wrong diet, sedentariness, alcohol abuse, over-eating, smoking);
- environmental conditions (home and work-place damp or cold);
- incorrect habits and forms of behaviour (e.g. excessive workload on a single joint);
- inevitable effects of the process of ageing;
- consequences of traumas;
- various types of metabolic imbalance;
- side-effects due to persistent hypertension.

Some findings confirming the results that emerged from the research

At the end of our work we distributed a questionnaire to those who had taken part, aimed at checking the results. Analysis of the data that emerged allowed us to confirm that the Delphi strategy had produced significant results and had contributed towards breaking down a pattern of relations involving little collaborative effort between the professionals and the management of the organisation. This aspect of the research was particularly important to us because our meta-aim had to do with finding decision-making strategies that would permit judgements expressed by the experts to be included in the decision-making process, thereby making a break with the incremental approach that was the norm in the organisation.

The data shown in Figure 6.4, obtained from the evaluation questionnaire administered to the judges at the end of the Delphi research programme, confirms the positive nature of the experience.

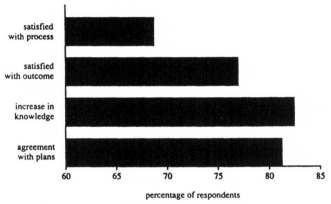

percentage of respondents

Figure 6.4 Family doctors' assessments of the Delphi exercises

Analysis of the results brings out the definitely positive opinion held by the professional groups involved. Eight-one per cent of the family doctors involved declare themselves completely in agreement with the directions taken in the plans that emerged from the analysis, and in 77% of cases declare themselves satisfied with the results of the work carried out. Even more significant is the fact of having been able to break down the wall of mistrust that existed in the relationship between the family doctors and the management of the organisation. In this respect some importance should be attached to the fact that 69% of them consider themselves satisfied with the research because, finally, their knowledge has been taken into consideration and included in the decision process. The last noteworthy element is the fact that 82% believe that the fact of taking part in the Delphi programme may have produced a reasonable increase in knowledge and may have unified the working practices of the doctors, reducing the difficulty of cooperation amongst professionals operating in different contexts.

Conclusions

The work we carried out enables us to confirm that the Delphi system can be considered a useful instrument for action intended to increase the rationality of the decision-making process in complex organisational contexts characterised by an inadequate information system. The structuring of the process of communication frees the exchange of views from conflict-creating prejudices and allows an analysis to be achieved that gets away from the stereotypes produced during day-to-day activities.

A further element that emerged concerns the possibility of linking up the Delphi Method with instruments of inquiry that can be effective in shorter time periods. The instrument in question here, the Nominal Group Technique, allows the speed of the inquiry process to be increased, but has to be applied in previously structured contexts. The structuring of the problem, in fact, requires the researcher to have greater freedom and cannot be rigidly predetermined, as is required by the organisation of the NGT itself (Gustafson, Cats-Baril and Alemi 1992).

The positive aspects mentioned can take shape only on condition that success is achieved in motivating the judges in their participation, and in removing the resistance connected with accepting such an unorthodox method of inquiry, and one that differs from the traditional canons of scientific research.

References

Alemi, F., Cats-Baril, W.L. and Gustafson, D.H. (1984) *Integrative Group Process* (working paper). Centre for Health Systems Research and Analysis. Madison, WI: University of Wisconsin.

Bertin, G. (1989) *Decidere nel Pubblico*. Milan: Etas Libri.

Delbecq, A.L., Van de Ven, A.H. and Gustafson, D.H. (1975) *Group Techniques for Program Planning: A Guide to Nominal Group and Delphi Process*. Glenview, IL: Scott-Foreman.

Gustafson, D.H., Cats-Baril, W.L. and Alemi, F. (1992) *Systems to Support Health Policy Analysis*. Ann Arbor, MI: Health Administration Press.

Kahnemann, D., Slovic, P. and Tversky, A. (1982) *Judgement under Uncertainty: Heuristics and Biases*. Cambridge: Cambridge University Press.

Linstone, H. and Turoff, M. (eds) (1975) *The Delphi Method: Techniques and Applications*. Reading, MA: Addison-Wesley.

Chapter 7

Alternative Approaches
to the Computerisation
of Social Security
Reflections on a Delphi Exercise

Michael Adler and Roy Sainsbury

Introduction

Over the past 25 years the Delphi Method has been adapted and used in an increasing number of ways. It has also been developed to take advantage of the opportunities presented by computer technology (see Chapter 3 above). In some ways the increasing technological sophistication of the Method may be off-putting for researchers and practitioners who do not have access to state-of-the-art computer equipment or are operating on modest budgets. In this chapter, therefore, we wish to describe our experiences of using the low-tech end of the Delphi methodology spectrum (what Linstone and Turoff (1975) call 'paper-and-pencil' techniques) in a study of the possible uses to which information technology can be applied in the delivery of social security benefits in Great Britain.

The chapter first describes the background to the research that we were commissioned to undertake by the Department of Health and Social Security (DHSS, as it then was). We then explain the terms of reference of the project and why we chose to use a version of the Delphi Method in preference to other techniques. The next section describes the essential elements of the research project: the people who participated, the structure of the questionnaires used, and our methods of analysis. We then spend some time reflecting on the strengths and weaknesses of our particular application of the Delphi Method and draw lessons for its future uses.

The Research Task

Background to the computerisation of social security

In 1982 the DHSS published its plans to computerise the whole social security system in *Social Security Operational Strategy: a Framework for the Future*, (DHSS 1982). Quoting an earlier Departmental working paper (DHSS 1980) it pointed out 'that social security operations were under considerable strain,...but that advances in computer and telecommunications technology were creating new opportunities for advance during the 1980s'. The Operational Strategy had three fundamental objectives (DHSS 1982, p.l):

1. to improve operational efficiency, reduce administrative costs and increase the flexibility of the operational system to respond to changing requirements;

2. to improve the quality of service to the public, e.g. by treating customers in a less compartmentalised benefit-by-benefit manner and more as 'whole persons' with a range of possible social security business, and by improving the provision of information to the public; and

3. to modernise and improve the work of social security staff.

In *A Framework for the Future* (DHSS 1982), the Department also outlined some of the main parameters of the programme. These comprised:

- movement towards a unitary claimant database which, in order to avoid excessive size, would be divided into geographical segments linked through a Departmental Central Index (DCI);

- the adoption of a functional approach to the processing of claims to benefit which would bring together the various functions which are common to all benefits, e.g. collating evidence, determining entitlement and implementing decisions;

- the development of a three-tier system comprising the DCI, area computer centres (where claimant records would be located) and a network of local offices containing interactive terminals which would constitute the main means of access to the system;

- a phased programme of implementation in which a number of discrete projects would be implemented in an incremental manner. Fourteen projects were identified at this stage and a number of additional projects were subsequently added in the light of changes to the social security system.

The Operational Strategy was summarised by O'Higgins (1984) as 'a response...to the problems of cost, size, duplication and complexity' which characterised the administration of social security.

Of the three fundamental objectives mentioned above, the first reflected the interests of the organisation, the second reflected the interests of the customer, while the third reflected the interests of social security staff. From the outset the Department of Social Security (DSS, as it had now become) paid greatest attention to the first – the technical task of setting up the necessary hardware and software (Dyerson and Roper 1989). It also attempted to construct job specifications which went some way to achieving the third objective (DSS 1988). Thus, there was an assumption that if the system was right and the staff happy, then an improvement in quality of service to the claimant would automatically follow.

Although the Department developed a number of initiatives designed to improve service to the public, they were largely pursued independently of the Operational Strategy. Furthermore, in spite of numerous rhetorical references to the 'whole person concept', the Strategy document contained little evidence that much thought had been given to what this might mean.

The impetus for the rediscovery of computerisation's potential contribution to quality of service came from the National Audit Office's scrutiny of the implementation of the Operational Strategy (NAO 1989). Its report criticised delays in the completion of individual projects and the Department's response to them. In particular it found a 117% increase in costs (which rose from £784m in 1982 to £1,700m in 1988) and a 54% decrease in savings (which fell from £1,006m in 1982 to £463m in 1988). The NAO considered that the escalating costs of the Operational Strategy were serious enough to call into question the financial viability of the entire programme unless improvements in the quality of service, which it had recommended in an earlier report (NAO 1988), were taken into account.

Putting the 'whole person' concept into practice

When the government became aware of the content of the NAO Report, it recognised that, since the publication of *A Framework for the Future* in 1982, little thought had been given to what the 'whole person' concept might mean in practice. In response, we were commissioned by the DSS to investigate its possible interpretations and implications. Our terms of reference were as follows:

- to give some substance to the notion of 'quality of service' by specifying those aspects of service to the public which are most salient;

- to identify the range of possible interpretations which can be given to the 'whole person' concept;
- to develop a small number of viable organisational models which could be run on an experimental basis in different local offices;
- to suggest a set of evaluation criteria in terms of which these models and the Operational Strategy as a whole could be assessed.

It is clear that these research objectives entailed a substantial modification of the DSS's implicit technological determinism, i.e. of the assumption, referred to above, that if the system was right and the staff were happy, an improvement in quality of service would necessarily follow, in that they implied that an elaboration of the notion of 'quality of service' could lead to experimentation and organisational innovation. They also involved a set of highly normative questions about which we ourselves held strong views and could quite easily have written about at great length. However, we thought the DSS would be more interested in an attempt to collect and collate systematically the views of a cross-section of informed and interested parties. The question for us was how best could we achieve this.

The opportunities presented by Delphi

Collecting data by a simple, one-off postal questionnaire, or by carrying out interviews, were two possibilities. However, we wanted our participants to generate ideas about the use of technology and thought that this could be achieved most effectively by bringing them into contact with one another in some way. Organising a panel of experts in, for example, a day conference would have been possible but, in our view, had several drawbacks. We were aware of the difficulties in getting the right people together at the same time and at reasonable cost, but more than that, we were concerned about the extent of the contribution each could make in a limited amount of time. Also we wanted to include relatively junior staff of the DSS (to give a view based on their experiences of working in local offices) and thought that they might have felt inhibited in the company of more senior officials. We wanted to encourage creative and innovative thought without the possibility (or probability) of hostilities breaking out between, for example, welfare rights workers and DSS policy makers.

We chose to adopt the Delphi Method because it promised all that we wanted without the limitations of one-off questionnaires or interviews or the problems of a face-to-face conference. It seemed to us to be a particularly effective means of canvassing opinion, identifying areas of agreement and disagreement, isolating ideas which called for further clarification, and developing and refining policy options. Moreover, its flexibility meant that it could be adapted to suit our particular research objectives.

Choosing our panel of experts

Our first task was to identify a set of respondents. Our selection reflected our wish not only to seek the views of those involved in the formulation or implementation of the Operational Strategy, but to canvass a much wider range of opinion. Sampling was problematic since there was no natural population which could act as a sampling frame. The participants were therefore selected to represent the main interest groups and all shades of opinion. We identified four main groups of experts from which to draw our sample:

1. DSS staff: including policy makers and systems analysts from the Operational Strategy team, local office staff and representatives from DSS trade unions;

2. welfare rights/pressure groups: this group comprised individuals who in some way represented claimants, including pressure groups, welfare rights workers, Citizens Advice Bureaux, Consumer Councils, and local authority Social Work/Social Service departments;

3. academics and researchers: including those with an interest in the administration of social security and in the application of information technology to case-level decision-making;

4. other organisations: this group included individuals with experience of large organisations, such as banks and building societies, and individuals with knowledge and experience of social security administration in the USA, Belgium, Australia and Norway.

It will be noted that we did not attempt to canvass the views of claimants directly. This is because the Delphi Method assumes a level of expertise that few claimants can be expected to have. This is not to deny that it would have been helpful to canvass their views by other means. Unfortunately, it was not possible to organise a claimant survey within the time and resources that were available to us. Nevertheless, many of our respondents, particularly those from welfare rights organisations and pressure groups, explicitly adopted a claimant perspective.

Designing the first Delphi questionnaire

It was clear from the outset that the time constraints under which we were working (we were funded for only twelve months) meant that we would have to restrict the Delphi exercise to two questionnaires (which we will refer to as Q1 and Q2 respectively).

Our task in designing our first Delphi questionnaire (Q1) was to formulate a set of issues to include and to devise an appropriate means of eliciting respondents' opinions. Our approach was based on an initial feeling that the 'whole person concept' could embrace a range of meanings depending on what are regarded as desirable and legitimate activities for the DSS in its administration of the social security system. It seemed to us that the Department could either restrict itself to a re-active approach (by merely processing the claims presented to it by claimants) or that it could, in addition, adopt some form of pro-active role (for example, by providing information, advice and guidance to individual claimants, developing multi-purpose claim procedures, providing help with budgeting or offering to refer claimants to appropriate welfare services). Furthermore, we felt that 'quality of service' had two distinct dimensions. On the one hand, it could be taken to refer to the range of provisions provided for the claimant as a social security customer; on the other hand, it could refer to the treatment of the claimant by the staff of the DSS, i.e. to the idea of being of service rather than providing a service. This distinction was used as the basis for Sections 1 and 2 in the first Delphi questionnaire.

All the issues or questions that we wanted to explore were presented in the form of policy options, such as 'The DSS should provide a more local service by opening more local offices which would serve smaller communities' or 'The performance of individual local offices should be assessed and the results made publicly available'.

Section 1 (comprising 12 policy options) referred to specific activities which the DSS either undertook at the time or could have undertaken in the future. Since we were interested in how broad a role our respondents thought the Department should adopt, and where they thought the boundaries between social security and other services and activities should be drawn, we included questions on the provision of money advice, help with budgeting, negotiation with creditors and referral to other agencies. We also included questions on the provision of information, the development of multi-purpose claim procedures, and the encouragement of participation in decision-making as well as questions on the prompt and accurate assessment of claims.

Section 2, which was primarily concerned with quality of service issues, addressed and covered issues such as courtesy, privacy, accessibility, convenience and impartiality (seven policy options in all).

It was clear that the operationalisation of the 'whole person concept' would be shaped by financial and technical considerations as well as by whatever was thought to be the legitimate or desirable span of Departmental activities. However, once a choice was made, there would be implications for the interface between the public and the staff of the Department and for the internal organisation of the office. The introduction of new technology would structure this interface and the internal organisation of the local office in such a way as to promote a particular version of the whole person concept. Sections 3 and 4 therefore addressed organisational issues.

Section 3 (13 policy options) explored a range of organisational issues and included questions on the integration of separate assessment procedures for unemployment benefit and housing benefit, the location of offices and their internal organisation, the provision of automated banking facilities, and the need for professional training of staff.

Section 4 (five policy options) asked respondents to assess four organisational models which the DSS put forward for discussion in a report on new technology, job design and organisation (DSS 1988). The four models all referred to the internal organisation of local social security offices and differed in the extent to which they maintained specialised roles.

Whatever version of the whole person concept the DSS chose to adopt, it would be important to evaluate its impact on the service provided to the public. At the time, the Department was using a number of 'performance indicators' to monitor its operations. However, these were mostly designed to meet the needs of management; the question of how service to the public should be measured had only recently been addressed. Section 5 explored some general policy questions concerned with evaluating performance, whilst Section 6 addressed the problem of what evaluation criteria would be suitable for assessing quality of service.

Section 5 (four policy options) examined possible ways in which the performance of the DSS could be assessed and raised questions about the relative merits of internal versus external audit and the use of objective versus subjective criteria.

Section 6 contained a list of 19 evaluation criteria which could be employed in the assessment of the performance of the DSS in its administration of the social security system.

In Q2, Section 6 was divided into two parts assessing objective and subjective evaluation criteria respectively. Section 7 appeared in Q2 only and explored a number of miscellaneous issues raised by the responses to Ql. Topics in Section 7 covered the structure and content of training courses for DSS staff, possible strategies to reduce waiting times in local offices, the relocation of benefit administration from central to local offices, and the integration of specialist functions with the processing of claims.

The task for our Delphi participants

Respondents were invited to comment in their own words on any or all of the policy options, to identify advantages and disadvantages, to modify the options, to argue in favour or against any of them, and to raise new policy options for consideration. Where appropriate, they were also invited to assess the desirability and feasibility of each of the policy options. In Ql, in an attempt to oblige respondents to make positive or negative assessments, we used two four-point scales (though, as we shall explain later, we changed to a five-point scale for the second questionnaire). The task of our respondents is illustrated in Figure 7.1 below which shows an extract from the first questionnaire.

3.4 The DSS should provide a more local service by opening more local offices which would serve smaller communities.

Comments:

Desirability assessment		Feasibility assessment	
very desirable	1	definitely feasible	1
desirable	2	possibly feasible	2
undesirable	3	possibly infeasible	3
very undesirable	4	definitely infeasible	4

Figure 7.1 Example of evaluation required in first Delphi questionnaire (overall importance asked separately)

Our interest was primarily in desirability but, in addition to rating the desirability of each policy option, we felt it was also important to assess the relative importance of each option compared with others. Where appropriate, therefore, respondents were also asked to rank the overall importance of the policy options within each Section. Since each Section contained a different number of questions, the extent of the ranking varied from Section to Section.

Analysis and presentation of results from Q1

Responses to Q1 were received from 56 of the 70 respondents who had agreed to take part. Completed questionnaires were analysed as follows:

- Where appropriate, we calculated the distribution of desirability and feasibility ratings and ranked the aggregate desirability and feasibility scores (after giving each rating a score of +2, +1, -1, or -2 on a four-point scale) within each Section or Sub-Section of the questionnaire. We also aggregated the overall importance scores for each policy issue, and likewise ranked them within each Section or Sub-Section.

- We collated all the comments on each of the policy issues and selected five or six which were representative of the range of comments made. Some respondents wrote at far greater length than others while a small minority rated and ranked all the policy issues but made no comments at all. 234 comments were selected from the 2,356 received – seven respondents were not quoted at all while the maximum number from any one respondent was 19. On average each respondent was quoted four times.

- In addition, we added our own summary of the ratings, rankings and comments of respondents in an attempt to provide a balanced overall assessment and indicated whether the option needed rephrasing, developing or relocating elsewhere in the questionnaire.

We produced a two-part Interim Report (Adler and Sainsbury 1988). Part I summarised the responses of the 56 respondents to the various policy issues raised in Q1. Part II analysed the responses to each policy issue in detail and included the quantitative assessments referred to above, a selection of qualitative comments, and our own summary of the main points raised by respondents. Figure 7.2 is an extract from the Interim Report illustrating the way in which we fed back the results of Q1 to our respondents.

Policy options 3.4: The DSS should provide a more local service by opening more local offices which would serve smaller communities.

Summary of responses

	+2	+1	-1	-2	Rank (out of 13)
Desirability rating	21	28	3	1	1st
Feasibility rating	8	29	17	0	7th
Overall importance of score 116					1st

Selection of comments

'No need for fully functional local offices in small communities, but a caller facility only (many offices already have this) for enquiries and information would be welcome in rural areas. With the direct access to benefit information arising from the Operational Strategy, this is even more feasible.'

'Could use existing district council offices or other public buildings at minimum cost, and post offices or banks on an agency basis. Mobile offices, like mobile banks, in rural areas, e.g. for Highlands and Islands.'

'The size of the office must be suited to its environment. For rural areas, offices should be smaller and more local. In more urban areas, larger offices may mean that more expertise on particular benefits can be built up.'

'There should be a gradual move away from the existing local offices towards more numerous, much smaller "social security centres" of the same size and appearance as Job Centres, and towards larger and fewer, perhaps regional, processing centres.'

Summary and response

Rated first in terms of desirability, seventh in terms of feasibility, and ranked first (of 13) in overall importance. Several respondents referred to the Moodie Scrutiny (an internal enquiry into Departmental administration) and the need to reverse the DSS's policy of concentration into larger Integrated Local Offices. They suggested that smaller offices, particularly but not only in rural communities, would provide a more personalised service, that they would reduce some of the pressures found in larger offices, and that they would be more convenient, especially for elderly and disabled claimants. Those who disagreed favoured a less personalised service. The movement towards a larger network of smaller offices, serviced by regional processing centres, was seen to be consistent with the Operational Strategy.

*Figure 7.2 **Example of analysis of responses to items in first Delphi questionnaire***

Designing the second Delphi questionnaire

On the basis of responses to Q1, a number of new policy issues appeared in Q2 and the wording of many of the original policy options was amended. Some policy options were moved to more appropriate Sections of the questionnaire. A new Section (Section 7) was included which allowed us to follow up some of the issues raised in Q1 in more detail (for example, about the content of training). Respondents were also asked to provide details of their employment history, their knowledge and experience of the Operational Strategy and of the administration of social security, their experience of providing a service to the public and in the use of computers in organisations, and the general perspective from which they approached the Delphi exercise.

Forty-three responses to Q2 were received. Forty of the 56 respondents who completed Q1 also completed Q2. In addition, three of the respondents who had not sent back Q1 were able to complete Q2. The 43 respondents to Q2 now comprised:

- 11 DSS personnel;
- 11 welfare rights officers and representatives of pressure groups;
- 11 academics and researchers;
- 10 persons with backgrounds in other organisations or overseas social security administrations.

The analysis of the responses and the presentation of the findings were similar to the first questionnaire. However, as we mentioned earlier, the desirability and feasibility scales were expanded to five-points (this time including a response for neutral or don't know answers) in response to requests from a number of respondents. We also aggregated the overall importance scores for each policy issue, and ranked them within each Section or sub-Section of the questionnaire.

At this stage we produced a two-part Final Report (Adler and Sainsbury 1990). Part I summarised the responses of the 43 respondents to the amended set of policy issues raised in Q2, and formulated a number of conclusions and recommendations relating to our research objectives. Part II reproduced the analysis of the responses to each of the policy issues in Q1 and presented a comparable analysis of the additional issues raised in Q2. While the two questionnaires were similar, they also had important differences, the implications of which we discuss later.

For the purposes of this chapter we do neither propose to present our findings in detail nor to discuss their wider ramifications (for a detailed discussion of our findings which attempts directly to address our terms of reference, see Adler and Sainsbury 1990; for a more wide-ranging discussion of the implications of our findings, see Adler and Sainsbury 1991). Instead we shall reflect on the Delphi Method and our use of it.

Reflections on the use of the Delphi Method

To begin with, we have a number of self-critical observations on the way in which we designed and carried out the Delphi exercise. First, we were aware from the literature that, ideally, Delphi exercises should consist of at least three or four rounds during which the questionnaires evolve from the relatively loose and unstructured to the more precise and structured. However, as we have already explained, it was clear from the outset that because of the time constraints of the project we could not afford the luxury of so many rounds and had to limit ourselves to two questionnaires only. This meant that we had to be more structured in our design of the first questionnaire than we would have liked, and although we were prepared to do this in order to reap the potential rewards from the Delphi approach, in retrospect we do see the disadvantages of collapsing the process into just two stages.

The main disadvantage of our approach is that there appears to have been a positive bias in the issues that our respondents were asked to consider. In only one of the Sections of the Delphi questionnaires did we require choices to be made between mutually exclusive options, i.e. between different organisational designs for DSS local offices. In the other Sections there were very few issues which attracted clear disapproval (even those which scored low on overall importance still attracted positive desirability scores). By structuring the policy issues as we did (with this inherent positive bias) and by asking the respondents to comment in any way they chose, including the option of not replying at all, we did not elicit systematically information on the relative advantages and disadvantages of each policy option. As a result we are suspicious of the apparent consensus that the responses to the two Delphi questionnaires suggest exists. When we compared the responses of the four groups of participants for Q2 we found them to be remarkably similar. For four of the Sections – on the span of Departmental activities (Section 1), the treatment of claimants (Section 2), organisational strategies (Section 4), and principles of accountability (Section 5) – there were no statistically significant differences amongst the four groups on any of the 34 policy issues. In the other two Sections – on organisational issues

Gazing into the Oracle

(Section 3) and follow-up proposals (Section 7) – a number of significant differences amongst the four respondent groups were found (see
Adler and Sainsbury 1990, Part 2).

Another way in which consensus can be artificially created by the
Delphi Method is that when the results of the first questionnaire have
been sent to the respondents, some of them may think that their views
are so at variance with the other participants that they consider their
further involvement a waste of time and hence do not reply to Q2.
Between Q1 and Q2, we lost 16 respondents, some of whom wrote us
to explain that they could not afford the time to complete the second
questionnaire.

When we first chose to use the Delphi Method, we were interested
to know, from a methodological viewpoint, how much the Interim
Report, which was the sole mechanism by which participants learned
of the views of the rest of the respondents, influenced the responses
to Q2. However, the changes that we introduced to Q2 (in the light of
the responses to Q1) render comparisons impossible. There are several examples of this. First, the wording of some of the policy issues
was amended. We could not therefore compare the answers to many
of the issues since we would not have been comparing like with like.
Second, there were eight additional policy issues in Q2 which meant
that the number of issues in some Sections increased. In some instances this necessitated ranking a different number of policy issues,
again rendering comparison between the two questionnaires impossible. A third change that we made to Q2 was to relocate some of the
issues that, from the responses to Q1, appeared misplaced in a
particular Section. A final problem, which was entirely of our own
making, were the differences between the desirability and feasibility
rating scales used in Q1 and Q2. In Q1 we adopted a four-point scale,
following the standard Delphi practice of not allowing respondents
to adopt a neutral position on any issue. What we did not do,
however, was to provide the opportunity to record a 'no judgement'
response which is, of course, perfectly valid, particularly when considering feasibility (for example, some respondents were clearly in
no position to assess whether some policy options were financially
possible). As a result, several respondents complained that they could
not record their genuine response to some issues. As referred to
above, we therefore decided to introduce a five-point scale for Q2
(with a '0' midpoint rating). In retrospect we are not convinced that
this was the best way of dealing with the problem since the zero rating
was used by a large number of respondents on some policy options.

For all these reasons we were unable to carry out what for us
would have been an extremely interesting piece of methodological
analysis. The only way, it seems, to measure the effect of the feedback

to the respondents would have been to make no changes between Q1 and Q2. This is of course not a particularly appropriate course of action in a policy-related research project. In what we may call this 'policy versus science' tension, policy concerns will almost invariably dominate.

A big attraction of the Delphi Method is that it combines both quantitative and qualitative elements. Since we were interested in the generation of new policy ideas as well as responses to our own suggestions, we were particularly keen to exploit the qualitative potential of the technique. However, both in our design of the questionnaires and in our presentation of the results, we now think that we may have unwittingly encouraged an emphasis on the quantitative element of the Delphi Method. Although some respondents wrote thoughtfully and at length on many of the policy issues, there were many who were cursory in their comments and some who did not comment at all. Almost everyone, however, did complete the requirement to rate and rank the issues, a much less demanding alternative to putting thoughts into words. In our presentation of the results to Q1 in the Interim Report we were perhaps at fault in putting the quantitative results at the head of each page (see Figure 7.2) above the selection of respondents' comments and our summary. This may have given too much prominence to the ratings and rankings. In retrospect we would have reversed the order and placed greater emphasis on the written comments.

Another reason for reducing the emphasis on the quantitative results is that there are potential difficulties in giving equal weight to the responses of people with widely varying knowledge and experience of social security administration, the Operational Strategy and providing a service to the public. Using a three-point (high, medium, low) scale, the 43 respondents to Q2 assessed their knowledge as follows:

Table 7.1 Self-assessed knowledge of Delphi response

Topic	Self-assessed knowledge		
	High	*Medium*	*Low*
Providing a service for the public	27	10	6
The administration of social security	14	15	13
The Operational Strategy	8	9	24
The use of computers in organisations	14	15	13

It will be seen that respondents rated their knowledge of providing a service to the public highest and their knowledge of the Operational Strategy lowest. There were differences in the ways in which respondents in the four sub-groups assessed their knowledge and experience of the four areas referred to above. The overall pattern was as follows:

Table 7.2 Self-assessed knowledge of four sub-groups of respondents by topic

Topic	DSS staff	Welfare rights orgs.	Academics/ researchers	Other orgs.
Providing a service to the public	high	medium-high	medium-high	high
The administration of social security	high	medium	medium	low
The Operational Strategy	medium-high	low	low	low
The use of computers in organisations	medium	low-medium	low-medium	high

The difficulties are probably more relevant for the assessment of feasibility, since there seems little reason for giving greatest weight to the desirability ratings regarding, for example, assessments by DSS staff of what activities the DSS should engage in merely on the basis of their greater knowledge of social security administration. Clearly, the views of welfare rights organisations and pressure groups are equally as valid on such issues.

Whether or not we could have devised a means of eliciting directly the views of social security claimants is unclear. As it was, we had to make do with proxy views. In the second questionnaire we asked respondents to indicate the general perspective which they adopted in their assessment of the policy options. Seven of the 43 respondents either did not answer or said they had adopted no particular perspective. Of the remaining 36, ten said that they had replied from a claimant perspective. However, we were criticised, not least by the DSS, for failing to elicit claimants' views directly and this may well have detracted from the impact of the exercise.

A final reflection concerns the impact of our Delphi exercise on the policy makers who commissioned the project. Many policy-related Delphi exercises, it seems, are carried out by organisations which are also responsible for implementing any resulting changes to policy. Such organisations will naturally have a large commitment to using the results of the exercise, and may involve the research team who carried out the exercise in later decision-making. Our relationship with the DSS was very different. As external researchers, we effectively persuaded the Department of the validity and potential usefulness of the Delphi approach, and thereafter were left alone to complete the project. After submitting our final report, our only direct contact with the DSS was limited to a formal presentation of the results to the relevant policy makers. This gulf between ourselves and the Department can be partly explained by the transfer of the civil servant who originally commissioned the research, but looking back we think it would have been wise to have maintained closer contact with his replacement and other key officials. Since we have not been involved in any subsequent policy discussions it is difficult to assess whether the exercise was a success from the DSS's point of view.

Conclusions

In this chapter we have described how we adapted the Delphi Method to address a particular set of research objectives, and reflected on the strengths and weaknesses of our approach and on the technique itself. Our reflections above are presented in the spirit of constructive self-criticism and as such we have concentrated on our mistakes and our doubts about some aspects of the Delphi Method.

However, we do not want to leave the impression that our overall assessment of the Delphi Method, or our use of it, is negative. We were particularly pleased at the range and calibre of our respondents, and are certain that we could not have recruited their assistance to a comparable extent in any other way. We are sure, for example, that many would not have been able or willing to attend a conference on the subject (even supposing that we had had the necessary funds to bring them together). In addition, we found that one of the promises of Delphi, that people with a lower status in organisations are not over-awed or intimidated by their superiors or by other eminent people, was entirely borne out. Some of our most diligent and assiduous respondents were administrative officers in DSS local offices, people who would not normally have the opportunity to participate in such a project.

We are certainly encouraged enough by our experience to consider the Delphi technique a useful methodological tool for certain types of research. Without the need for sophisticated computer facilities we were able to harness the knowledge and experience of a range of informed individuals, and generate and appraise a diverse number of policy ideas. We have also been able to assess the strengths and weaknesses of our use of Delphi in this exercise which we hope will serve to help others achieve the potential of a highly versatile research technique.

References

Adler, M. and Sainsbury, R. (1988) *Putting the Whole Person Concept into Practice: Interim Report* (Parts I and II). Edinburgh: Department of Social Policy, University of Edinburgh.

Adler, M. and Sainsbury, R. (1990) *Putting the Whole Person Concept into Practice: Final Report* (Parts I and II). Edinburgh: Department of Social Policy, University of Edinburgh.

Adler, M. and Sainsbury, R. (1991) 'The social shaping of information technology: computerisation and the administration of social security'. In M. Adler, C. Bell, J. Clasen and A. Sinfield (eds) *The Sociology of Social Security*. Edinburgh: Edinburgh University Press.

Cm 288 (1988) *Government's Expenditure Plans 1988–9 to 1990–1*. London: HMSO.

DHSS (1980) *A Strategy for Social Security Operations*. London.

DHSS (1982) *Social Security Operational Strategy: A Framework for the Future*. London.

DSS (1988) *New Technology, Job Design and Organisation*. London.

Dyerson, R. and Roper, M. (1989) *Computerisation at the DSS 1977–89: The Operational Strategy* (Technology Project Papers No.4). London: London Business School.

Linstone, H.A. and Turoff, M. (eds) (1975) *The Delphi Method: Techniques and Applications*. Reading, MA: Addison-Wesley.

National Audit Office (1988) *Department of Health and Social Security: Quality of Service to the Public at Local Offices*. London: HMSO.

National Audit Office (1989) *Department of Social Security: Operational Strategy*. London: HMSO.

O'Higgins, M. (1984) 'Computerising the social security system: an operational strategy in lieu of a policy strategy'. *Public Administration 62*, 201–210.

Otton, G, (1984) 'Managing social security: government as big business'. *International Social Security Review 2*, 158–170.

Chapter 8

The Use of the Delphi Method in Forecasting Accidents in the Year 2000

Ed van Beeck

Introduction

Long-term planning is an important part of health policy. Many policy measures in this area are characterised by a long time-lag between development and implementation, and, after being implemented, may need a long time before they ultimately achieve their desired effect. Therefore, some strategies should be prepared far in advance, e.g. to keep the supply and demand of health care facilities in balance and to reduce the major health problems facing modern society.

In the process of long-term planning, the application of forecasting techniques (e.g. the Delphi Method) can be of value (Brouwer and Schreuder 1986). This chapter describes the methodology, the approach and the results of a Delphi study into the future of accidents and traumatology in the Netherlands. This study was initiated by the Steering Committee on Future Health Scenarios (1986), a body advising the Dutch government on long-term developments in health and health care.

Accidents were selected because of their frequent occurrence and serious consequences. They constitute one of the major health problems in the industrialised world (Committee on Trauma Research 1985; ECMT 1986; Geus 1987). At the time the study was conducted, there were almost 4,000 deaths and 100,000 hospital admissions per annum from traffic accidents, occupational accidents or home and leisure accidents in the Netherlands (see Table 8.1).

Home and leisure accidents accounted for more than half of the accidental deaths and for almost three-quarters of the hospital admissions due to injuries. Many of these accidental deaths and hospital admissions concerned elderly people who sustained a hip fracture (without performing a specific activity).

**Table 8.1 Annual numbers of deaths and hospital admissions
related to accidents, by type of activity, the Netherlands c. 1984**

	Deaths		Hospital admissions	
	Absolute number	Per 100,000 of population	Absolute number	Per 100,000 of population
Traffic	1752	12.1	23,500	162.6
passenger car	774	5.4	5500	38.0
moped	125	0.9	3300	22.8
bicycle	360	2.5	6400	44.3
pedestrian	212	1.4	2600	18.0
other traffic	281	1.9	5700	39.5
Occupation	75	0.6	3000	20.7
industry	12	0.1	800	5.5
building trade	10	0.1	800	5.5
services sector	24	0.2	1000	6.9
other occupations	29	0.2	400	2.8
Home and leisure	2068	14.2	71,500	494.7
house-keeping	157	1.0	3000	20.7
do-it-yourself activities	62	0.4	1500	10.4
sports	78	0.5	16,500	114.2
other home and leisure activities	1771	12.3	50,500	349.4
Total	3895	26.9	98,000	678.0

Source: Adapted from data published in various CBS publications

Although traffic accidents accounted for fewer victims than home
and leisure accidents, they also constituted a large problem. Most
road traffic casualties were passengers in private cars or cyclists. On
the other hand, occupational accidents appeared to be a public health
problem of relatively minor importance.

In the period directly preceding the study, there had been a
remarkable reduction in the number of accidents in the Netherlands.
Between 1970 and 1984, a tremendous drop in mortality due to traffic,
occupational and home and leisure accidents was observed (see
Table 8.2).

Table 8.2 The development of accident mortality in the Netherlands, by accident category, 1970-1984 (indirectly standardised for age and sex)

Year	Mortality rates (per 100,000 person-years)			
	All accidents	Traffic accidents	Occupational accidents	Home and leisure accidents
1970	51.3	26.7	1.6	23.0
1975	39.6	18.5	1.2	19.9
1980	30.5	15.0	0.8	14.7
1984	25.5	12.3	0.6	12.6

Source: Adapted from data published in various CBS publications

The decline in traffic accident mortality was most impressive. Policy measures aimed at preventing accidents (speed limits, compulsory wearing of seat belts and crash helmets, alcohol legislation, etc.), taken by the Dutch government in the period 1970–75, made a major contribution to this development (Kampen and Edelman 1979; Noordzij 1980). On the other hand, factors considered 'autonomous' by health policy makers were also important (Beeck and Machenbach 1988). For example, the economic recession after the first oil crisis (1973) had an important (negative) influence on the growth rate in traffic volume; furthermore, technological progress improved the safety of roads and road vehicles.

In the 1970s, reductions in accident mortality were also observed in many other countries (Lamm, Chouieri and Kloeckner 1985). However, despite this development, in the early 1980s accidents still constituted a major health problem in the industrialised world. This is why in 1984 the European Member States of the World Health Organisation formulated as a target a 25% reduction in accident mortality between 1980 and the year 2000 (WHO 1985). The Delphi study on 'Accidents and Traumatology in the Future' was set up to investigate the possibility of achieving this reduction. Because of the potential influence of both autonomous developments and policy measures, the study had two aims:

1. to explore those autonomous developments that might take place before the year 2000, and their likely effects on the incidence and outcome of accidents;

2. to list policy measures which might be implemented before the year 2000, and estimate the potential effects of different strategies on the incidence and outcomes of accidents.

In this chapter, the methodology and main results of the Delphi study 'Accidents and Traumatology of the Future' are presented, and the implications of the study for long-term health planning in the Netherlands are discussed.

Methodology

The Delphi study was undertaken between June and November 1986. The subject was divided into four areas: traffic accidents, occupational accidents, home and leisure accidents and medical care for accident victims.

In selecting the panellists, priority was given to obtaining a balanced distribution of expertise in the four specific subject areas. In order to avoid 'common bias', experts belonging to different sections of society (government, trade unions, business, private organisations, research institutes, etc.) were chosen.

Eighty Dutch experts were asked to participate. Anticipating potential non-response, four samples of twenty panellists were formed. Our intention was to achieve panels of about 15 respondents, on which experts from all important sections of society were represented.

Considerable attention was paid to the design of the questionnaire. Four questionnaires were designed, all of which had the same structure. This structure was based on a conceptual model of the processes behind accidental injuries and their outcomes (see Figure 8.1).

The conceptual model distinguishes a number of separate 'variables' which are influenced both by autonomous developments (demographic, economic, socio-cultural and medical technological developments), and by policy measures (in the fields of accident prevention and medical care). The following 'variables' were included:

- Exposure (e.g., the number of passenger kilometres travelled in the population).
- Accident risk (e.g., the number of injured persons per passenger kilometre).
- Case fatality (the number of accidental deaths per 100 injured persons).

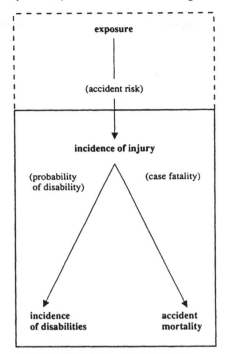

Figure 8.1 The central variables in the Delphi study

- Probability of disability (the number of newly disabled persons per 100 injured persons).

The questionnaires presented to the experts asked them to attach probabilities to one or more of the 'variables' concerned, under a number of different conditions:

1. A combination of minimal government intervention (no new initiatives in the fields of accident prevention and medical care for accident victims in the period 1985–2000); modest economic growth (1–1.5% per year, at that time regarded by experts as the most likely economic development); the respondent's assessment of the socio-cultural and (medical) technological developments resulting from this situation.

2a. A combination of minimal government intervention; rapid economic growth (4% per year); the respondent's assessment of socio-cultural and (medical) technological developments resulting from this situation.

2b. A combination of minimal government intervention; economic stagnation (0% growth per year); the respondent's assessment of the socio-cultural and (medical) technological developments resulting from this situation.

3. As (I) but with strong government intervention in the fields of accident prevention and/or medical care for accident victims (assuming the implementation of a number of policy measures mentioned by the respondent).

All the combinations had to be based on the demographic 'middle variant' of the population forecast of the Dutch Central Bureau of Statistics of 1985 (Cruijssen 1986), featuring an increase in the number of people over the age of 65 years between 1985 (12% of the total population) and the year 2000 (14% of the total population).

Combination 1 aimed to display the most likely development according to the Delphi respondents (the so-called principal expectation). The possibilities classed under combination 2 were meant to give a picture of the likely range of autonomous developments. Combination 3 aimed to give an impression of the maximum that government policy could achieve.

The experts were asked to give quantitative estimates of the rate of change of the variables concerned, as well as verbal statements. The experts on traffic, occupational and home and leisure accidents had to express their opinions on possible changes in exposure (where other sources of information did not exist), and accident risk. Both variables were subdivided according to the principal activities in which accidents occur. The experts in the field of medical care for accident victims were asked for their expectations of case fatality and the probability of disability. These two variables were divided according to the principal types of injury. In giving their quantitative estimates the experts were asked to use the scale represented in Table 8.3.

Table 8.3 The answer categories in the questionnaires used in the Delphi study

	Annual rate of change	*Situation at 31/12/1999 compared with 1/1/1986*
++	> 5% increase	+ 100% or higher
+	1-4% increase	between +15 and +80%
0	< 1% increase/decrease	+/-15%
-	1-4% decrease	between -15 and -45%
--	> 5% decrease	-50% or lower

In designing the questionnaire, we tried to avoid aggregating developments for which quite different future trends might be expected in the following ways:

- by constructing a separate questionnaire for each of the four areas;
- by distinguishing exposure, accident risk, case fatality and the probability of disability;
- by distinguishing a large number of separate activities (see Tables 8.4–8.6) and separate types of injury (see Table 8.7).

This does not mean, however, that aggregation could always be avoided. For example, the questions did not specify different age groups.

Considerable attention was also given to avoiding ambiguity. The questionnaires were accompanied by a pack of explanatory material, containing definitions of the terms used and detailed instructions on how to complete the questionnaire.

In the first round, the Delphi study used a structured questionnaire. After the results of the first round were analysed, a second questionnaire was given to the respondents, who were given the opportunity to redefine or to elaborate upon their earlier responses. The second questionnaire informed the respondents about their own answers and the group's collective opinion, as expressed in the first round.

Results

The response to the two questionnaires was highly satisfactory. Of the panellists (all panels combined) 82% returned both questionnaires. Amongst the four panels there were no important differences in response rates (variation from 75%–85%). All panels consisted of 15 or more respondents.

For a selection of questions we present the expectations of the experts in the fields of traffic accidents, occupational accidents, home and leisure accidents and medical care for accident victims. The group's collective opinions on different questions are set out in the Tables below. In describing the results, the verbal statements given by respondents are also referred to. The group's collective opinion was defined as the smallest number of contiguous categories chosen by at least two-thirds of the respondents. If, for example, a two-thirds majority of the panellists chose two contiguous categories, these answers indicate the group's collective opinion (e.g. 0/- if 5 of the 15 respondents chose 0, and 6 of the 15 respondents chose -).

In nearly all the questions, a high level of consensus was reached after the first round. Although the second questionnaire led to changes in individual answers, e.g. by respondents who interpreted certain terms correctly only in the second round, it had little influence on the collective opinions of the group. Only a few questions led to considerable disagreement. In a few cases, two groups of about equal size could be identified, choosing quite different (not contiguous) categories: e.g. where 7 of the 15 respondents chose + and 8 of the respondents chose -. These cases are indicated by the term disagreement.

Traffic accidents

The panel's expectations of developments in exposure and accident risks, as expressed by experts in the field of traffic safety, are presented in Table 8.4.

Table 8.4 Expected trends in exposures and accident risks in traffic, under different conditions, 1985-2000 (group answers of the Delphi panel on traffic safety, second round (n=15))

	Principal expectation	Alternative autonomous developments		Strong government intervention
		Rapid growth	Stagnation	
	1	2a	2b	3
Exposure (passenger km per inhabitant per year)				
passenger car	+	++/+	+/0	not asked
moped	0/-	0/-	0/-	not asked
bicycle	+/0	+/0	+	not asked
Accident risk (injured persons per passenger km)				
passenger car	-	+/0/-	0/-	-/--
moped	+/0	+/0	0	0/-
bicycle	0/-	+/0	0	0/-/--
pedestrian	0/-	+/0	0/-	-

We comment first on the principal expectations. The panel thought that modest economic growth would lead to growing use of passenger cars, and that a growing attention to 'health' would lead to a shift from the use of mopeds to the use of bicycles. According to the panellists, for most traffic modes the risk of accidents would be reduced by the introduction of new safety technologies. The only exception was moped drivers, where the risk of accidents was expected to rise because panellists expected that the use of mopeds would be more and more restricted to people in the 16–17 year-old age group who are inexperienced in traffic and exhibit a high propensity for risk-taking.

According to the panel, rapid economic growth would lead to some unfavourable developments. A higher level of economic activity would not only lead to a growing use of passenger cars, but also to a rise in the risk of accidents, because of a higher level of risk acceptance in society under these circumstances. Economic stagnation would have quite different results. The use of passenger cars would be restricted. The risk of accidents would increase compared to a situation of modest economic growth, because no new safety technologies would be introduced.

This panel expected that the risk of accidents would be substantially reduced by strong government intervention. In particular, occupants of passenger cars would profit from a number of policy measures aimed at improvements in road behaviour, roads and road vehicles. These might include a national policy in the field of traffic-safety education, the introduction of new safety technologies, and measures aimed at the separation of traffic modes.

Occupational accidents

For occupational accidents, Table 8.5 shows the expectations of trends in accident risks. The experts in the field of occupational safety were not asked for their expectations of changes in exposure, because estimates of this variable were already available from the Dutch Central Planning Bureau (CPB 1985).

Table 8.5 Expected trends in accident risk at work, under different conditions, 1985-2000 (group answers of the Delphi panel on occupational safety, second round (n=15))

	Principal expectation	Alternative autonomous developments		Strong government intervention
		Rapid growth	*Stagnation*	
	1	*2a*	*2b*	*3*
Accident risk (injured persons per person-year)				
industry	0/–	0/–	+/0	–/––
building trade	0/–	+/0/–	+/0/–	–/––
services sector	0	0	0	0/–

According to the principal expectations of this panel, the accident risks of workers in manufacturing and the building trade would fall on account of the introduction of new technologies for controlling work-related injuries.

Rapid economic growth would lead to the same developments, whereas economic stagnation would result in the absence of investment in new technologies and lead to increasing accident risks in manufacturing.

The panel was optimistic about the influence of strong government intervention. Many policy measures which could reduce the accident risks in those areas were mentioned, e.g. compulsory occupational safety services, extension of the capacity and powers of safety inspectors, extension of the powers of work councils, etc.

Home and leisure accidents

Table 8.6 sets out the opinions of the experts in the field of home and leisure accidents. This panel expressed the following principal expectations: people would spend less time on housekeeping; do-it-yourself activities and sports would grow in importance. In contrast to the expectations in the fields of traffic safety and occupational safety, unfavourable trends in accident risks were anticipated on the assumption of modest economic growth. Accident risks at home were expected to rise because of the ageing of the population. The accident risk associated with do-it-yourself activities was expected to grow because of the use of more dangerous equipment. Sports would be accompanied by higher accident risks because of a shift towards more hazardous types of sporting activity and because people were expected to exhibit more 'aggressive' behaviour.

Both rapid economic growth and economic stagnation were expected to have effects on the exposure to the risk of accidents. Contrary to what was expected in the fields of traffic safety and occupational safety, accident risks would hardly be influenced by alternative economic conditions.

This panel was also optimistic about the effect of strong government intervention. Whereas without government intervention accident risks were expected to rise, according to this panel the implementation of a number of policy measures aimed at changes in behaviour and improvements in product safety would lead to a reduction of these accident risks: for example, a national policy in the field of safety education, legislation in the fields of product recall and product liability.

**Table 8.6 Expected trends in exposures and accident risks
at home and during leisure activities, under different conditions,
1985-2000 (group answers of the Delphi panel on home
and leisure safety, second round (n=17))**

	Principal expectation	Alternative autonomous developments		Strong government intervention
		Rapid growth 2a	Stagnation 2b	
	1	2a	2b	3
Exposure (activity hours per inhabitant per year)				
house-keeping	0/-	-	+/0	not asked
do-it-yourself activities	+	+/0	+	not asked
sports	+/0	+	0	not asked
Accident risk(injured persons per activity hour)				
house-keeping	+/0	+/0	+/0	0/-
do-it-yourself activities	+	+	+	0/-
sports	+/0	+/0	0	0/-

Medical care for accident victims

The expectations of trends in case fatality and the probability of disability, as expressed by the experts in the field of medical care, are represented in Table 8.7. This table only shows the expectations under the assumption of modest economic growth, either with or without government intervention. The experts in medical care were not asked to consider the consequences of alternative economic conditions.

It was expected that, even without government intervention, the case fatalities for most types of injury would drop as a result of progress in the field of medical technology. All injuries except those of the central nervous system would benefit from new diagnostic and therapeutic methods. With the exception of injuries of the central nervous system, this panel had an equally optimistic view about the future probability of disability.

It was expected that case fatalities of severely injured patients, especially those with injuries of the central nervous system, would be greatly reduced by the introduction of policy measures aimed at improving the system of trauma care in the Netherlands. This would consist of measures in the fields of pre-hospital care – such as introducing a national emergency phone number and staffing ambulances with nurses who have supplementary training in trauma care; in hospital care, such as regionalisation of trauma care; and rehabilitation, such as increasing the volume of rehabilitation medicine.

Table 8.7 Expected trends in case fatalities and probabilities of disability, under different conditions, 1985-2000 (group answers of the Delphi panel on medical care for accident victims, second round (n=16))

	Principal expectation 1	Strong government intervention 3
Case fatality (deaths per 100 injured persons)		
skull fractures and intracranial injury)	0	-
spinal cord injuries	0	0/-
hip fractures	-	-/--
burns	-	-/--
internal injuries of abdomen, chest and pelvis	0/-	-/--
multiple injuries	0/-	-/--
Probability of disability (disabled persons per 100 injured persons)		
skull fractures and intracranial injury	0	disagreement
spinal core injuries	0	0/-/--
peripheral nerve damage	0/-	disagreement
hip fractures	0/-	0/-/--
other fractures	0/-	-/--
soft tissue injuries	0/-	-/--

Little agreement was reached about the influence of these measures on the probability of disability resulting from some types of injury. For example, in the case of skull fractures and intracranial injury, about half the panellists expressed the opinion that a reduction of case fatality would be accompanied by an increase in the probability of disability based on an increasing number of very severely injured patients as survivors. The other half expected a decrease in the probability of disability based on the prevention of secondary brain damage by the new policy measures.

Variation

In our description of the results of the Delphi study, we have focused on the opinions of two-thirds majorities of the panels. These panels showed a high level of consensus in their expectations of the future under four different combinations of autonomous developments and policy strategies.

Only a few items where there was considerable disagreement were identified, for example, the panel on medical care could not agree on change in the probability of disability arising from some types of injury in response to improvements in the system of trauma care. The lack of consensus may, however, provide important information for health policy since it can show where further research is needed.

In addition, for nearly all items one or two respondents formulated answers which were quite different from the group's collective opinion. This is illustrated in Figure 8.2, which shows the distribution of opinions on the expected trend in accident risks (by activity type) and case fatalities (by type of injury), assuming the most likely course of economic development (modest economic growth) and minimal government intervention.

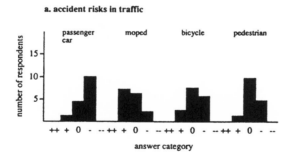

Figure 8.2 The distribution of answers to questions about the development of accident risks, by type of activity (Delphi panels on traffic, occupational, and home and leisure safety) and case fatality, by type of injury (Delphi panel on medical care for accident victims), under conditions of modest economic growth and minical government intervention.

b. accident risks at work

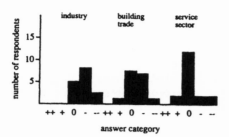

c. accident risks at home and during leisure activities

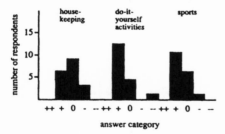

d. case fatality by type of injury

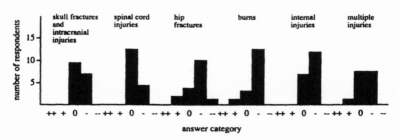

Figure 8.2 (continued)

In the field of traffic safety, two respondents expressed more pessimistic views concerning the development of accident risks. Contrary to the group's collective opinion, these respondents believed that risk consciousness would be reduced as a result of favourable trends in the preceding period, and that this would lead to increasing risk behaviour. In the other panels, small minorities with quite different opinions were also found.

These 'dissident opinions' might also be useful in health policy-making because they help identify 'low probability/high-impact developments'; that is, future developments which are not very likely but which might have a very high impact on the problem if they did occur.

Discussion

To facilitate long-term health planning, a Delphi study was carried out on possible future developments in the field of accidents and traumatology. The results of this study provide information about autonomous developments which might take place between 1985 and the year 2000, as well as about policy measures which could be implemented in this period.

The Delphi study provided interesting new information which could be used in formulating a national strategy in the framework of the World Health Organisation's 'Health for All by the Year 2000' strategy.

However, the results were obtained by a method which is not beyond criticism (Sackman 1975). The Delphi Method is characterised by a number of problems concerning the selection of panellists, the size of the sample, the design of the study and the structure of the questionnaire. The ways in which these problems were dealt with have been described above, but none of these problems could be completely solved.

In selecting the panellists the problem is that there are really no 'experts on future developments'. This probably explains why many respondents stressed that their opinions were to be regarded as 'speculations' rather than as 'predictions'.

In considering the size of the samples, it must be recognised that most panellists did not have expert knowledge of all the subjects in the questionnaire. For a few specific questions, the number of true experts was probably far lower than the number of overall respondents.

In a Delphi questionnaire it is very difficult to avoid aggregation and ambiguity. In conducting our study, considerable attention was given to this problem. The questionnaires were designed with care, using a conceptual model of the processes underlying accidents and their consequences. Although many different sub-areas were distinguished, and all key variables in accident epidemiology were treated separately, aggregation could not be entirely avoided; that is, no questions were asked about specific age groups. Moreover, it is quite possible that some questions may have had more than one interpretation.

A final problem concerns the structure of the Delphi questionnaire. In order to reduce the number of approaches to the panels, we started with a pre-selected set of questions. This may have reduced the number of ideas obtained.

These methodological problems indicate that the results obtained in our study should be considered as 'well-informed speculations on the future'. Treated as such, they nevertheless provide valuable information.

A Delphi study, if executed with care, should be recognised as a well-developed and systematic procedure for tapping expert opinion. It avoids some of the problems of group processes which employ face-to-face interaction. Our Delphi study illustrated consensus, but also displayed disagreement where it existed. It paid attention to the group's collective opinion as well as to 'dissident' opinions of individual participants. And because the questionnaires used rather 'extreme' combinations of autonomous developments and policy strategies, its results provide a good picture of the range of possible future developments which need to be considered by health policy makers.

A disadvantage not mentioned so far concerns the inherently fragmented nature of the results. A Delphi study leads to many separate estimates of different variables in different sub-areas. In our study we asked for expectations on exposures, accident risks, case fatalities and the probability of disability for 13 activities in the fields of traffic safety, occupational safety and home and leisure safety. Possible interactions between the different sub-areas were not investigated. This produces the danger of the results being inconsistent. We therefore decided to conclude the Delphi study with a workshop for sub-samples of panellists who could then check the consistency and critically. review the methods and results of the enquiry. No inconsistencies were, however, identified by the participants, who regarded the results as plausible and coherent descriptions of future developments under different sets of conditions (Beeck *et al.* 1989).

Another problem resulting from the fragmented nature of the procedure is that a Delphi study provides information on developments of separate variables without providing a clear view of the 'net effects' of these developments; for example, accident mortality in the population. In order to calculate these net effects, we constructed a computer model (Mackenbach *et al.* 1989). Some of the results obtained with this model have already been reported elsewhere (Beeck *et al.* 1989). The model consisted of two parts: a demographic sub-model which simulated changes in the population structure as forecast by the Central Bureau of Statistics, and an epidemiological sub-model. In the latter model, the accident mortality of a future year, to take one example, was calculated by multiplying the population numbers by age and sex as computed in the demographic sub-model, and the exposures, accident risks and case fatalities of the principal types of activities and principal types of injuries. The data on exposures, accident risks and case fatalities derived from routinely available statistical information from the Netherlands. For future years, these data were adapted as suggested by the Delphi panels.

The results of these calculations confirmed the impression based upon inspection of the separate calculations. The principal expectations of the respondents implied that health policy makers would have to anticipate a combination of developments both favourable (e.g., technological progress) and unfavourable (e.g., the consequences of an ageing population, a growing amount of traffic and a growing participation in hazardous sports). The net effect of these developments would, according to our computer calculations, be a stabilisation of accident mortality rates at 1985 levels. It was further shown that rapid economic growth and economic stagnation would both probably lead to 'trend reversals'. Rapid economic growth, for example, was expected to lead to increasing risk behaviour in society while economic stagnation was expected to result in the absence of (medical) technological progress. We calculated that the net effect of both situations would be a rise in accident mortality between 1985 and the year 2000.

In the way described above, the results of our Delphi study were used as input for computer model calculations, and formed the basis for a number of 'future health scenarios', both with and without government intervention.

These scenarios were presented to health policy makers in 1988. It was demonstrated that the favourable trends of the period 1970-1985 would probably not continue if the government abstained from new policy measures in the fields of accident prevention and/or medical care for accident victims.

This pointed to the necessity of developing new policy strategies. It was shown that the vigorous continuation of present government policies in the field of accident prevention and the implementation

210   Gazing into the Oracle

of new initiatives in the field of medical care for accident victims could both lead to a reduction of accident mortality, as the World Health Organisation has stipulated as a goal.

The Delphi study yielded a number of ideas about policy measures, which at that time had not yet found a place in policy documents. Since then, many of these ideas have been incorporated in policy plans on the part of the government. For example, in 1989 the intention to implement measures aimed at the improvement of trauma care, as formulated by the Delphi respondents, had been expressed (Ministerie van WVC, 1989). Before the study, no policy document had been formulated in this field. We can therefore conclude that our Delphi study had made some contribution to health planning in the Netherlands.

There is, however, a gap between an expression of intent and the implementation of policy measures. So far, none of the new initiatives has been implemented. This illustrates the long-term nature of developing, implementing and evaluating the effects of policy measures referred to at the beginning of this chapter.

Since our Delphi study was conducted, almost nine years have passed. In this time, many industrialised countries, including the Netherlands, have seen accident mortality trends become less favourable than in the preceding period (Beeck and Mackenbach 1992). The year 2000 is now getting nearer so pressure is increasing on our ability to achieve a reduction in accident mortality by that year, as envisioned by the WHO. The information generated by our Delphi study 'Accidents and Traumatology in the Future' can still contribute to the formulation of a strategy to achieve that aim.

References

Beeck, E.F. van, Mackenbach, J.P., Habbema, J.D.F. and Maas, P.J. van der (1989) 'Delphi Study: accidents and traumatology in the future'. In R.M. Lapré and J.P. Mackenbach (eds) *Accidents in the Year 2000*. Dordrecht/Boston/London: Kluwer Academic Publishers.

Beeck, E.F. van, and Mackenbach, J.P. (1988) 'Trends in de sterfte ten gevolge van ongevallen in Nederland sinds 1950'. *Tijdschrift voor Sociale Gezondheidszorg 66*, 89–95.

Beeck, E.F. van, and Mackenbach, J.P. (1992) *Accidents Monitoring Report 1992: Developments since 1985*. Rijswijk: ST6.

Beeck, E.F. van, Mackenbach, J.P., Oortmarssen, G.J. van, Barendregt, J.J.M., Habbema, J.D.F. and Maas, P.J. van der (1989) 'Scenarios for the future development of accident mortality in the Netherlands'. *Health Policy 11*, 11–17.

Brouwer, J.J. and Schreuder, R.F. (eds) (1986) *Scenarios and Other Methods to Support Long-Term Health Planning*. Utrecht: Uitgeverij Jan van Arkel.

CBS *Diagnosestatistiek ziekenhuizen 1983*. (Hospital diagnostic statistics 1983.) (1986). Voorburg: CBS.

CBS *Overledenen naar doodsoorzaak, leeftijd en geslacht serie A1, diverse jaartallen*. (Deaths by cause of death, age and sex, series A1, several years.)Voorburg: CBS.

CBS *Statistiek der bedrijfsongevallen 1984*. (Occupational accident statistics 1984.) (1985). Voorburg: CBS.

CBS *Statistiek der bedrijfsongevallen, diverse jaartallen*. (Occupational accident statistics, several years.) Voorburg: CBS.

CBS *Statistiek van de verkeerongevallen op de openbare weg 1984*. (Statistics on road accidents on public highways 1984.) (1985). Heerlen: CBS.

CBS *Overledenen naar doodsoorzaak, leeftijd en geslacht in het jaar 1984, serie A1*. (Deaths by cause of death, age and sex in 1984, series A1.) Voorburg: CBS.

Centraal Planbureau. *De Nederlanse economie op de langere termijn* (1985). Den Haag: CPB.

Committee on Trauma Research (1985) *Injury in America: A Continuing Public Health Problem*. Washington, DC: National Academy Press.

Cruijssen, H.G.J.M. (1986) 'Bevolkingsporgnose voor Nederland 1985–2035'. *Mndstat. Bev.* CBS 3, 33–41.

European Conference of Ministers of Transport (1986) *Statistical Report on Road Accident Trends in 1984*. Paris: OECD.

Geus, G.H. de (1987) *An Inventory of Surveillance Systems and Studies on Home and Leisure Accidents in the European Community*. Amsterdam: ECOSA.

Kampen, L.T.B. van, and Edelman, A. (1979) *Legislation and Research in the Field of Traffic Safety Regarding Seat Belts and Crash Helmets*. R-79–52. Voorburg: SWOV.

Lamm, R., Chouieri, E.M. and Kloeckner, J.H. (1985) 'Accidents in the US and Europe: 1970–1980'. *Accident Analysis and Prevention 17*, 429–438.

Linstone, H.A. and Turoff, M. (eds) (1975) *The Delphi Method: Techniques and Applications*. Reading, MA: Addison-Wesley.

Mackenbach, J.P., Oortmarssen, G.J. van, Beeck, E.F. van, Barendregt, J.J.M., Habbema, J.D.F. and Maas, P.J. van der (1989) 'Projections of the epidemiology of accidents: a computer model for calculating the future incidence of accidents and their consequences'. In *Accidents in the Year 2000*. R.M. Lapre and J.P. Mackenbach (eds). Dordrecht/Boston/London: Kluwer Academic Publishers.

Ministerie van WVC (1989) *Ontwerp kerndocument Gezondheidsbeleid; dicussienota Ongevallen en Traumatologie*. Rijswijk.

Noordzij, P.C. (1980) *Recent Trends in Countermeasures and Research Concerning Drinking and Driving in the Netherlands*. R 80–34. Voorburg: SWOV.

Sackman, H. (1975) 'Summary evaluation of Delphi'. *Policy Analysis 20*, 694–718.

Steering Committee on Future Health Scenarios (1986). *STG: Structure and Terms of Reference*. Utrecht: Uitgeverij Jan van Arkel.

World Health Organisation (1985) *Targets for Health for All*. Copenhagen: WHO Regional Office for Europe.

Chapter 9

Delphi Estimates
on Clients' Perceptions
of Family Planning Services

Mauro Niero and Alex Robertson[1]

Introduction

Since their inception in 1974, public-sector family planning services
(FPSs) have grown in importance within the Italian health and welfare system. Though their organisation varies according to the needs
of different regions of the country, they now share a number of
difficulties in common. They face competition from a range of private
services and agencies; they seem to have failed in their goal of
becoming a community resource for handling family problems; and
they are criticised as mere pill dispensers and organisers of easy
abortions. In short, they seem to be losing the positive perception and
public trust that are crucial to services providing for needs in such a
sensitive area (see, for example, Donati 1980).

In this chapter we shall describe a pilot programme carried out in
Venice, where a new FPS policy is the subject of debate among
politicians, professionals and users. The debate was itself assisted by
a Delphi investigation, in conjunction with surveys of people's preferences concerning ways of dealing with family planning problems
(for the results of these surveys see Folin and Niero 1990).

---

1   The research on which this chapter is based was carried out by Mauro
     Niero. He also wrote the first version of this chapter, but the version
     which appears here was a collaborative effort involving both Mauro
     Niero and Alex Robertson. A special acknowledgement must be given to
     Stefano Campostrini (University of Padova) for his contribution to the
     design and realisation of the Delphi research and to the Director of the
     Venice School of Social Work for permission to use data from the
     original research report.

Gauging Public Preferences: A Research Framework

Generally speaking, the decision to use public FPSs represents a choice between a range of alternatives available at either primary level (family, neighbourhood, etc.) or secondary level (public and privately-provided such as hospitals, etc.) (see, for example, Barnes 1972; Boissevain and Mitchell 1973; Maguire 1983). This is why, perhaps more than for any other health or social service, clients' decisions to use FPSs are sensitive to the effects of and balance between the following factors:

- the availability of alternative solutions;
- the nature and extent of information at the user's disposal;
- public perceptions and attitudes regarding the service.

These are the basic elements involved in people's decision to use the service (see, for example, Bettman 1979; Brinderg and Lutz 1986; Calvi 1977; Belk 1975; Howard and Seth 1969). Any investigation in this area must obviously address these elements within its research design.

Some issues in clients' decision-making

Competing solutions: Previous surveys have shown that, in Venice, people's use of FPSs is very much less than expected for a population of its size and composition. For some of the more important services offered by FPSs, the situation is as follows:

- gynaecological consultations – a mere 10% of women referred to the FPS as the agency they would approach first for such consultations: the great majority would resort to a private practitioner;
- contraceptive consultations – FPSs constitute the first choice of only 14.3% of the relevant population: the majority of individuals again reported they would prefer to go to a private professional for such services;
- sexual counselling – 13% of respondents referred to FPSs as their most likely first point of contact for assistance: the other main sources of help were found within the family itself;
- marital problems – 14.1% saw themselves as likely to resort first to the FPS: the main solution to such problems was seen as coming from the couple themselves 'absolutely without' any external help;

- cancer prevention in women – 10.1% nominated FPSs: hospitals were seen as the main service providers in this respect.

It is thus apparent that although FPSs occupy an honourable position in the 'market', this is perhaps insufficient to justify the effort involved in ensuring that a costly service remains alive and viable.

Information: With regard to information, several studies have shown that usage of certain public services is particularly heavily concentrated in the upper and more educated sectors of the population. This clearly adds to any existing inequalities in the distribution of these services.

Tudor-Hart's (1975) 'inverse care law' is particularly relevant to the situation under consideration, since the survey we are about to describe shows 37% of the female population of Venice aged between 14 and 60 years to be ignorant of the FPSs' existence. The survey also demonstrates that those least likely to know about the service were disproportionately drawn from the less educated lower class and unemployed sections of the female population. A further 40% knew about the existence of the services but did not know how FPSs could cater for their problems.

Perceptions: Further problems are raised by values, attitudes and understandings: what are generally called 'perceptions' (see Cohen 1971; Gutek 1978; Shaw 1976, 1984). Public services are perceived in very negative terms, at least in Italy. Public administration is synonymous with sluggishness, inefficiency and impersonal service. For certain services, this attitude goes further, developing into a perception of public services as intrusive. This view has formed the basis for some of the principal criticisms of comprehensive welfare state policies in the seventies (see, among many authors, Habermas 1976; Luhmann 1981; Flora and Heidenheimer 1981). For the FPSs, this is a quite dangerous and damaging inheritance, since positive public attitudes and perceptions are crucial to the successful implementation of their programmes. The 'compliance', for instance, that is essential to successful communication between patients and practitioners (Dunnell and Cartwright 1972; Conrad 1985), would in the case of FPSs be undermined by negative perceptions of this type.

Their involvement in problems of social and physical reproduction makes FPSs an extraordinarily sensitive and emotional topic. Stereotypes (both positive and negative) about the service therefore grow quickly and spread easily. This is why FPSs must remain conscious of the need to promulgate positive and active information about their work.

Towards a theoretical framework

It is generally accepted that policy makers must address two versions of reality: the situation as it actually exists, and the situation as they would like it to be. The first is clearly a descriptive, the second a prescriptive task. The same holds true for measures geared to changing public perceptions of a service. To present the issue in terms similar to those used immediately above, decision-makers have to cope with the difference between people's expectations of the service and their actual perception of it.

In the case of family planning services, policy had never been articulated in these terms, although FPSs had always been conscious of the fact that, in the course of their everyday activities, they were both providing a service and shaping people's perceptions of it. In other words, practitioners have always acted as if they had a clear idea of what people were expecting of the service; whilst in the course of their professional experience, they try to establish what people actually think of it.

Given this, it was considered that the most appropriate initial step to gauging public attitudes to FPSs would be to ask practitioners and other people involved in the service what they thought clients' and the general public's perception of FPSs would be. Whilst such material could not be regarded as a statement of the actual goals of FPSs, it would be useful for our purposes because it is affected by:

- professionals' views of what people wish the service to be like;
- experience of the recent history of FPSs and the areas in which they are thought to have been successful or unsuccessful;
- professionals' perceptions of the rumours, stereotypes and attitudes they encounter among the people they meet in the course of their current daily work.

These results could form the main point of departure for other types of perceptual analysis; in particular, people's actual perceptions of FPSs themselves.

The research project thus comprised a first phase, implemented by means of a Delphi exercise, in order to obtain a picture of what those involved in some official capacity with the FPSs thought were the public's views of the services they offered; and a second phase consisting of a survey of a sample of the population of Venice, which aimed to tap people's actual perceptions of FPSs.

Before developing these basic ideas further, it may be useful to refer to Figure 9.1, which presents the framework underlying the two phases of the research project. This aims to follow through the stages involved in a decision about whether or not to use the service, with the client

- experiencing specific needs;
- having to deal with competing types and sources of information; and
- developing views on appropriate solutions.

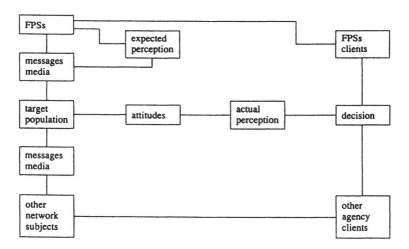

Figure 9.1 Flow chart of clients' decisions

Competing Groups: Research Design and the Delphi Process

From the inception of the project, different points of view emerged amongst politicians, lay people with some involvement in the activities of the FPSs (participation committees), and the staff of the FPSs themselves –psychologists, social workers, medical practitioners and nurses. Each of these groups had its own opinion about the factors leading to a 'good' or 'bad' perception on the part of clients, which were likely to be strongly related to their reasons for becoming involved in the programme.

It was also clear that there were conflicts of interest amongst these groups and that their aim was not only to assist in a research project, but also to suggest specific measures of intervention. This was why it would not have been sufficient to undertake a random survey of people's opinions; it was also necessary to confirm or refute competing hypotheses about the policy measures themselves.

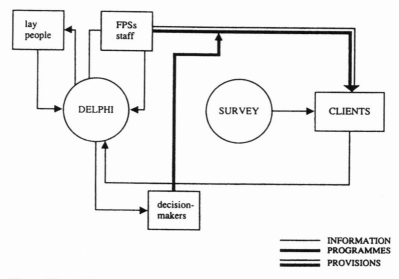

Figure 9.2 Delphi process and communication networks

These considerations led to the adoption of a model of the research as based on a communication network, with a Delphi exercise at its core. The Delphi exercise was designed as a tool for linking the various groups involved in the policy, while a system of sample surveys on the general population would permit comparisons with the clients' point of view. This is illustrated in Figure 9.2, where the surveys and the Delphi process provide the links between the different parties with an active interest in the work of the FPSs. It should be noted that the entire system is conceived as a continuous communication flow, supporting both decision-making and evaluation of the impact of new policies. As such, its features go far beyond what will be discussed in this chapter.

The role of the Delphi component within this scheme was influenced by more than one of the 'Inquiry-Systems' paradigms identified by Mitroff and Turoff in 1975. The main aims of the Delphi study in this process were as follows:

1. to create an efficient communication network between subjects with potentially competing interests;
2. to provide a sound theoretical frame of reference for identifying differing perceptions and decisions within the client population;

3. to integrate surveys of client opinion on these matters more effectively into the decision-making process;

4. to identify the main policy solutions for responding to clients' perceptions and priorities.

The survey itself aimed to test current public perceptions, and in particular to:

- assess the extent of public knowledge about the service;
- evaluate the degree to which different media have an effect on clients' decisions about using FPSs;
- study the main factors leading to a positive decision by clients to use the service;
- gauge the general perceptions held by clients of the service.

The following discussion refers specifically to the first phase of the research, namely, the contrast between professionals' perceptions of what clients thought of the service and the views held by the clients themselves of the service they were actually receiving. We shall, in other words, be looking at the relationship between the results yielded by the Delphi exercise and the sample survey.

The Delphi Project: What Service Providers Expected Clients to Think of the FPSs

The Delphi investigation consisted of two basic parts: a first, 'ideas creation' phase, and a second phase of quantitative data collection. Let us first briefly consider four decisions that had to be taken concerning the conceptual area, the target population and the membership of the Delphi panel.

1. Since FPS users' needs tend to vary according to their stage within the life cycle, it was agreed that the Delphi statements should differentiate amongst the views providers attributed to clients in three age-groups, namely: 14–25; 26–45; and over 45.

2. Individual services had, moreover, to be analysed in terms of the specific perceptions held of them. The following were selected as the most typical:

   family planning consultations

   gynaecological consultations

   abortion counselling

   pregnancy assistance

> psychological counselling/therapy
>
> health and sexual counselling
>
> adoption counselling
>
> legal advice.

3. The questions identified as appropriate to studying clients' expected views of services concentrated on three main topics:

   media and advisors directing people to the FPSs

   factors encouraging people to use the FPSs ('motivators')

   factors discouraging people from using FPSs ('de-motivators').

4. The composition of the Delphi panel had to take into account the different groups involved in planning and delivering services, but excluding those responsible for planning at the local level, who had shown no particular knowledge of people's various concerns. The groups represented on the panel were therefore: lay people (members of the official participation committees); and practitioners (members of the various professions) in the FPSs. The first panel accordingly comprised a total of 43 people, 31 of whom stayed through to the end of the project.

The size of the panel and the conceptual dimensions of the research suggested the list of questions should be split between separate questionnaires and administered in a double round. The final design of the Delphi project thus consisted of four rounds, with two rounds in each stage. The logic and procedures underlying this design will be discussed in the following section.

Generating ideas: the first stage

As may easily be deduced from the above discussion, and as confirmed in Figure 9.3, this made for rather a long questionnaire. The total number of questions was in fact 78, which would clearly have required considerable time and effort on the panel's part. It was accordingly decided to divide the different areas of investigation among the panellists, in order to minimise the amount of work involved for any one individual. The life cycle questions (see the 'tree' in Figure 9.3), for example, were divided between different questionnaires, concentrating in each case on an average of three services, with a total of about nine or ten questions in each questionnaire.

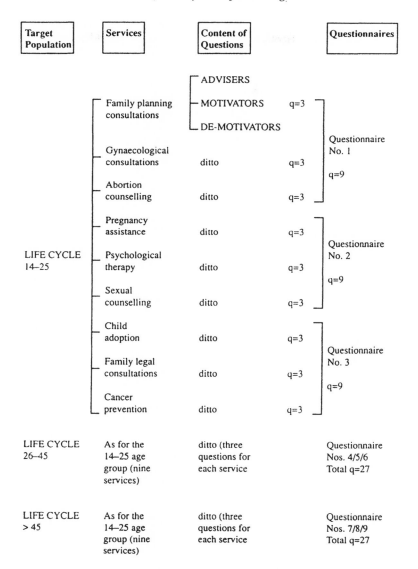

Figure 9.3 Questionnaire design (q=number or questions)

This resulted in a total of nine questionnaires which, given there were 43 persons on the panel, would have meant each questionnaire being completed by four or, at most, five panellists. This was regarded as too restrictive and the first stage was therefore designed as two rounds, the first round consisting of five and the second of four questionnaires. This meant that each questionnaire was completed by a sub-panel of ten persons. The total panel was therefore divided into five sub-panels of 8–9 members, the sub-panels being so selected as to ensure they were as different as possible from each other in the social status of their members (mainly lay people and representatives of the various professions). This procedure is illustrated in Figure 9.4.

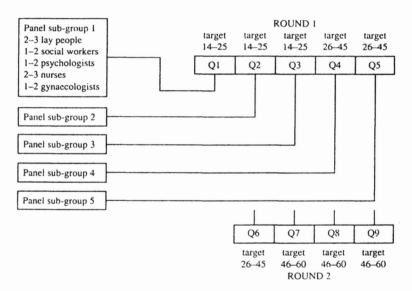

Figure 9.4 The allocation of the questionnaires to panel sub-groups

Panellists were instructed each time to think of a potential client (representing a particular client group) in need of one of the services specified in the list. The questions were based on the items listed above. In accordance with the classic Delphi Method, results were processed with a view to using all items that emerged as pertinent. This yielded the material for the second-stage questionnaire.

Second stage: first round evaluation

The findings from the previous round showed there to be no great difference amongst the three target age-groups when considered service by service. In other words, all age groups were thought by panel members to be affected by the same 'motivators' and 'de-motivators' in their use of individual services. It was thus decided to group all the services together in one evaluative questionnaire, to be administered to the entire panel.

The questions were the same as those used in the previous stage, though each member had for obvious reasons to be presented with a shortened list of the items 'created' in the first stage. These related to the nine service areas, each being covered by three questions pertaining to 'Advisers and Media', 'Motivators' and 'De-motivators', as follows:

Advisers and media: These could be divided into four general categories: neighbourhood and family; clients of FPSs; family doctors and other practitioners; and advertising and other public media. The complete list comprised twelve items. Panellists were asked to respond using a ten-point scale (1 = minimum; 10 = maximum).

Motivators: Motivating factors differed quite markedly amongst services. Nonetheless, it was possible to group them into the following categories:

- whether or not charges were imposed: this was a factor mentioned by most panellists;
- consulting hours and the extent to which these were or were not convenient for clients;
- waiting lists: this tended to be seen as more of a de-motivator, although practitioners said this was less of a shortcoming than in other services and that people would appreciate this fact;
- bureaucracy: as in point above;
- setting and 'atmosphere': comfortable surroundings and acceptable service;
- perceived competence of practitioners: this was thought by panel members to be one of the most important reasons for using FPSs;
- team work: particularly effective approaches to dealing with clients' problems;
- availability: the degree to which professionals were able to modify their approach in order to facilitate access by clients;

- privacy: this was expressed in various ways in the first round, and it refers to the extent of clients' confidence that personal records or problems would be kept strictly within the confines of the agency;
- ideology: this related to the claims, made by the women's movement during the 1970s, that FPSs should be the front-line service for dealing with female problems;
- stereotypes: these were generally seen as linked to a good 'reputation'.

Each item was placed in the questionnaire by indicating in parenthesis the original text used by the panel in the first-stage survey. Respondents were also asked to evaluate items in this section of the questionnaire on a ten-point scale (1 = 'non-motivating'; 10 = 'highly motivating').

De-motivators: De-motivating factors followed the same general pattern as the motivators. In other words, 'de-motivators' could be grouped under the categories listed above. These items can in fact be easily translated into negative terms: 'stereotypes', for example, may be positive or negative; judgements on practitioners might be positive or negative, etc. Certain less self-evident points must nonetheless be mentioned:

- a service being free of charge is obviously a motivator, but certain panellists felt that many people would not attend a free service because they see this as indicating superficial and inferior treatment;
- timetable: there is a need to ensure consulting hours do not make access to the service difficult for individuals holding jobs;
- teamwork: according to some panellists (chiefly doctors and nurses), teamwork could sometimes be perceived as an unwanted intrusion in the treatment process;
- confidentiality: according to certain panellists, fears concerning lack of confidentiality could be exacerbated by the physical location of certain clinics in neighbourhoods away from the town centre, with the attendant possibilities of gossip or unwanted encounters with certain people;
- ideology: can be a powerful demotivator, raising as it does the possibility of disagreement over ethical and political beliefs.

As before, the items were evaluated on a ten-point scale (1 = not de-motivating; 10 = most de-motivating). It should also be noted that not all of these concerns were raised in relation to every service. For certain services, only two or three motivators or de-motivators were relevant.

Data processing: Motivators and de-motivators were processed together for all subjects on a scale from +10 (most motivating) to -10 (most de-motivating). Results were presented as means and standard deviations, on the scores obtained by the life cycle 'tree' (Figure 9.3), type of service, and professional status of the panellists. The results of this round will be presented later.

Second stage: second round evaluation

A quite lengthy questionnaire had been administered in the previous stage of the research and it was felt panellists' patience had perhaps been tried enough. A further questionnaire was nonetheless necessary in order to allow panellists both to think further through their answers (in the light of the results of the first round) and to seek an appropriate level of consensus.

Serious consideration was at this juncture given to the possibility of administering a new long questionnaire. In addition, it was essential to completion of the Delphi exercise that some estimate be reached on the functioning of the Family Planning Service as a whole, rather than its various specialist services. The final questionnaire was therefore broadly the same as the previous one, but without its questions on the media and including only questions relevant to the services judged most typical of the FPSs: gynaecological and family planning consultations, psychotherapy, and pregnancy assistance.

These four services had been selected with the object of including both medical and psycho-social components of the services offered by FPSs. As before, responses were calibrated on a ten-point scale. Motivators and de-motivators had also emerged as very similar in these services and it was thought this would ease data processing.

The figures given in Figures 9.7–9.10 represent the overall mean scores with reference to the four services. Results have been transformed into 'z' scores to facilitate comparison.

Delphi and the sample survey

The overall design of the second stage is presented in Figure 9 5. In this, it is possible to see that, from the starting point of the first-round questionnaire which dealt with nine FPS services ('A' to 'I'), the second-round questionnaire included questions on motivators and

de-motivators with regard to four services: gynaecological consultations; family planning advice; psychotherapy; and assistance with
pregnancies.

This procedure could be regarded as unorthodox from a 'classic'
Delphi point of view. In fact, whereas the first round (of the second
stage) aimed to yield estimates on each specific service, the second
round was intended to provide an overview of perceived expectations. A 'strict' Delphi approach would therefore have applied to only
one aspect of the information collected up to this point.

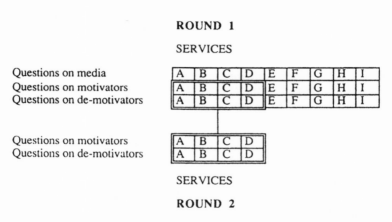

ROUND 1

SERVICES

Questions on media
Questions on motivators
Questions on de-motivators

Questions on motivators
Questions on de-motivators

SERVICES

ROUND 2

Figure 9.5 Second stage Delphi design

The second-round format was influenced both by the finding that
people tend to form generalised perceptions of the services they
receive (though normally linked to particular aspects of the service),
and by practical considerations. The Delphi process had caused
fatigue among the panellists and another long questionnaire would
have been regarded as something of a burden. Second-round results
should nevertheless prove very useful to future applications of the
Policy Delphi. We shall not deal with this further here because it has
still to be implemented, but shall discuss later in the chapter some
ideas concerning its possible design.

The survey design was itself influenced by the anticipated outcomes of the Delphi investigation, particularly with regard to motivators and de-motivators. Once the Delphi exercise had shown that
some of these should be considered in a positive and others in a
negative light, a series of questions was devised along the lines
outlined above. Unlike the Delphi instrument, however, the items on

the survey questionnaire were rated on a scale from 1 to 10 (1–5 being positive; 6–10 negative). We shall make some comparisons between the Delphi exercise and the survey results in the next section.

Research Results

This section will focus on the results of the two related investigations. An analysis of the differences between *expected* and *actual* perceptions requires comparison of the Delphi and survey results. Although our attention will focus mainly on the Delphi investigation, we shall also review certain aspects of the overall research design. Where appropriate, we shall also comment on the peculiarity of Delphi results and the Delphi's particular mode of constructing reality.

Information flows and the media

Since the publication of Shannon and Weaver's (1949) well-known article, a medium is generally seen as an instrument of communication. McLuhan (1964), however, has argued that a medium can sometimes enhance the message by spreading messages of its own. This is the sense in which 'medium' will be used in this part of our discussion. In fact, we shall consider as 'media' not only the classic instruments of mass communication, but also persons involved in transmitting the messages that form part of the information processed by clients in arriving at their own individual decisions.

This section also provides us with our first opportunity to compare the Delphi and survey data. It will concentrate on those individuals who used, or the occasions on which clients had the opportunity to refer to, an FPS.

The aims of the two investigations were rather different. In the Delphi exercise, the main concern was who or what had been the primary influence on the decision to use the FPSs, the aim being to list the media which influenced or were involved in individual decision-making. The survey, on the other hand, was intended to explore the degree to which the various media connected with the FPSs had penetrated people's thinking. Sample members were thus asked from where or whom they had obtained information on the existence of the FPSs and were provided by them.

It was therefore not surprising that the preliminary results revealed substantial differences between the two sources. According to the Delphi responses, the main influences on decision-making were neighbours, followed by other clients, doctors and other professionals and, finally, advertisements. By contrast, 42% of the survey sample referred to neighbours; 29% to medical and welfare practitioners; 41% to advertisements; and 38% to other clients (respondents could give more than one response). There were thus substantial differences between the significance accorded these items in the separate surveys. The difference was particularly marked in the case of advertisements, which the Delphi panel had placed last, whereas the survey sample rated it close to first.

The survey data relate, however, to people's awareness of the advertisements, not to the effects advertisements had on their decisions, which had been the focus of the Delphi study. Once the survey data were re-processed using only subjects who had actually been clients, an attempt was made to isolate the effects of the media from those of other potential influences on individuals' decision-making. The results are presented in Figure 9.6.

Figure 9.6 shows clearly not only that the rank order is the same, but also that the distribution of the two sets of z scores is very similar. The 'z' score measures the distance from the mean measured in units of standard deviation. Thus,

$$z = \frac{x - \bar{x}}{s}$$ where 'x' is the score, '$\bar{x}$' the mean and 's' the standard deviation

The differences lie mainly in the greater significance attached to family doctors and other medical practitioners and the lesser importance ascribed to the role of advertising in panel members' judgements. The panellists did, however, seem to have a fairly accurate perception of clients' actual decision-making. Further analysis of the survey data showed that, for certain media, there was an inverse

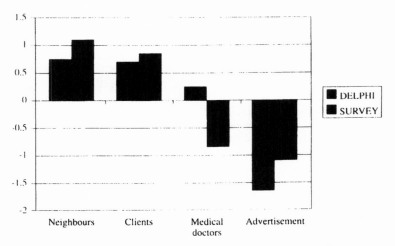

Figure 9.6 The influence of different sources of information on the decision to use FPSs: comparison of 'z' scores for Delphi and Survey

relationship between diffusion and the effectiveness of information in changing people's behaviour. In fact, the most widely diffused advertisement was unable on its own to persuade people to refer to FPSs.

From what has been presented thus far, one might conclude that the Delphi exercise and the social survey yielded relatively similar types of data. As has been shown by the above discussion, such similarities were not, however, immediately apparent. Any links had to be elicited by scrutinising and re-analysing the survey data from the perspective of the individual client.

In what follows, we shall see different results emerging from the perceptions contained in the two sets of data. In this, the disjunction between a prescriptive and a descriptive purpose will become clearer.

Motivators and de-motivators

The final results proved very interesting both in relation to the Delphi Method itself and to the whole research process. Let us first review the changes occurring in the final two Delphi rounds.

Figure 9.7 highlights the way in which the panel's estimates changed. The numbers along the bottom axis in this and subsequent figures refer to the following factors:

   1 = free of charge

   2 = consulting hours

   3 = waiting lists

   4 = bureaucracy

   5 = location and atmosphere

   6 = practitioners' degree of expertise

   7 = teamwork

   8 = availability

   9 = confidentiality

  10 = ideology

  11 = stereotypes.

The trends identified in Figure 9.7 suggest that the perceptions which panellists expected clients to hold of the FPSs were rather negative. Thus, they were pessimistic in the expectations they predicted users would have of such objective features as consulting hours and wait-ing lists. They also saw people as coming to the FPSs because the service was free. They anticipated positive perceptions of the practi-tioners' degree of expertise (their skills and knowledge, ways of

dealing with problems, and teamwork). They were decidedly negative in what they saw as the views likely to be possessed by clients
over such emotionally-charged features as confidentiality and the
role of ideology.

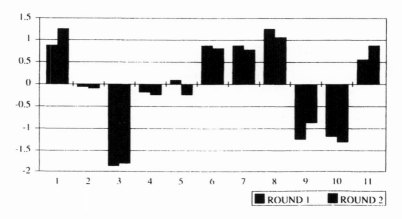

Figure 9.7 Delphi estimates of 'z' scores in rounds 1 and 2

No significant differences emerged between the evaluations obtained
in the first and second rounds of the Delphi study. As a motivator,
freedom from direct charges increased somewhat in importance;
location and atmosphere declined, and views on the stereotypes held
by clients became more optimistic.

As mentioned above, however, the panel contained various types
of professionals. Data were processed for the following sub-groups:
lay people; medical doctors; nurses; psychologists; and social
workers. Comparisons between these groups revealed fairly clear
differences, as can be seen in Figure 9.8.

Figure 9.8 reveals that lay members of the panel saw clients as
likely to be highly critical of objective aspects of the service, particularly waiting lists, bureaucratic procedures, and location and atmosphere. They expected clients to have positive views of practitioners'
skill levels and ability to work in teams (though not their availability).
They were also more optimistic than other groups about confidentiality and ideology, but rather more pessimistic about the role of
stereotypes.

Social workers and psychologists were decidedly optimistic about
clients' views concerning the effectiveness of teamwork whereas
doctors, and more especially nurses, were not. This highlights one of
the sharpest areas of disagreement within the FPS teams. Nurses are

generally the most pessimistic. Doctors show particularly low expectations for clients' views on such important factors as confidentiality, counterbalanced by a belief in the potential for mitigating stereotypes about the service.

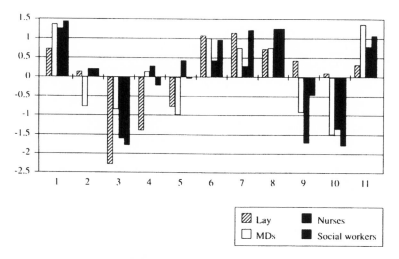

Figure 9.8 Delphi estimates of 'z' scores by sub-group

To summarise, the opinions held by the various professions within the debate are fully reflected in the Delphi results. Health professionals do have less faith in the effectiveness of teamwork which, they argue, leads to perceptions of intrusiveness and damages people's faith that confidentiality will be respected. Social workers and psychologists, on the other hand, lay emphasis on what they hold to be the most important characteristic of the FPSs: team work.

Some detail should be added to this picture of a change in the extent of agreement amongst the various groups represented on the panel. Figure 9.9 shows a consistent and substantial reduction in standard deviations between the two rounds, especially for expected views on bureaucracy, availability and confidentiality. It should be remembered that the final scores relate to questions presented in the first phase in a positive (motivator) and in the second in a negative (de-motivator) form, each measured on a ten-point scale, making for a possible range of twenty on the scores obtained. Bearing this in mind, a reduction in the size of the standard deviation from more than 3 to 2 for ideology and from 3 to 1.4 for confidentiality may be regarded as a very impressive result.

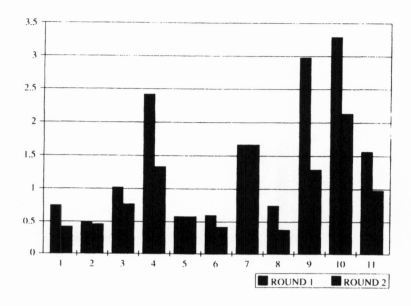

Figure 9.9 Standard deviation of 'z' scores in rounds 1 and 2

It must, however, be conceded that this outcome may not be attributable to the Delphi process. A certain number of panellists dropped out between the first and second rounds, which might obviously have affected the results by removing certain of the more extreme instances of disagreement from the sample. In addition, the sub-panels were for the most part made up of people who communicated regularly with each other for professional reasons. A degree of communication and discussion of the Delphi results inside the teams might therefore have produced a kind of 'consensus overload'.

However, the most interesting result arises from a comparison between the actual and expected perceptions. Figure 9.10 presents the final set of data, using 'Z' scores in order to facilitate comparison.

The differences are quite striking. The attitudes of clients and members of the general public seem more benevolent than those of the practitioners themselves. People in the first place claim that freedom from direct charges is not necessarily a reason for choosing a FPS service. Second, they agree with practitioners over the impor-

tance of waiting lists, but hold extremely negative views about bureaucracy. The panel, on the other hand, saw FPSs as much less
bureaucratic than any other public service.

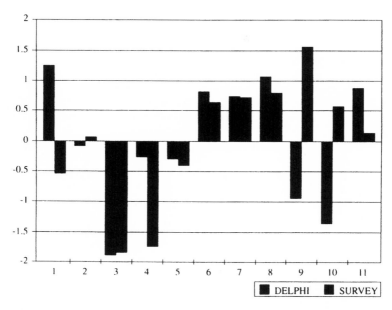

Figure 9.10 Comparison of 'z' scores derived from Delphi and survey

Members of the public also agree with professionals in their perceptions of those aspects (skills, teamwork and availability) which affect
the professional functioning of the service. Perhaps the most surprising result, however, is the divergence between the two samples over
the last three items. Lay users do not see ideology as a de-motivating
factor and are entirely satisfied with the degree of confidentiality
which FPSs are seen as capable of guaranteeing. These opinions are
shared by non-clients (as reflected in the survey results) even though
this group in particular scored lower than the general sample on the
last three items. This could mean that these factors have a particularly
important bearing on people's decision to use FPSs.

Overall, FPSs seem to enjoy a good image. Their perceived problems in general relate to such physical and organisational matters as
bureaucracy, waiting lists, etc. One final brief comment is required,
however, concerning why such differences should exist between the

points of view of different groups. It also confirms the wisdom of the decision to ask practitioners to specify what they perceived the public as likely to think of the services on offer.

In our view, the perceptions panel members imputed to the public were a mixture of descriptive and prescriptive assessments of the situation. Practitioners take heed of messages emerging from their own everyday experience. What was particularly perceived by practitioners (in their discussions with both clients and the general public) was the dissatisfaction expressed by people when comparing their experience against an ideal 'image'. This is why 'confidentiality' and 'stereotypes' achieved much better scores than (for instance) 'bureaucracy', which was rated very negatively by the survey sample. On any objective criterion, however, this hardly constitutes a legitimate cause for anxiety among practitioners.

An alternative interpretation would be that negative messages are processed by professionals irrespective of how frequently they are expressed, thus causing exaggerated estimates to form of the number of dissatisfied people. Practitioners may, for example, believe that individual complaints will be transmitted to a wider audience, spreading bad perceptions among the public as a whole. In other words, they may mistakenly regard what are in fact sporadic and isolated occurrences as part of a much wider informal communication network.

A third explanation relates to disagreements that may arise among staff as a result of clients' complaints about confidentiality, stereotypes, ideology, etc. From this viewpoint, the Delphi Method would counter such a pattern of relationships by presenting an alternative way of interpreting the situation. We have already seen how 'stereotypes' and 'confidentiality' showed a greater reduction in the size of their standard deviation between rounds 1 and 2 of the Delphi exercise. This could be attributed to the 'blind communication' the Delphi says takes place between individual panellists and a group they are part of, in their search for estimates on which to base their own individual judgements. This would, in other words, be an outcome of the way the Delphi process operates, creating a new consensus in what were previously conflicting situations.

Some Issues for a Perception-Oriented Policy

The items pertaining to motivating and de-motivating factors are not arranged randomly in the Figures reproduced above. On the contrary, their ordering seems to reflect an underlying taxonomy. At the lowest level of this taxonomy are physical and objective motivating factors (timetable, waiting list, etc.); at the next highest level are located factors to do with human relationships within the service (bureaucracy; practitioners' skill; teamwork); while on the highest level one finds factors more concerned with feelings and current stereotypes (ideology, 'image', unobtrusiveness, etc.) which are likely topics of conversation among the clients inside and outside the service. The higher we go in this taxonomy, the more abstract the content of the judgements tends to be.

This taxonomy is very important for policy planning. At the first level it includes judgements that people can give as a result of personal experience or knowledge of the service. Of course, the mass-information process may well exaggerate the importance of timetables or the inconvenience caused by waiting lists; but such problems can be addressed by good organisation of the service and/or objective counter-information.

At the second level are factors linked to the network of relationships inside the service. Direct experience is not in itself sufficient to ensure practitioners will be recognised as good and reliable; it must be reinforced by an exchange of information with other people or clients or intermediaries (other practitioners, institutions, etc.). And although the items pertaining to this part of the taxonomy are in our case clearly positive, it is possible to anticipate certain concerns that might arise in this connection. These are mostly to do with the presence of intermediaries in the communication process. This suggests that besides the advice of clients or other people, it is extremely important to know how other practitioners know or evaluate FPSs. This therefore provides a basis for identifying issues connected to the way other agencies become involved.

The factors emerging at the third level are the most general and unfocused, and are often not matters of any special concern. They do, however, weigh heavily on people's minds and are often an amalgam of various different types of perception. This is the area of people's perceptions which is the most difficult to deal with and which also (when negative) presents the greatest dangers for the development of the service, since it tends to become part of people's everyday assumptive framework. The previous elements of our taxonomy exert a strong influence on the way generalised perceptions of this type develop over time. Nonetheless, the survey has shown that, in the present case, any such influence was far from negative.

In any case, certain of these issues have to be developed through more intensive presentations in the classic media, and in ways appropriate to a service of this type. But among the findings already mentioned for both the survey and the Delphi exercise was that one of the most important ways of doing this is via primary networks. This is the means by which FPSs can develop not only a new policy, but also a new vocation.

Table 9.1 FPSs' perceptions and policy issues:
a starting point for a Policy Delphi

Kind of Perception	Symbolic Content	Settings of Interaction	Possible Policy Issues
On material comfort or discomfort	Low	Within the FPS themselves	Organisational
On health outcomes and technical reputation	Medium	Within the health system	Organisational
Image-based	High	Towards the external environment	Primary networks

Table 9.1 depicts a possible frame of reference for the first stage of a Policy Delphi, linked specifically to decision-making in the environment under study. The problem for a new Delphi process is that of setting priorities for the new policy: in other words, and in the language we have been using in this chapter, the new perceptions of what users and the public want.

There is also the problem of deciding on the new policy measures to give effect to these new perceived expectations. One further aspect could be considered a corollary, justified by the diverging results of the Delphi exercise and survey reported above. It concerns the 'internal perception' of the FPSs. It would not be useful to work out new perception-oriented policies when FPSs contain such differing perspectives within themselves. The need for a new, agreed perception among the FPS staff should therefore be the first concern of any policy. The Delphi Method could be invaluable in developing such an approach.

Concluding Comments

This chapter has shown that the Delphi Method can be used in conjunction with other data sources, as a communication tool for a policy making and evaluation process. In the course of the chapter we have also confirmed that the Delphi technique contains its own particular method of reality construction, and that only in very special circumstances can it be used in place of other data sources.

The experiment we have described indicates that the Delphi Method encourages a prescriptive emphasis and this must be borne in mind in its different applications. We have also shown that a Delphi exercise linked to a communication network can offer a useful tool for policy-making and control (Niero 1993). In concluding, we must nonetheless point out certain shortcomings.

While the Delphi Method at first sight seems simple and cheap to apply, it is in fact extremely complex and time consuming, and also fairly expensive. The costs are not the staff or resource costs involved in the Delphi and questionnaire design, but the costs generated by complete involvement of the panellists. Each round took much more than a month and the experience we have been describing lasted about seven months.

The Delphi round was considered interesting and stimulating by those involved in it, although further rounds (especially those repeating the same questions as appeared in previous rounds) risk being seen as a burden, and ultimately as a waste of time. People have little time to fill in questionnaires, or forget to do so and so have to be pressed by the researcher. Moreover, the length of each round is determined by the time taken not by the average but by the last person to complete the questionnaire, and, since few people are likely to express a clear intention to withdraw, there is always the possibility that the researcher will simply wait in vain. This tends to be self-perpetuating: as time passes, the initial interest in seeing the results obtained from such an exercise, which is one of the factors helping to keep panellists' interest alive, begins to flag.

Nor would it necessarily be better to adopt a simplified Delphi design, since complex issues can be expressed clearly, but seldom succinctly. The search for more efficient methods should therefore be encouraged. The use of 'real time' Delphi approaches might be a sensible strategy, since these tend to exploit the moments of greatest motivational interest on the part of the panellists and enable the process to be finished within a relatively short time (Linstone and Turoff 1975, Ch. 7). But this highlights the question of who should be selected for the panel. Not all people will have a PC with modem at their disposal, and it may thus be impossible to connect up large panels because of the difficulty of finding enough people ready at the same time. For a further discussion, see Chapter 3 above.

In short, it is clear that the Delphi Method, as used in this context, raises issues that are worthy of serious discussion.

References

Barnes, J.A. (1972) *Social Networks*. Reading, MA: Addison-Wesley.

Belk, R.W. (1975) 'Situational variables and consumer behaviour.' *Journal of Consumer Research 2*, 3, 157–164.

Bettman, J.R. (1979) *An Information Processing Theory of Consumer Choice*. Reading, MA: Addison-Wesley.

Boissevain, J. and Mitchell, J.C. (eds) (1973) *Network Analysis: Studies in Human Interaction*. Den Haag: Mouton.

Brinderg, D. and Lutz, R.J. (eds) (1986) *Perspectives on Methodology in Consumer Research*. New York: Springer.

Calvi, G. (1977) *Valori e Stili di Vita Degli Italiani*. Milan: Isedi.

Cohen, A. (1971) 'Consumers view.' *Social Work Today 1*, 12, 39–43.

Conrad, P. (1985) 'The meaning of medications: another look at compliance.' *Social Science and Medicine 20*, 29–37.

Donati, P. (1980) *Consultorio Familiare e Bisogni Sociali*. Milan: Angeli.

Dunnell, H. and Cartwright, A. (1972) *Medicine Takers, Prescribers and Hoarders*. London: Routledge and Kegan Paul.

Flora, P. and Heidenheimer, J. (eds) (1981) *The Development of Welfare States in Europe and America*. New Brunswick, NJ: Transaction Books.

Folin, R. and Niero, M. (1990) 'L'immagine dei consultori familiari a Venezia'. In A.R. Genazzani and L. De Cecco (eds) *Il Consultorio Familiare*. Rome: CIC edizioni internazionali.

Gutek, B.A. (1978) 'Strategy for studying clients' satisfaction.' *Journal of Social Issues 34*, 4, 44–56.

Habermas, J. (1976) *Legitimation Crisis*. London: Heinemann.

Howard, J.A. and Seth, J.N. (1969) *The Theory of Buyer Behaviour*. New York: Wiley.

Linstone, H.A. and Turoff, M. (eds) (1975) *The Delphi Method: Technique and Applications*. Reading, MA: Addison-Wesley.

Luhmann, N. (1981) *Politische Theorie Im Wohlfahrtsstaat*. Munich: Olzog Verlag.

Maguire, L. (1983) *Understanding Social Networks*. Beverly Hills, CA: Sage Publications.

McLuhan, M. (1964) *Understanding Media*. New York: McGraw-Hill.

Mitroff, I.I. and Turoff, M. (1975) 'Philosophical and methodological foundations of Delphi'. In H.A. Linstone and M. Turoff (eds) *The Delphi Method: Technique and Applications*. Reading, MA: Addison-Wesley.

Niero, M. (1988, 1993) *Paradigmi e Metodi di Ricerca Sociale: l'inchiesta, l'osservazione e il Delphi*. Vicenza: Nuovo Progetto.

Shannon, C.E. and Weaver, W. (1949) *A Mathematical Theory of Communication*. University of Illinois Press.

Shaw, I. (1976) 'Consumers' opinions and social policy.' *Journal of Social Policy 5*, 1, 19–32.

Shaw, I. (1984) 'Consumers' evaluation of the personal social services.' *British Journal of Social Work 14*, 277–284.

Tudor Hart, J. (1975) 'The inverse care law'. In C. Cox and A. Mead (eds) *A Sociology of Medical Practice*. London: Collier-Macmillan.

Turoff, M. (1970) 'The design of a Policy Delphi.' *Technological Forecasting and Social Change 2*, 2, 141–171.

US Bureau of the Census (1992) *Statistical Abstract of the United States: 1991*. Washington, DC: US Government Printing Office.

User's Guide for Introducing Genetically Engineered Plants and Micro-Organisms (1991) Washington, DC: US Department of Agriculture (Technical Bulletin No.1783).

The Washington Post (1991) Tuesday 10th December, 1991, p.A12.

Chapter 10

Concluding Remarks

Michael Adler and Erio Ziglio

In this final chapter we use the case studies to assess the actual and potential contribution of the Delphi Method to issue exploration and decision-making in social policy and public health. As we approach the 21st century, the need for this has, for a number of reasons, never been greater. Unprecedented changes in the labour market, family structures, lifestyles, ill-health, environmental conditions, values and expectations are bound to have an enormous impact on both health and social policy. And yet there are enormous difficulties in extrapolating from recent trends. Different outcomes reflect different assumptions which are associated with different experts. It is, of course, possible for planners and policy-makers simply to rely on the advice of a few well-placed individuals. However, it is clearly preferable to consult more widely and to subject the views of experts to critical scrutiny. The aim should be to identify a consensus, where one is achieved, and the degree of uncertainty associated with it. Where there is no consensus the aim should be to characterise alternative scenarios and the arguments for and against each option.

For example, it is important to assess the new challenges public health (defined as the science and art of promoting and maintaining health) will face in the 21st century. What new body of knowledge, which reflects social, economic, cultural and ecological change, do we need to develop an appropriate set of policies to deal with these changes? How can policy-makers ensure that public health measures are implemented with a commitment to equity, public participation, sustainability and accountability? How can local initiatives be better supported by global strategies? These are policy issues which require policy makers, planners, professionals and the wider community not simply to respond to the past but to base their thinking on the best available information about the future.

The social, economic, cultural and ecological changes referred to above have had a profound effect on the quality of life. Understanding the origins, complexities and far-reaching implications of these changes is a prerequisite for building a 21st century social policy which will protect and develop the well-being of citizens. Economists, sociologists, behavioural scientists, social policy experts and community representatives must find better ways of pooling their opinions to reveal fresh insights and new possibilities for intervention. There is a pressing need to move from purely theoretical discourse towards practical strategies for action, based on policies for investing in health, well-being and quality of life.

The Delphi Method is, of course, not the only technique for gazing into the future. There are many different methods which meet different aims and objectives. Scenario generation can help communities to envision healthy futures as the first step to identifying health and welfare-promoting measures. Forecasting and simulation can help local, national and international agencies to fulfil their roles better. Cross-impact analyses can help policy-makers to better understand the consequences of their decisions and Delphi-produced scenarios can contribute to broadening their vision of 'what might be'. We realise, of course, that different cultural and social traditions among countries will inevitably call for different strategies. In thinking about the future of public health and social policy, at local, national and international levels, it is clear that much work lies ahead. This is particularly true in closing the information gaps, in monitoring key economic and social changes, in problem definition, and in evaluating options on interventions.

This is the context in which the Delphi Method, in spite of its limitations, can make a major contribution to preparing for the future. As the case studies in this book suggest, it probably works best as a means of characterising the possible impact and likely implications of past, present and future trends and developments under different sets of assumptions and as a preliminary stage to deciding how society should respond to them. Examples here are to be found in Goldschmidt's study of the ethical, legal and social implications of biomedical and behavioural research and technology in the USA (in Chapter 4), in Bijl's analysis of future scenarios for mental health and mental health care in the Netherlands (in Chapter 5), and in van Beeck's investigation of accidents and injuries in the same country (in Chapter 8). The Delphi Method can be particularly useful where it makes sense to canvass the views of different groups of experts who may have little contact with each other and as a result be mutually antagonistic. An example of this can be found in the involvement of family doctors and hospital doctors in Bertin's study of services for the elderly in Italy (in Chapter 6).

More difficulties are likely to be encountered when the Delphi Method is used in the policy-making process. Where it is generally recognised that improvements need to be made, that innovations are required and that a policy shift is desirable, and where policy-makers are willing to be guided by expert opinion, the Delphi Method can have a major impact on the policy-making process. However, where certain outcomes are ruled out on ideological grounds, or where vested interests are allowed to determine the course of events, this will not be the case. For example, the recent failure of the US government to implement comprehensive national health insurance, despite very high levels of agreement about the need for it from experts and the general public, suggests that no Delphi consultations would have any significant impact.

It is important to stress that the outcome of a Delphi process is only one among many factors which can influence policy making. It can, however, be particularly important at a national level where, as in the Netherlands, there is a commitment to planning for the future on an informed basis (see Chapters 5 and 8 above) and at an international level where expertise is diffuse and there is a commitment to formulate policies based on a broad consensus. An example here might be the World Health Organisation's 'Health for All' strategy (WHO 1991). Where these conditions are not met, Delphi outcomes may be sidelined but, even here, the process may not be in vain since they can be used to formulate a set of criteria by which policies and programmes can be evaluated. Examples can be found in Adler and Sainsbury's analysis of the organisation of social security in the United Kingdom following computerisation (in Chapter 7) and in Niero and Robertson's study of family planning in Italy (in Chapter 9).

With the exception of the Goldschmidt study, all the Delphi applications described in Part 2 of this book have been relatively small-scale and involved little technology. These applications have not, for a number of justifiable reasons, utilised the techniques designed further to improve group participation which are described by Rotondi and Gustafson (in Chapter 2) or the new interactive possibilities made possible by recent developments in computer technology advocated by Turoff and Hiltz (in Chapter 3). Nevertheless, they have all proved to be effective in clarifying issues and/or appraising options. In thinking about possible future applications of the Delphi Method, the possibility of harnessing it to these new and exciting developments can only enhance its usefulness. In a period of rapid and accelerating social and economic change, the need for this could hardly be greater.

List of Contributors

Michael Adler is Reader in Social Policy and Director of the Edinburgh Centre for Social Welfare Research at the University of Edinburgh.

Giovanni Bertin is Professor of Social Policy at the University of Trento, Italy. He is one of the founders of Emme & Erre, a non-profit organisation undertaking research and consultancy for the public sector.

Rob Bijl is Research Coordinator (Epidemiology) at the Netherlands Institute of Mental Health in Utrecht.

Peter Goldschmidt is President of the World Development Group Inc. (WDG) Bethesda, Maryland. WDG provides business development assistance to health care and biotechnology companies.

David Gustafson is Professor in the Department of Industrial Engineering at the University of Wisconsin, Madison.

Starr Roxanne Hiltz is Distinguished Professor of Computer and Information Science at the New Jersey Institute of Technology and a member of the Faculty of the Graduate School of Business at Rutgers University, New Jersey.

Mauro Niero is Professor of Social Research Methods at the School of Social Work, University of Venice. He is one of the founders of Emme & Erre, a non-profit organisation undertaking research and consultancy for the public sector.

Alex Robertson is Reader in Social Policy at the University of Edinburgh.

Armando Rotondi is Assistant Professor of Health Systems Engineering in the Division of Critical Care Medicine at the University of Pittsburgh Medical Centre.

Roy Sainsbury is Senior Research Fellow in the Social Policy Research Unit, University of York.

Murray Turoff is Distinguished Professor of Computer Science and Management at the New Jersey Institute of Technology and a member of the Graduate Faculty at Rutgers University, New Jersey.

Ed van Beeck is Assistant Professor of Public Health at the Netherlands Institute for Health Sciences, Erasmus University, Rotterdam.

Erio Ziglio is Regional Adviser for Health Promotion and Investment at the World Health Organisation's Regional Office for Europe in Copenhagen. He was formerly a Consultant in Public Health for the European Community.

Subject Index

accident forecasting
     study
  aims of 195–6
  conceptual model 196–7
  future scenarios 209–10
  generally 193–6
  home and leisure
     accidents 193, 194,
     202–3
  medical care for
     accident victims
     203–5
  methodology 196–9
  occupational accidents
     193, 194, 201–2
  questionnaire
     design of 196–9, 208
     results 199–207
        home and leisure
           accidents 202–3
        medical care for
           accident victims
           203–5
        occupational
           accidents 201–2
        traffic accidents
           200–201
        variations in 205–7
     selection of panellists
        207–8
  traffic accidents 193,
     194–5, 200–201
advances in research
     and technology
  implications of see
     biomedical and
     behavioural
     research and
     technology study
anonymity 6, 20–1, 57,
     60–3, 141

computer-based
     Delphi processes
     and 60–3, 80
  lessening 38–9
  pitfalls of 39
  pseudonyms, use of 62
  reasons for 61
  team building and 37
Arrow's paradox 70, 71
asynchronous interaction
  characteristics of 10, 58
  computer-based
     Delphi processes
     and 20, 58–60, 64
  need for 10

biomedical and
     behavioural research
     and technology study
  advance, implications
     of government, role
     of 115
  background to 90–2
  computer technology
     108, 119
  conduct of 127–8
  consultant panels
     selection 95–6
  context of 89–90
  data banks 108, 119
  ends and means 112–13
  ethical issues 112
  evaluation workbooks
     99, 101–2, 103–5
  extension of life 109,
     120
  final report,
     preparation of 106
  findings about
     advances 108–10,
     119–22
  first policy evaluation
     instrument
     background papers 99
     evaluation workbook
        99
     introductory
        materials 98–9
     pre-test 98
     purpose of 97–8
     scope of 97–8

genetic screening
     109–10, 120–1
  implications of
     advances 112
  ends and means
     112–13
  freedom 115, 118
  for individuals 111
  justice 115
  moral and ethical
     issues 112
  need for controls
     114–15
  need to mediate
     value conflicts 113
  public participation
     116
  for society 111
  individuals,
     implications for 111
  introductory materials
     98–9, 100, 102
  issues, selection of 96–7
  key findings 107–8
  mediating value
     conflicts 113
  methods 93–106, 125–8
  moral issues 112
  objectives of study 91–2
  participants, selecting
     125–7
  policies
     autonomy of
        researchers and
        providers 117
     coordinated national
        policy 116
     findings about
        113–14, 122–5
     individual
        responsibility and
        freedom 118
     public participation
        in 118
  pre-testing 98, 100, 102
  public participation
     and 116, 117–18
  reproductive
     engineering 110, 121
  second policy
     evaluation
     instrument

245

Author Index

Printed in the United Kingdom
by Lightning Source UK Ltd.
134912UK00001B/287/A

Printed in Great Britain by
Amazon.co.uk, Ltd.,
Marston Gate.